The
SEX
TALK
You Never Got

The SEX TALK

You Never Got

RECLAIMING THE HEART OF MASCULINE SEXUALITY

SAM JOLMAN, MA LPC

NELSON BOOKS

An Imprint of Thomas Nelson

Published in Nashville, Tennessee, by Nelson Books, an imprint of Thomas Nelson. Nelson Books and Thomas Nelson are registered trademarks of HarperCollins Christian Publishing, Inc.

Published in association with The Bindery Agency, www.TheBinderyAgency.com.

Thomas Nelson titles may be purchased in bulk for educational, business, fundraising, or sales promotional use. For information, please email SpecialMarkets@ThomasNelson.com.

Unless otherwise noted, Scripture quotations are taken from the Holy Bible, New International Version®, NIV®. Copyright © 1973, 1978, 1984, 2011 by Biblica, Inc.® Used by permission of Zondervan. All rights reserved worldwide. www.zondervan.com. The "NIV" and "New International Version" are trademarks registered in the United States Patent and Trademark Office by Biblica, Inc.®

Scripture quotations marked CEB are taken from the Common English Bible. Copyright © 2011 Common English Bible.

Scripture quotations marked ESV are taken from the ESV® Bible (The Holy Bible, English Standard Version®). Copyright © 2001 by Crossway, a publishing ministry of Good News Publishers. Used by permission. All rights reserved.

Scripture quotations marked KJV are taken from the King James Version. Public domain.

Scripture quotations marked MSG are taken from THE MESSAGE. Copyright © 1993, 2002, 2018 by Eugene H. Peterson. Used by permission of NavPress. All rights reserved. Represented by Tyndale House Publishers, a Division of Tyndale House Ministries.

Scripture quotations marked NLT are taken from the Holy Bible, New Living Translation. Copyright © 1996, 2004, 2015 by Tyndale House Foundation. Used by permission of Tyndale House Ministries, Carol Stream, Illinois 60188. All rights reserved.

Scripture quotations marked RSV are taken from the Revised Standard Version of the Bible. Copyright © 1946, 1952, and 1971 National Council of the Churches of Christ in the United States of America. Used by permission. All rights reserved worldwide.

Emphasis in Scripture quotations is added by the author.

Any internet addresses, phone numbers, or company or product information printed in this book are offered as a resource and are not intended in any way to be or to imply an endorsement by Thomas Nelson, nor does Thomas Nelson vouch for the existence, content, or services of these sites, phone numbers, companies, or products beyond the life of this book.

This book is intended for informational and educational purposes only. It does not constitute professional therapy or medical advice, diagnosis, or treatment, and should not be used as a substitute for seeking guidance from a qualified mental health professional or medical practitioner. The author and the publisher assume no responsibility for any injuries suffered or damages or losses incurred during or as a result of the use or application of the information contained herein. Names and identifying characteristics of some individuals have been changed to preserve their privacy.

Library of Congress Cataloging-in-Publication Data

Names: Jolman, Sam, 1979- author.
Title: The sex talk you never got : reclaiming the heart of masculine sexuality / Sam Jolman.
Description: Nashville, Tennessee : Nelson Books, [2024] | Summary: "Men today are starved for sexual formation. They've been failed by parents, churches, and culture alike, leading to widespread shame, confusion, and brokenness in the area of sexuality. In The Sex Talk You Never Got, therapist Sam Jolman helps men reconnect their God-given sexuality with innocence, awe, and joy, and shows readers how to celebrate--instead of struggle against--the gift of sexual desire"-- Provided by publisher.
Identifiers: LCCN 2023050383 (print) | LCCN 2023050384 (ebook) | ISBN 9781400243907 (tp) | ISBN 9781400243921 (epub)
Subjects: LCSH: Men--Sexual behavior. | Sexual ethics. | Sex--Religious aspects--Christianity.
Classification: LCC HQ36 .J656 2024 (print) | LCC HQ36 (ebook) | DDC 306.70811--dc23/eng/20240110
LC record available at https://lccn.loc.gov/2023050383
LC ebook record available at https://lccn.loc.gov/2023050384

Printed in the United States of America

24 25 26 27 28 LBC 5 4 3 2 1

To Brandt, Simon, and Westley.
Your innocence and aliveness inspired me to write this.
May you always know the wild goodness of your lover hearts.

Contents

Contents

Contents

Contents

Foreword

At last.

A kind, wise, and poetic guide to the complex and beautiful issue of our sexuality, and a path toward the wholeness every man longs for.

I'm serious—this is the most important book on sexuality you will ever read because of Sam's *approach*.

Most boys—including the boys-now-men reading this foreword—had no one to initiate them into wholehearted, masculine sexuality. If we received any guidance at all, it was the barren and confusing "here are the mechanics" talk delivered by an uncomfortable father or father figure plus the cold, moral warnings of the church, or it was the random cocaine hits of hyperstimulation and undernourishment punching us in the gut from out of a dark culture.

This has left many of us wondering if our sexuality can ever be wildly good again.

But somewhere down deep in our souls, we remember Eden. We ache for sexual fulfillment that is exotic, intimate, and utterly without shame. Even when we are lost in fantasy, pornography, or prostitutes, we know in our heart of hearts that those things aren't touching the real need inside. Not even close.

So we stumble on, completely unfathered and uninitiated in this most sacred, most fabulous part of our humanity. Left to work things out on our own.

Yes, there are truckloads of books for men on sexuality. But nearly all of them leave out the most essential part. Masculine sexuality emanates from and expresses with thunder the deepest places of our masculine *heart*, and only by going to those places can we hope to heal, strengthen, and release our sexuality into all it was meant to be. Wildly good.

This is why I'm thrilled with the approach Sam is offering in this book. He gently steps right past all the barren mechanics, sterile moralizing, and volatile sexual politics to guide us into the Edenic terrain of the lover deep within our heart. Oh, the lover is there—the truest part of our masculine heart and soul—beautiful and powerful, just waiting to be fathered and released.

For only in that release comes redemption.

You're in for a wonderful journey here. I've known Sam for many years. He's truly a good man and trustworthy guide, and this book has been long in the making. Come with an open heart, and you will not be disappointed.

John Eldredge
Colorado Springs, Colorado

The Most Neglected Part of a Man's Life

Three things are too wonderful for me;
four I do not understand:
the way of an eagle in the sky,
the way of a serpent on a rock,
the way of a ship on the high seas,
and the way of a man with a maiden.
—PROVERBS 30:18–19 (RSV)

Kyle stood in the kitchen holding a pack of condoms, the ones his father had just tossed to him. It was Saturday morning, and he hadn't even finished his cereal yet. Minutes earlier he'd lumbered down the stairs, as fourteen-year-olds are prone to do when their body gets big and they're still learning to animate those man-size movements. He found his father milling about the kitchen drinking coffee.

As Kyle rummaged for cereal and milk and made his way to the table, his father turned and wordlessly threw something to him. Kyle caught it, and that's when he found himself holding the condoms.

What does this mean? His eyes, now wide-awake, darted from staring at the condoms to searching his father's face for an answer. "Just don't get a girl pregnant," his dad said and walked out of the room. It seemed Kyle's dad thought he'd come of age. And that was his sex talk. It turned out to be his only sex talk, the sum total of the words Kyle would ever get from his dad about sex.

———

Brian turned down another row of peas, his strong hands picking the pods ripened by summer rain. His fingers were well trained from tending the seven acres of corn, peas, and tomatoes sprawled around him. What was once a small family garden had grown into this cornucopia. Later that day Brian would drive the family tractor down the two-lane road to sell their produce at the small farm town's grocery store. Being trusted with that trip as a thirteen-year-old filled Brian with pride and joy.

But for now he picked. And so did his dad, working one row over. His dad broke the silence unexpectedly: "So if you ever have any questions about sex, let me know."

Brian looked up, startled to a stop. Of *course* he had questions—questions he didn't even know to ask yet. Yes, he knew what sex was, but he and his father hadn't talked about it. He looked for his father's face, hoping he'd continue. But his dad did not look up or stop working. The moment was gone. His father's turned face remains branded in Brian's memory and still cuts him to his core. He wasn't even worth his father's eyes. And his father never spoke another word to him about sex.

Isaac lost his words. For the better part of a week he could not talk to his mom. Something weird had happened to him, and he was dying to talk about it with someone, but he felt so scared and embarrassed that he couldn't bring it up. So he avoided his mom, hoping she'd get curious.

One day she found him in his room, lying on his bed with his feet propped up on the wall. "Honey, what's wrong?" she asked. He stared at the poster in front of him, unable to look her way. After a long silence he worked up the courage to say something.

"It's about . . ." he started.

"What? You can tell me."

Isaac found the word. "Sex."

"Ah, okay. I'm guessing you're ready for 'the talk.'"

No, that's not it. He wanted her to keep asking questions. Something had happened at the campout last weekend with the youth volunteer, and he needed to let it out. But he didn't know how to get his mom to ask those questions.

"Well," his mom continued, "we both know your father isn't going to talk to you about it. Let me get the book I gave your brother. And if you have any questions, feel free to ask your brother since I'm not a guy." And she left the room. Isaac did not mention his experience again until ten long years later, when a wise counselor chose to stay curious and guided him to finally name the weird thing that had happened as sexual abuse.

A Crisis of Sexual Abandonment

As men, our sexuality is one of the most neglected and abandoned parts of us. Despite the overwhelming ways our culture elicits and arouses male sexuality (often to sell us something), most men live with enormous sexual malnourishment. We don't nurture our sexuality at all. We don't cultivate it. We assume it runs by itself, I guess. Or we treat it like the lions at the zoo and spend all our effort caging its wildness. That's about it.

By saying our sexuality is neglected, I am not implying that we just need more sex or titillation. No, we need the cultivation and recovery of something deep within. Being sexual is not the same as being sexually mature. And we live with the madness of being oversexualized yet sexually undernurtured. Most men I talk with are starving for sexual formation and aching for guidance into a healthy and alive sexuality. It may never even get put into words because talking *well* about sex is hard to do. All too often when men talk about sex, they speak in proverbial locker-room talk or dirty jokes. And that lack of healthy conversation becomes an embodied ache or frustration we carry within our sexuality.

It's a story we've been living for years, since long before we became full-grown men. Journalist Peggy Orenstein has dedicated a portion of her career to studying trends in sexual development and culture among high school and college-age men and women. In an interview on NPR about her book *Boys & Sex*, she observed that while other areas of masculine culture are getting less macho, sexuality is still channeling the 1950s *Playboy* era.[1] Our sexuality is not growing with the rest of us.

Let's return to Kyle and his condoms for a moment. There were a thousand questions behind Kyle's stare, a longing for more than mere information. He probably knew full well what a condom was from his friends at school, Google, or porn—the latter being an all-too-common source for information about sex. But pornography is about as "realistic as pro wrestling," says Peggy Orenstein.[2] It makes madness of sex. The actors often aren't even enjoying themselves. It's about as nourishing as licking a toilet.

Think about the message Kyle's father sent him. It gave permission, but it held no blessing. It made sexuality seem instinctive, requiring no conversation, which left Kyle to assume he would automatically know what to do and how to pursue a woman. His father's face said as much as his words—resignation that male sexuality was uncontrollable, so just "do what you want, but keep it in a rubber and don't screw up." The silence implied that Kyle and his sexuality were not worth a real conversation. Far from a blessing, this sex talk surely landed more like a curse. It offered nothing that would guide Kyle's heart through the risky and adventurous terrain of sexuality and romance, condemning him to figure it out alone.

A single, isolated sex talk isn't ever enough. But that initial discussion should be a threshold moment, a sacred ritual, a rite of passage. I know men for whom it was so awkward and rare for their father to talk at all that the sex talk left them too shocked to speak, let alone ask questions. Often such talks amounted to little more than a shoddy anatomy lesson that addressed some basic questions but did not reach the heart. For some men, it became a moralistic lesson on lust or purity so quickly that there was no room to anticipate the goodness of sexuality. There was no blessing.

Some men got no discussion at all. When I told my father-in-law about this book, he bravely confessed that he had not given his son a sex talk. And with an edge of grief, he added, "Come to think of it, I didn't get one either." And on and on it goes. Sexuality is one of the most unfathered places in our lives.

But there may be indications that this is shifting. A study from 2014 revealed that about 82 percent of parents have given their children some sort of sex talk.[3] Yet a Harvard study released in 2017 stated that 70 percent of young adults aged eighteen to twenty-five wanted more conversations with their parents about sex and romance.[4] That's a huge discrepancy. It shows that what parents are doing is not enough. We need more.

And as mentioned above, we don't need just one conversation. We need hundreds. We need an ongoing *dialogue* about sex throughout our life. We need discussions about the goodness of our bodies, arousal cycles, consent, and mutual pleasure, but also about sexual abuse, broken hearts, shame, pornography, and masturbation. We need romance talks, too, like how to have a first kiss, ask a girl out, pursue a woman's heart, or know if (or when) you should get married. And we especially need to talk about the underpinnings of our sexuality: our capacity for beauty, sensuality, and love.

In other words, young men's sexuality needs to be fathered *and* mothered. Our sexuality needs to be cared for, nurtured, and blessed. The absence of care in this area is worse than mere neglect; something like a curse lands on our hearts. When we don't talk about or acknowledge something, we make a statement about its value—or lack thereof. As one man told me, "When I came of age, I felt a huge disconnect between how little I was taught and all the feelings I had inside. I had nowhere to go with my questions and curiosity and hormones. It felt like I had to hide all that. I wanted one—just one—place where my sexual coming of age was celebrated."

And so in this age of abandonment that leaves us feeling as if our sexuality is a curse, burden, or place of conflict, it needs to be acknowledged, healed, and freed. We really can't live without that blessing. I wrote this book to engage, cultivate, and bless male sexuality because the dangers of not doing so are severe. We cannot afford to banish our sexuality, because what is left *unformed* will only become *malformed*. In the absence of intentional formation, other forces will always step in to fill the void.

Is Male Sexuality Fundamentally Broken?

If I told you that the world needs more virile men, you might be tempted to laugh at me or stop reading right now. I get it. It's easy to doubt that male sexuality could be *that* important or that good for the world.

If we've learned anything from the #MeToo movement, it's the staggering amount of awful harm that has been done in the name of male sexual desire. Millions of women (and men too) have since shared their stories of sexual harm at the hands of men. Over 90 percent of perpetrators of sexual abuse are men.[5] As a therapist, I've heard hundreds of these stories from people I sit with in counseling.

Yes, a lot of harm has been done in the name of male sexuality. We know all too well about the men who slake their thirst for power with sexual conquest. We read these stories time and again and hear the agonizing pain of victims who have suffered under this abuse. History is replete with men who have committed atrocities in the name of sexual desire. And these are just the stories we know about, not accounting for the myriad of women who've suffered in silence.

Even for women who have not experienced outright sexual trauma, many likely face the daily realities of catcalls, lustful looks, or degrading sexism from men—harm that they endure at work, in public, or at home. These stories are ever present. They exist in the DNA of every one of us, men and women alike.

The world groans under this harm.

And we can't ignore the suffering of men whose sexuality has been a place of immense personal struggle. So many men have sabotaged their own lives—their careers, marriages, or creative energy—for the sake of sexual thrill. These men suffer a silent sense of failure, shame, loneliness, and numbness.

I am deeply aware of the dangers close at hand in writing a book to rouse and bless male sexuality. So much harm, self-destruction, and violation of others have been done in the name of male sexual pleasure. Should we really try to do anything that risks further stoking men's sexual desire?

When the dominant picture of sexuality in our culture is the male sex addict, we may be tempted to believe that male sexuality is inherently bad, that life works well only when a man has corralled or caged its savage nature and resolved to keep it in check. Maybe it's a fundamentally broken thing, downright sinful at its core. That suspicion toward sexual desire—and bodily passions and appetites in general—is woven throughout history, including in Christian thought. We've disowned male sexuality because we don't know what to do with it, as men or as a society.

A few weeks ago, a woman lamented to me her experience of online dating. She shared a few stories that ranged from being fairly bonkers to absolutely horrific. It started with men who used profile pictures that were decades old (or not even real pictures of themselves). It got worse from there.

One man staged his own version of the show *The Bachelor* by inviting three women on the same date—without mentioning it was a group date. He wanted, in his words, to "save time" because he was "busy." Never mind the obvious narcissism. At the sight of the other women around the table, my friend walked out, only to have the man chase her to her car to announce she had "won" the date and now had a chance to have the night with him. She burst out laughing. This guy had turned romance into a clown show.

We both laughed, and then her face went somber as she said, "I have another story to tell you." She described a man who made advances at the end of a date. She turned him down only to have him assault her. The police did intervene and the man landed in jail, but the harm had been done.

But that wasn't my friend's final story. Toward the end of our conversation, she shared that one man—only one man—honored her request to talk over the phone several times before they ever met in person (a technique she'd learned to weed out the awful candidates). He was more than happy to do that. He got it. That man became her husband.

I had no words as she ended. Despite hearing the happy ending of my friend finding her husband, I couldn't get past the ridiculous and terrible encounters she'd experienced. It was like a tour of the bombed-out state of men, masculinity, and romance in our world. As I sat staring in shock, this very wise woman asked the question that most needed to be asked: "What happened? What happened to men?" Her question held no disdain but simply expressed an imploring curiosity. She repeated it like she knew the whole world was asking the very same question. It was a lament we can all join, men and women alike.

What happened to men?

"They Were Being Cut Off from Their Hearts"

For her book *Boys & Sex*, journalist Peggy Orenstein interviewed more than a hundred young men about their sexual upbringing and experience, hoping to get her finger on the pulse of what has gone awry in men's sexuality. She summarized her diagnosis in the NPR interview we mentioned earlier: "The core issue with girls was that they were being cut off from their bodies. With boys, it felt like they were being cut off from their hearts."[6] One college-age man she interviewed told her, "I've had two one-night stands in college, and both of them have left me feeling empty and depressed. I have no idea what I gained from those experiences other than being like, 'Yeah, I had sex with someone.' There were no feelings of discovery or pleasure or intimate connection, which are really the things that I value."[7]

This man was able to name what was missing—a rarity. Even when they lack the words to describe this struggle, most men know when something is out of sorts. Yet we settle for the struggle. We resign ourselves to living in silence and shame, maybe getting off but hating ourselves without bothering to try to discover what's missing.

The problem isn't too much sexual desire but rather too little heart. There is nothing inherently wrong with an aroused man. But somewhere along the way, we lost the heart of male sexuality. Our hearts and our sexuality have become disconnected. Dissociated. Forsaken. We've lost our awe and wonder and innocence toward life, beauty, and sexuality and exchanged them for a masculinity that is about as movable as stone.

Yet if sex and our hearts are meant to be so closely connected, how did they ever get separated? Every man has his story (or stories) of when this disconnect occurred. Ever since humanity was expelled from Eden, we have all suffered harm to our sexuality. We are all the brokenhearted. It may be the trauma of overt sexual abuse or the more subtle harm of emotional pain. Maybe we felt our sexuality was condemned by our family or spiritual community, or maybe it was simply ignored and unaddressed.

But it's not pain alone that severs the connection between our heart and sexuality. In the absence of care, shame always comes to haunt us. And the realm of evil hopes that, with enough shame, we will disown our sexuality. Shame wants us to believe we are bad, dirty, or foolish and must stay hidden so we don't get exposed or rejected. So we tuck our sexuality away deep inside, along with its underpinnings of sensuality, relationship, and aliveness. We disown the heart connection. Remember when I said that in the absence of love or care something like a curse settles on male sexuality? This shame is the curse.

The Shadow Self and Becoming Savage

I believe almost all men have disowned their sexuality to one degree or another, pushing it into the shadows. This is rarely conscious. We split or dissociate in the places where we've suffered. Like surviving a war wound, we just find a way to live with sexual fragmentation. These splits, these broken places in our hearts, can heal only if we address them by pulling them into the light, into our conscious awareness, and into vulnerable relationship. If we don't, the things we hold in shame stay in the shadows with tremendously negative consequences. They become our shadow self. By "shadow," I don't mean something that is entirely bad, dark, monstrous, or evil. Our shadow self is simply all the parts of us we're ashamed of that we keep hidden out of sight—in the shadows, we might say.

These parts of us don't disappear or cease to exist. They just take on a life of their own in the wilderness of our being. As Robert Bly said, "Every part of our personality that we do not love will become hostile to us."[8] Our shadow selves have a way of jumping us when we least expect it, asking us to pay attention to them. This may show up in our lives as anxiety, flashbacks, or angry outbursts at our kids or spouse. It could be not knowing what to say or shutting down inside. It could feel like we have a separate self, an alternate personality that overtakes us. Often we act out sexually in some way.

If we continue to ignore our heart's requests for engagement, that shadow part will grow more savage, more unruly. While we keep the exterior polished, the part we've disowned and exiled begins to mutate. As Bly puts it, "When we put a part of ourselves in the [shadow] it regresses. It de-evolves towards Barbarism."[9] A man's split can become a double life, a secret sexual self that he lives out in destructive ways. We get stuck with a sexuality that Johan Huizinga calls puerile: a "blend of adolescence and barbarity."[10] When a grown man's sexuality remains stuck in junior high even though he ages, what was once just immaturity becomes increasingly savage. And the nearer he drifts toward becoming a savage, the further he gets from being a lover. By savage, I mean "an unfeeling, brutal, or cruel person . . . whether civilized or uncivilized."[11] A savage has no empathy. He lives driven by every impulse other than love: lust, hate, anger, selfish desire. In a word, he becomes increasingly *heartless*. Left unchecked, the shadow self may eventually become known by other names. The predator. The abuser. The monster.

Most men don't grow savage to this extreme. Their sexuality just wanders lost in the wildlands of their inner world, uncared for and uncultivated. Barbarism for them looks far more *underdeveloped* or *unsophisticated* than monstrous. They resemble an immature and selfish brute. But that kind of barbarism is still wounding and destructive. It often leads to low-grade suffering for these men and those around them.

Recovering Your Sexuality from the Wild

Consider this book the sex talk you never got. Only you're a little older now, so we've got more to talk about. And more to fight for, because there's a good chance you've suffered a lot in this area of your life. I've written this book not as an instruction manual on the mechanics of sex but as an attempt to get to the heart of sex. Or, to borrow a phrase from Esther Perel, we're going to talk about the "poetics of sex"—the desire that drives it, the mystery and meaning of it, the way it's meant to move you and color and shape your whole life.[12] Because the mechanics of sex do not work without the poetics of sex.

Put simply, I want to help you recover your sexual innocence and aliveness. Sex holds a connection to all the awe and wonder you have not just for other human bodies but also for the beauty of the world. Just recovering that awe-ability would be a great accomplishment. But I want more than helping you recover something. We are not going to simply *talk* about sex. We are going to *bless* your sexuality.

Your sexuality is a good part of you. It's the artwork of God that he declared good on the sixth day of creation. A lot has happened since that original blessing, both in the story of the world and in the story of your life. We all plunged with the world into sin and darkness, muck and mire, pain and sorrow. We need to talk about that story—not just the story of the fall long ago but the way we still suffer it today.

But despite that fallenness, you need to know that your sexuality never lost its original blessing or its capacity to return to its original glory with the help of God. Believe it or call me a liar, but your sexual aliveness and innocence can be recovered. It's actually one of the most important things you can do to change the world for good. The world needs men who've recovered their sexual aliveness and, with it, their awe and innocence.

Blessing is not the same as enabling or permitting, though I hope you find empowerment and freedom to explore. Maybe "blessing" comes across as an empty religious term you've heard from a priest or pastor. Or something your aunt from the South might say to you in the "bless your heart" sort of way. You've probably been blessed every time you sneeze. That's not the kind of blessing I'm talking about.

Have you ever had somebody really see you and name something good in you? This is more than just a blanket offer of encouragement or a passing "Good job!" or "I'm proud of you," which passes for affirmation these days. This is what I mean by *blessing*: To bless is to behold something or someone, to tell the story, and to give the good a name. It's when somebody catches you doing something brave, beautiful, bold, or alive, and they take the time to tell you the story of what they see. They let their own vulnerable wonder show even if they struggle to find the words. A blessing is an active recollection of the delight they felt in seeing you. A blessing nurtures, grows, shapes, and affirms. It helps some part of you become more fully alive.

It can be a little frightening when someone blesses us like this. It sometimes makes us want to pull away because to truly receive a blessing is to accept that there is glory in us. In the blessing, we are called to own in a deeper way the goodness and beauty within ourselves. Every blessing comes with a calling, some charge to live it out or foster it.

God saw something in our ancestors' sexuality. He beheld something in Adam and Eve that moved him, and he called it good. And with this blessing came the charge to be fruitful and multiply, to be virile and alive. He sees goodness in your sexuality too. He wants to bless it, and he charges you to become fully alive in this long-neglected area of your heart.

We're going to help you recover your sexuality. Though it may feel like walking into darkness itself, we can't afford *not* to take this journey. And we must find a way to reconnect your heart to your sexuality. We're going to walk into the wild, unknown places of your self and your story to recover your sexual innocence. It is not gone. No matter what your story has been or how hopeless you feel, your innocence is not lost for good. It can be recovered. But, to paraphrase author Joseph Campbell, we need to go into the darkness we fear to find the treasure we seek.

Can we do this? Not only can we, we *must*.

ONE

You Are a Lover

Love . . . its flashes are the flashes of fire,
The very flame of the LORD.
—SONG OF SONGS 8:6 (ESV)

Human beings are fundamentally erotic creatures. . . . To
be human is to be a lover and love something ultimate.
—JAMES K. A. SMITH

I am the lover of uncontained and immortal beauty.
—RALPH WALDO EMERSON

I crawled on hands and knees in the underbrush of a big pine. An elk the size of a horse trotted a stone's throw in front of me through an aspen grove. Armed with a bow, I worked to get a shot. With no time to range for distance, I sighted my forty-yard pin on the thick patch of fur behind her front shoulder and released my bowstring. The elk ducked a few inches and I heard the thwack of my arrow hitting a tree.

She trotted a safe distance away from any further volley, paused, and then thundered down the mountain.

I sat waiting for my heartbeat to slow down. My hunting partner joined me. He had been working the elk calls a hundred yards back.

"Did you get a shot?" he asked.

"Uh, sort of," I said.

We found my arrow a minute later. No blood.

Here was my first shot on an elk, and I'd missed.

The disappointment hit me hard. We reshouldered our packs and trudged on, hoping to make our destination of the tree line in time for an evening hunt. It was late August, when the hot weather pushes the elk to the rugged but cooler high alpine. I looked up at that twelve-thousand-foot-elevation edge of timber and felt every heavy step ahead. I walked somber. Hunting these mythic creatures often feels like trying to find unicorns. Shots are rare, but it felt like the point of being here was to get an elk. And I suspected that I'd lost my best chance.

A rainstorm pushed us to find tree cover and a nap before pressing on to the glistening meadows of the high country. When we arrived, we were not alone. As I focused my binoculars, I spotted an entire herd of elk feeding its way out of the tree cover into the lush, open meadow. We'd struck absolute gold. My whole being felt giddy. Elk in rut are *loud*. The bulls scream and bugle with a deep guttural mating call, slamming antlers into their competition, while the cows chirp and squawk. It was glorious hormonal madness.

For the next several hours we did our best to commingle with the elk and line up another opportunity to take aim. Despite being close enough to smell them, we never got another shot.

I will never forget our trek back to camp. You'd think I'd be awash with the agony of near-misses. But something had shifted. My body buzzed with the energy of witnessing an ancient ritual as old as Eden—elk in the play of mating. It opened my heart to something bigger than a successful hunt would have. I thought that God might initiate the warrior in me through this hunting trip. But he knew I didn't need more warrior. He had a far more urgent part of my heart to initiate. He was getting ready to initiate the lover in me.

We crested the ridge as the day's last light set remnant clouds ablaze in fire red, the sound of the elks' revelry still echoing behind us. I gasped. The beauty pierced me. On the top of a mountain, the world immersing us in its glory, I felt purely alive. I thanked God that we didn't get an elk. Instead, we inherited the world.

The Power of Beauty

Do you know those moments when the beauty and the goodness of life catch you off guard and take your breath away? Maybe you sought them out, like a trip to the Grand Canyon, a day at an art museum, or fathering children. But then you stand at the South Rim of the canyon, gaze at a famous painting, or hold your newborn for the first time, only to find that nothing could have prepared you for the wonder of the moment. Or maybe it came out of nowhere, like a dazzling sunset as you left Costco or a song that tugs at your heart. Either way, beauty has a way of surprising us, getting past our defenses, and undoing us.

My friend John Blase calls it being slack-jawed. It's the *wow* that leaves us jaw-dropped and speechless. It's the whole-body sensation of beauty that overwhelms us—chills or goose bumps or a stomach flutter. Beauty moves us. We were *made* to be moved by beauty. "Awesome" is a word worn tired from years of overuse. It means almost nothing now. Anything can be awesome, including that awesome burrito you had yesterday. I don't know, maybe it was *that* good. But "awesome" was originally intended to describe something that overcomes us with its goodness and beauty.

If you're ever going to have an alive sexuality, this is lesson number one—a lesson that few of us ever got. We must learn how to handle and receive the power of beauty within us. As Jay Stringer warns us, "If we do not marvel at and honor beauty, we will inevitably bend it toward our control."[1] Whether your sexuality is controlling or coercive or marvelous and awe-inspiring hinges on what you do with beauty.

Beauty Beyond Appearance

Sometimes beauty moves us with its bigness, its grandeur. The thunder of a waterfall reverberates through your body and elicits awe. So does the unfathomable expanse of the Grand Canyon or the staggering presence and power of a bull elk with antlers four feet in span. But beauty does not have to be big to be moving. You can be arrested by the beauty of a wildflower or a sentence from a book. The bigness comes not from the thing's physical dimensions but from its impact on us, the quality of its presence. The orange glow of painted-cup wildflowers in summer can take my breath away. A Yo-Yo Ma cello solo can split my heart wide open.

Beauty is not just something pretty to look at. Beauty is about presence, not simply appearance. When experienced fully, it impacts our whole being. It may thrill the eyes, but to be fully grasped it must stir the rest of the senses. It must rumble the heart and the mind—and even quicken the soul. Author John O'Donohue said, "Beauty isn't all about just nice loveliness. Beauty is about more rounded, substantial becoming . . . an emerging fullness, a greater sense of grace and elegance, a deeper sense of depth."[2] When we've taken in the *essence* of a thing, then and only then have we beheld its beauty.

How does something or someone move us? Both the hearts of the beheld and the beholder matter in this experience. There is a family of sea otters at our local zoo that have learned to play in front of the glass water enclosure. They seem to revel before the audience as they show off their rhythmic turning and flipping. During our last visit as we all wowed and laughed, it struck me that I was beholding the true glory of these animals. They showed up, and so did I.

When it comes to how we treat human beauty, we've reduced the beauty of a person down to physical appearance at great harm to us all. We think "hot" people are beautiful, which reduces them to cardboard props and misses everything else that factors into genuine human beauty—the life we create, how we think and love, the things that make us laugh or cry, how we sing or dance. We lose this broader sense of human beauty when we reduce it to surface-level sex appeal. We propagate the notion that men are more visually stimulated than women (which research has proven false).[3] And, driven by the beauty industry, we distort true beauty into an emaciated version—a burden for women to achieve rather than an innate quality they can cultivate.

I watched a climbing competition once, amazed at how deftly the men and women moved on the wall. The grace and balance of their bodies was astounding. It looked more like vertical ballet than climbing. I once heard a friend read a poem about her wrestling with God that undid me and left me in tears. These are examples of sensual beauty, which is distinct from sexuality per se. But our sexuality is built on the capacity to take in the true and full beauty of a person.

When researcher Dacher Keltner asked, "What brings people the greatest experience of awe?" he imagined it would be the grandeur of nature or the overwhelming power of good music or the transcendence of religious experience. But as it turns out, we humans are most moved to awe by other people living with what he called "moral beauty."

When people display courage, kindness, strength, or perseverance, we are wowed most fully. "Exceptional virtue, character, or ability— moral beauty—operate by a different aesthetic."[4] Presence, not just appearance. It's why we wow at the Olympics, become gluttons for survival stories, or marvel at the kindness of a good person. These events stir this deeper aesthetic, that of the whole body and being.

Beauty of Presence

I saw my wife, Amanda, for the first time years before she noticed me—our Christian college was just big enough that you couldn't know everyone. One day as we filed out of chapel, her flowing golden hair arrested me, and as she turned to talk to a friend I caught a glimpse of her profile. *Be still my heart.* But then she disappeared into the crowd and was gone—my heart dizzy in the wake of her presence.

A few weeks later, this golden-haired woman ascended the stairs to the stage in our chapel to preach. She shared her story of coming to faith at a Christian camp. With no immediate faith background, she'd dug out an old heirloom King James Bible from her basement and Lysoled off the mildew so she could have a Bible with her at camp. For years after, she hid that same Bible under her pillow as if it was forbidden, afraid of what her faith might provoke in her agnostic home. Her sole determination to pursue God led her to a small local church that for years she drove to alone.

I was riveted by her story, in awe of her tenacity and grit. There stood a woman of rich and deep faith who knew the weight of suffering but shined far brighter for it. What started as simple attraction exploded into a rich, full-person awe. She embodied the full beauty of presence, not simple appearance.

I journaled about her that day. But it would take me nearly two years to finally get the courage to introduce myself and ask her out.

That's another story—there was a part of me that I had not yet owned. I was a divided man who struggled to rise to what beauty called forth in me. I was the uninitiated, the uncourageous. And I believed I was *too* attracted to her beauty for it to be God's will. My sexuality still lived in the shadows.

Moved by Beauty

We were made to be moved by beauty. To receive it in all its fullness, and thereby to receive sexuality for all it was meant to be, we must learn to embrace the fullness of our body's design for pleasure. When God gave us our senses, he meant for us to really take creation for a ride. Our senses are how we experience the world. We taste, touch, see, smell, and hear our way through life. God made creation to play on our senses like a musician on an instrument. Our whole basis for living is sensual. We really cannot turn our senses off. They are our interface with the world.

God intended so much more than simple survival when he made our senses. Think of taste buds. Most studies estimate we have two to four thousand of them.[5] And though they do alert us to danger if something is too hot or cold, rotten, or poisonous, they exist largely for us to experience pleasure when we eat. They let us savor a well-prepared steak and distinguish a good bourbon from a bad one. The same goes for all your senses. Smelling smoke may help you survive a fire, but your nose also lets you savor the earthy smell of rain in the woods or take in the intoxicating scent of your wife. Your ears allow you to hear the cries of a distressed child in need of help, but they also let you relish the reverberation of good jazz. Life is not just for surviving but for tasting and seeing and enjoying too. God made his good world to be pleasing. The poet Rainer Rilke put it this way: "Body delight is a sense experience . . . a great boundless experience which is given us, a knowing of the world, the fullness and splendor of all knowing."[6]

John, the disciple beloved by Jesus, began his first letter with the witness of his sense experience of Jesus:

> From the very first day, we were there, taking it all in—we heard it with our own ears, saw it with our own eyes, verified it with our own hands. The Word of Life appeared right before our eyes; we saw it happen! And now we're telling you in most sober prose that what we witnessed was, incredibly, this: The infinite Life of God himself took shape before us.
>
> —1 JOHN 1:1–2 MSG

Even the truth is sensual by God's design. Our bodies bear witness to the beautiful and the pleasurable in a world full of God's glory. This is actually what it means to be a sensual person: not just the capacity for and orientation to the world through our senses but the ability to take *delight* in it all. We don't often talk about sensuality in this way, too easily making the mistake of equating sensuality with sexuality. But they are different. All of life can be sensual. Not all of life is sexual.

It turns out our sexuality is built on our sensuality. It would be impossible to enjoy the fullness of sexuality without the embodiment of our senses. Therefore, if we cannot bless the fullness of sensual pleasure, we will not embody our sexuality well.

Much like taste buds, the design of our genitalia stands as witness to the fact that God cares about our pleasure. Recent research found that men have around eight thousand nerve endings in their genitalia (in the dorsal nerve of the glans penis) and women have around ten thousand (again, in the dorsal nerve of the glans clitoris).[7] This over-abundance of nerve endings, taste buds, and other sensory gifts reveals that men and women alike are designed to experience the beautiful, including the beauty of sex. We are meant to be moved by beauty. We are sensual beings through and through. And we can never hope to recover the innocence and awe of a fully alive sexuality unless we are attuned to our identity as sensual beings designed to behold and experience beauty in all its manifestations.

Meet a Sensual Man

I'd like to introduce you to a man named Nordstrom, who will help us see this connection between sensuality and sexuality. He's the main character in a Jim Harrison novella called *The Man Who Gave Up His Name*. Nordstrom has entered midlife with the grace of a car crash. (He would be furious if he found out I put him in a book on sexuality.) He's not trying to be anyone's hero—he's just a broken man, finding his way and messing it up all at the same time. But as such, some things emerge from his life that are just more honest than someone who puts on a facade of keeping it all together.

At one point Nordstrom goes for a walk in New York and stops by a park. He's trying to clear his head by drinking in the world around him. He notices a woman playing in the grass with her toddler son. Their innocent play entrances him. While he's watching, a gust of wind blows the mother's skirt up a little bit, revealing her thigh. The glimpse of her flesh stirs him. Harrison writes, "Nordstrom felt more aroused generally than sexually, though there was that too, but added was the feeling of good food, good wine or another perhaps stranger feeling, that of letting a beautiful trout go after you had caught it."[8]

This episode reveals a huge difference between awe and lust. Awe becomes more expansive in our bodies and hearts. Lust narrows, obsessing on very specific body parts or fantasies. Nordstrom saw more than this woman's thigh. He saw her playful love for her son. He felt the breeze blowing through the city. The lover in him went from being moved by her to being moved *beyond* her. She aroused him not to lust but to the sensual memory of beauty. He returns to things he *loves*.

Does it feel like I'm excusing away a man's lust? It would help to clarify that *sexual arousal is not the same as lust*. Arousal is a body response to sexual stimuli (the mechanics). But lust happens in the realm of desire, in the heart (the poetics). Desire and arousal are separate and distinct (known as "arousal non-concordance"). So many of us men get this confused in our bodies. Arousal can *become* lust if our hearts move there. But it can also become reverence and awe. Nordstrom does not fantasize about her, but gets carried away with memories of beautiful moments in his life.

In marriage, of course, a beautiful moment can lead to actual sex. But vows alone don't mitigate lust. For arousal to move to awe, the heart must awaken with the loins to all that the heart loves. The poet's verses in Song of Songs reveal this kind of lovemaking. As the poet takes in his lover's body, his being bursts with sensual connections to all that he loves—fine wine, mountains, pomegranates, spices, flowers, and flocks of goats. The sensual commingles with the sexual.

Where Beauty Will Lead You

All this pleasure from the beautiful world God made is meant to take you somewhere. More than simply making you feel good, beauty is meant to rouse you to something greater than yourself. Sensual pleasure is meant to help you fall in love with the beautiful things of this world and the God who made them.

In encountering and knowing the taste of a good steak, you will come to *love* a good steak. In developing your instincts hunting in the rugged mountains, you'll come to love its peaks, elk, and wildflowers. Sensuality allows you to experience a woman's beauty and can lead you to fall in love with her. That same attraction can help you hear the sorrow in her voice when she walks in the room and stir you to offer care. When you revel in a good sunset, you'll want to fall in love with the divine artist who shaped the play of light at dusk. Beauty stirs the body to pleasure, and pleasure stirs the heart to love, body and heart in unison.

And here is another lesson that few of us learned during our sexual formation. Sex is never just a body thing, because you aren't just a body. Whether a man knows it or owns it, at his very center is a heart. And hearts are meant to do one thing: love. Hearts love like lungs breathe. Your center is your love. You have a heart—a big one actually—and it drives all you do, or at least everything that's most important to you. You work because you love. You play because you love. You get discouraged or sad or angry because your heart is out there.

That makes you a lover. You heard that right. I'm saying every man at his core, his very essence, is a lover.

As a man, your most fundamental sexual identity is as a lover. No other description will ever capture the essence of your sexuality. You are a lover.

Male Stereotypes of the Lover

We don't often think of men as lovers—not in this earnest, deep, meaningful sense. We respect men as workers and warriors wearing uniforms, being covered in sweat or grease, or donning a suit and tie. And this respect fits these men for the most part. Something is right about men who sweat and labor and risk their lives for a good cause, including the cause of supporting their family. We celebrate men who achieve great things. We applaud fighters and athletes and entrepreneurs. Sadly, we've also grown familiar with the much less chivalrous versions of these qualities. We know men who are too driven, too lost in work or a war. They become angry or withdrawn, distant or dangerous. They turn into impenetrable brutes, someone we hope not to run into anytime soon. And we ache for a little more heart in these men.

But when we think of a man as a lover, we may laugh. We've got almost no imagination for it. A few cultures do celebrate the idea of men as lovers, but it's a complicated legacy to say the least. For example, Hispanic cultures know the sexually machismo man, the Don Juan, the fictional legend revered for seducing thousands of women. I knew a man whose Spanish father made it his goal to turn his boy into such a lover. But for this father, that only meant teaching his son to size up every woman they passed based on her breasts or butt. This father gave his son no ability to appreciate and love a woman. The Don Juan archetype may embody elements of the sensuous, but it also teaches a man to seduce—but not love—a woman. In America, we've got the frat boy and the playboy, which embody almost nothing redemptive. None of these archetypes invite men to the risk and vulnerability of real love and passion.

The lover in a man is the part of him that connects to his world and enjoys it for all its goodness. It lets him laugh, play or dance, hug or weep, reminding him that love isn't just something we do; it's something we feel. It's the part of him that's not merely getting work done, fighting some battle, or hashing out his plans, but a part that relates deeply to the people, places, and stuff of his life—anything from his dog and lawn to his friends, wife, and kids. The lover in a man also fuels the things that make him shake his head or break his heart. The interior lover is the source of our spiritual longing, too, giving us a desire to connect with the great mystery of existence, the spirit realm, and God.

As psychologists Robert Moore and Douglas Gillette state,

> The Lover is deeply sensual—sensually aware and sensitive to the physical world in all its splendor. . . . It is the Lover, properly accessed, that gives us a sense of meaning—what we have been calling spirituality. It is the Lover who is the source of our longings for a better world for ourselves and others. He it is who is the idealist, and the dreamer. He is the one who wants us to have an abundance of good things.[9]

Men who truly love may make us feel awkward. It disrupts us to see a man whose heart is so *out there*. We may even be tempted to emasculate him by calling him cute or smitten or by saying he's succumbed to "the old ball and chain." Yet we secretly envy men who are comfortable with being lovers. Don't you admire a man whose heart is alive toward his kids, who may even well up with tears of pride for his sons or daughters? Think of those soldiers reunited with their families who weep with joy as they give out hugs. A client who just returned from a destination golf trip with some buddies confided in me how jealous he was of the guys who really missed their wives and seemed to really be in love when they called home.

We've been conditioned to think men just want sex, but that's simply not true. When men in counseling tell me they want love, they often preface it by saying, "I guess I'm more like the woman in the relationship. I actually want the emotional stuff." What a broken, warped world it is when a man who wants affection, emotional connection, or romance thinks he's acting like a woman.

In our culture the word "lover" and the idea of a fully alive heart have been exiled miles away from the world of masculinity. Take the word "libido," which we define as a person's sex drive. The word, which comes to us through the Latin *libido*, can be traced back to the Proto-Indo-European root *leubh*, which means "to love." The German word for love, which is *liebe*, still holds this imprint. Libido can capture the intensity of our sexual desire. But by definition your libido doesn't begin in your loins; it arises from your heart, from love. We've lost that connection.

Even the word "virility" extends beyond our simple definition of sexual potency. The word comes from the Latin word *vir* ("man"), which happens to be the same Latin root from which the word "virtue" (*virtus*) also derives. Like virtue, in antiquity virility was often associated with courage and self-control. In *A History of Virility*, the editors make this summary statement to begin the book: "The virile is not simply what is manly; it is more: an ideal of power and virtue, self-assurance and maturity, certitude and domination . . . courage and 'greatness' accompanied by strength and vigor."[10]

In other words, being a lover is about way more than your sex drive.

The connection between sex and the heart is inextricable. I want you to recover this image of a truly virile man, a man with virtue and vigor and courage and strength, because it gets us closer to identifying what's missing in many men today. Being a lover involves a lot more than asking a girl out or trying to get laid. But I suspect you knew that already, deep in your gut. To be a man is to have heart. And sex that doesn't require your heart, that doesn't put your heart on the line, lacks virility.

My senior year of college I sat at a bar drinking a beer with my friend Dan, talking about life as we always did. On this occasion our conversation took on a seize-the-moment kind of tone. The last year of college will do that to you, I suppose. We both knew that in May a really responsible world awaited us. But it was only September. And for now we were plotting how to wring the towel of time and draw the most out of life's next few months.

In the spirit of the moment, I brought up the woman I'd seen around campus. The Golden Haired Woman. Dan rolled his eyes. This was far from the first time he'd heard about her. No joke—it had been two years of adoration. Two years since I stood a few people behind her as we filed out of our chapel auditorium, her golden curly hair lying on her shoulders just so. And I was smitten. Every time I spotted her since then, Dan got the news—usually from my elbow in his side as he stood next to me. "Dan, Dan, there she is!" He was so over me. Come to think of it, I was sick of me too.

In two years she had inspired a lot of bad poetry and a few good piano songs—hints of my lover heart's attempts at showing up. But she had not inspired me to overcome my fear and ask her out. Not that the problem was her. It was me. I could not seem to find enough courage inside to make my legs walk toward her. To rise to the occasion, as they say. I was a shy junior-higher in a young man's body.

So back to Dan and I at the bar talking. "You know, maybe I'll ask her out this year," I said and sat back, proud of myself for being so courageous in the moment.

"Okay," said Dan. "You've got a month."

"A month—what do you mean, a month?" I asked.

"If you don't ask her out in a month, I'm going to deeply and significantly embarrass you in front of her."

Now I was backpedaling. I didn't mean I was actually going to ask her out. I was just caught up in the moment, keeping the conversation going, playing around. He smiled as I squirmed. He was not going to budge.

Four weeks later, with two days left until my month deadline, we spotted her in the library. Before I could say a thing, Dan just took off walking toward her. He was dragging me into a conversation with her. If I was going to save my dignity at all, I had no choice but to follow. So I did. And in that conversation, I finally asked her out. Two years later, I married her.

Thank God Dan got annoyed with me. It called out something in me that was unformed. God used that to initiate me as a lover. It grew my courage to become the lover who puts his heart out there.

Rediscovering the Romantic

Okay, we need to mess with your understanding of the word "romance," too, because it's been lost to the world of men and we need it back. Did I just lose you? At the very mention of romance, some of you might be rolling your eyes out of your head. You're used to it being "the stuff women want." Your mind probably flashes to date-night planning and trying to find that available babysitter, or Valentine's Day and the commercial ploy to take your money for a dozen roses and chocolates. But I want you to hear as clearly as possible that *you need and want romance too*. You just don't know to call it that.

The word "romance" is derived from a fourteenth-century French word that originally had little to do with love pursuits. It described tales of knights and heroes on adventures likely written in classical Roman style (hence the *romance* moniker).[11] A romantic was thereby one who "partook of the heroic or marvelous."[12] Think hero's journey stuff. Only later did the literary category of romance come to involve pursuing the fair maiden, which eventually culminated in our modern usage of the term.

But this means that, in its origins, romance described adventure.

Romance is the adventure of love. We need to recover this much fuller meaning for the sake of your heart. Romance can be the literal adventures you go on in the course of your love relationship with your beloved, from skydiving to train hopping in Europe. In can also be the wild risk of going to counseling together and learning to explore each other's inner worlds. Hawaii can be romantic, but so is your couch when you're pursuing your lover's heart. I think of all the wild places love has carried me and my wife—from the day I first asked her out, to witnessing her birth three man-children into the world, to grieving with each other as we wrestled with our childhood stories, to exploring new vistas in Colorado. All of that is romance. And in light of that, it's no wonder you cringe at the Hallmark version of it.

Love is a wild journey, far more harrowing and elating than a simple date night.

And by the way, this romance is the only story sex was meant to live within, the only place your sexuality can thrive.

You want this adventure because it's far bigger than even love for a partner. There's a God romancing you, too, inviting you into the adventure of his love. All the beauty in the world screams it. God wants to adventure with you in so many ways that may never involve what we typically think of as a romantic relationship. As Robert Moore and Douglas Gillette write, "If we are appropriately accessing the Lover . . . we feel related, connected, alive, enthusiastic, compassionate, empathic, energized, and romantic about our lives, our goals, our work, and our achievements."[13] Did you catch that? To feel romantic about your life means to feel the spirit of adventure within it, how God is pursuing and wooing your heart.

Men rarely receive a blessing on the lover within, the part of you that was made for sensuality and romance. But we need that blessing more than ever.

Did your heart flinch through some of those last few pages? We just talked about the stuff of our senses—*sens*uality and *sens*itivity—and how our bodies respond to beauty. And if that wasn't enough, I called you a lover and said you need romance. Shouldn't I just be talking about sex more?

But this is the stuff that makes good sex, the stuff we don't talk about in the masculine world. Most of this is not *allowed* in the masculine world. Admitting something has power over us—even if it's beauty—is to relinquish our man card. We men are conditioned to be known for our toughness, our grit, our ability to endure the hardest of things. We have almost no room to talk about the things we love or the things that move us.

And to be fair, much of a man's life is lived in the grind and hustle of hard work. We are workers and warriors. We fight and labor for life. A man with grit and drive and fight is a good thing. Moses described life as full of "toil and trouble" (Psalm 90:10 ESV), and we need something within us to weather that. Beauty will always commingle with suffering. As author Frederick Buechner put it, "Here is the world. Beautiful and terrible things will happen. Don't be afraid."[14] A man needs his fight and his drive to push through hard things.

But a man's fight and drive and rule are never his true power. A man's true power will always be his love. As Augustine said of himself, "My weight is my love."[15] You may not believe me, but I guarantee that it's already how you think of men. You remember men for their passions—what they love and what they don't. You know Andy loves fly fishing. You heard Austin talk down to his wife and it bothered you. You smile when Eric revels in mountain biking and talks about how much he loves taking his kids on adventures. You cringe when Kyle gives his kids anger instead of patience. Bill always shares racist jokes. Ethan always hugs you. You remember when a man is arrogant or treats people badly. And you remember the guys who are generous or helpful or friendly.

Long after we're gone, people will talk about our love or lack thereof.

Without the lover, we become savage, cold, detached, mechanistic, or even sadistic. Neglecting the lover within eventually makes us heartless. But nourishing and cultivating the lover humanizes a man. The lover gives us our center. There's an ancient Proverb that says, "Never give a sword to a man who can't dance." A man who has a weapon but no dance, no play, no laugh, no love, would be a savage.

We are made to love. That is our whole life's North Star.

I am not talking about mere bodily pleasure. Robert Moore and Douglas Gillette warn that a man immersed in sensuality alone is a boundaryless addict. He's at the mercy of his feelings.[16] But for the man who is a lover, moments of sensual beauty and play inspire his labor: "The Lover keeps the other masculine energies human, loving, and related to each other and to the real life situation of human beings struggling in a difficult world."[17] Beautiful moments, sensual play, and adventure with the people we love—that's what we really live for.

Men are not honored for being sensual. We are honored for our suffering and working and warring. That's what the world expects of us in the mash of its gears. We need to produce. Meet that deadline. Shoulder the weight of leadership. Take no breaks. When do we have time for the beautiful? The sensual man is the outcast even though the sensual man is *every* man. We've lost him. Or, better put, we've disowned him, abandoning him to the wilds within. He shows up here and there. We relegate sensuality for a good beer or cigar after work, maybe the thrill of a good movie, or a walk in the woods.

Or sex.

Within the masculine world, sex is the primary place you are allowed to be sensual. (Part of this is right and good. Sex is *meant* to be sensual, a full-body experience of beauty.) But just don't talk about it like a lover. Make sure it's about "getting some."

The poet Rainer Rilke mentored a young military cadet aspiring to become a poet. For a number of years they wrote letters back and forth, about writing, life, sex, love, God, spiritual practice. It really became a father-son relationship. Rilke wrote this to him about the sensuality of sex: "Almost all men misuse and squander this experience, and apply it as a stimulus for the weary places of their life, a dissipation instead of a rallying for the heights."[18] Don't over-hear Rilke here. It's okay and good that sex is comforting. But he's asking, Is this the outflow of a lover or a squandered moment of quick comfort for a desperate man? Do you rise to it, does it call you up, or do you collapse into it? Is it a painkiller or the overflow of your heart?

Rilke actually believed good sex ought to make you want to become a poet the next day. "Those who come together in the night time and entwine in swaying delight perform a serious work and gather up sweetness, depth and strength for the song of some poet that is to be who will rise to tell of unspeakable bliss."[19] He was calling forth the lover in the young man.

Sex Is Not a Need

It's not a given that a man will engage in sex from the overflow of his lover heart.

Take, for example, the fact that we call it a "sex drive." Sex is not a drive. A bodily drive is one that is *necessary* for your survival. You need oxygen. You need food and water. You need sleep and shelter. You even need love and connection. You don't need sex. As sex researcher Emily Nagoski points out, no one has ever died from lack of sex—though some have surely felt they might![20]

Sex is a desire, not a drive. It's a want, not a need.

Calling sex a "drive" isn't just bumbled wording. It encourages us men to treat sex as a need, something akin to life and death, which confuses our relationship with our bodies. Men get stuck relating to sexuality as a necessity, an urge they have to answer, something they are powerless to stop. This perspective keeps men from having a conversation with their bodies and sexuality, and puts them in survival-reaction mode.

Furthermore, given that men on average have a higher sex "drive" (i.e., a more frequent desire for sex), a woman may feel pressure to give a man his "required" dose of sex. It is sometimes even said that if she doesn't, he will succumb to the temptations of porn or seeking another woman to meet his need. This mindset obligates women to a duty and keeps men immature, at the mercy of an urge.

And then sex loses its beauty.

But what if sex is a desire? Well then, a whole world opens up for you. Emily Nagoski says it so well: "Your partner is not an animal to be hunted for sustenance, but a secret keeper whose hidden depths are infinite."[21] That makes sex an act of exploration and adventure (there's that word again), full of heart and relationship, discovery and freedom. Sex may be powerful, but you are not simply at its mercy. The lover in you gets to play and grow and change. Nagoski says we need to think of sexual desire more like curiosity.

We are not taught this as men. And I daresay, in the absence of this teaching, we lose our sensuality, too, resulting in a confused and difficult relationship with our bodies and our sexuality.

Unraveling Lust and Desire

The church is often guilty of perpetuating this "drive" model for understanding sexual desire, reading it into Paul's words to husbands and wives in 1 Corinthians 7:5: "Do not deprive each other." This perpetuates what author Sheila Wray Gregoire has called the "obligation sex message,"[22] which teaches that we must never say no to our spouse's expressed interest in sex. But if no one is dying from a lack of sex, Paul's instruction against deprivation reads a lot different. With the proper context of sexual desire rather than the drive model, not depriving each other still leaves lots of room for saying no.

It gets worse. There are other ways many churches have driven a wedge between us and our sensual connection with our bodies. If you got a sex talk at all or found one in a Christian book on male sexuality, there's a good chance you were heavily warned about the terrifying nature of sexual lust. Don't get me wrong: lust is a real thing. Jesus warns strongly about it, identifying it as a form of covetousness (Matthew 5:27–28). We should be on guard against it.

But what is lust? It's rarely defined outright. In many religious contexts, it's implied that lust is that feeling you get whenever you see a beautiful person. If an attractive woman stands next to you at Starbucks and you look at her and feel good feelings in your body, you've lusted. And the solution is usually some version of, "Run! Flee! Bounce your eyes. Shut it down. Never be alone in a room with a woman. Freak out." And by the way, the teaching goes, since lust is also every man's albatross, you can be assured you are guilty.

Not content with this conclusion that all men lust continuously, Gregoire did a study on just how many men actually struggle with lust on a daily basis. Of the three thousand men she polled, 76 percent self-reported that they struggled with lust every day.[23] Not quite every man, but the majority. Yet when asked pointed questions about specific *behaviors* that would confirm this reality, more than half (56 percent) of the lust confessors showed no discernible lust behavior. In other words, only 33 percent of the three thousand men surveyed actually struggled with lust in any conclusive way.

Her absolute salvo of a conclusion reads,

> Sexual attraction is a hardwired state of being over which you have no control. . . . Noticing that a woman is beautiful or has an attractive figure is instinctual. It's not good or evil; it's biological. It happens in a part of our brains we don't control. But once our conscious brain registers and starts to weigh in on the situation, we can handle ourselves in many different ways. That's where morality comes in.[24]

That thing that stirs inside you in the presence of a beautiful woman is sexual attraction. It's a man's sensual response to beauty. Let's even call it arousal. Because again, *sexual arousal is not the same as lust*. And it is not wrong. You are made to be moved by the beautiful. Even sexually moved. And calling it lust only shuts down the part of you God hardwired to respond to his good world.

Dan Allender has said that "lust is desire gone mad."[25] What begins as desire can be turned in the heart to a slobbering hunger, savagery, or consumption. But since it's a desire we're talking about (not a need or a drive), we get to decide. We're *responsible* to decide. And if we choose anything other than love, we've lost sensual engagement and started down the path of lust. God made you to be moved by beauty. What you do next is where morality begins.

A young man gave this account to journalist Peggy Orenstein, whose work I've mentioned several times:

In middle school, porn was considered cool. Guys knew the names of porn stars. And I watched it almost because it was like the unknown—like the same impulse that makes me want to climb a rock or go to a forest. But pretty quickly, I was like "This is just so f—ed up." What's on the screen isn't actually sensual, not for either person. So I stopped.[26]

We will get into how a man stops lust. But for now, listen to this young man's self-reflection. Can you hear the spirit of adventure that initially led him to porn? He recognized it as the same curious exploration that led him into the beauty of nature. His heart began with sensual wonder. And his heart felt the difference. When he says there is no sensuality in porn, he seems to be describing the quality of engagement. Something about the performers seemed absent. These people didn't bring the same innocent wonder to sex. It's like tasting a truly good cup of single-origin coffee versus Folgers (sorry if you drink that stuff). You can down shots of whiskey to get drunk, or you can sip it simply to savor its oaky sweetness. You can have sex to get off or you can let it play out for all its sensual layers.

When your heart can be present to your sexuality, noticing a beautiful woman can become appreciation for her, not lust. And sex becomes so much more than how much you get or don't get. It's about the wonder you experience. Sensuality is a whole other world waiting for the innocent of heart.

Hookup Culture

In case you wonder if the culture at large is doing better at sensual sexuality than the church, I give you hookup culture, the casual-sex culture made infamous on college campuses.

"It's always nice," said a college student to professor Lisa Wade, "to have a clean, emotionless hookup."[27] Lisa is the author of *American Hookup*, a book dedicated to deciphering hookup culture. She writes that possibly the most essential rule to hookup culture is this: *Don't feel it*. Whatever you do on your hookup—from making out to oral to intercourse with anyone from a friend to a stranger—make sure it does not move you. Wade calls it "compulsory carelessness."[28] Another student said the goal was to have "fast, random, no-strings-attached sex."[29] Hooking up should bring no emotions and mean nothing so that it's no big deal.[30]

In hookup culture, emotions are talked about as if they're an STD. You don't ever want to catch feelings. "Catching feelings meant developing an emotional attachment and was, for many girls, something to protect against when hooking up, just as they would guard against catching herpes or chlamydia," says Peggy Orenstein in her book *Girls & Sex*.[31]

Don't feel it. What a bizarre endeavor to eradicate something that seems implicit in the experience of sex itself. Why would you *not* want to feel it? "Saying we can have sex without emotions is like saying we can have sex without bodies," says Lisa Wade.[32] But if emotions and feelings were allowed, then hookup culture would collapse on itself. Hookups wouldn't work anymore. They would be too moving and invoke too much care and mutual connection. And that would force people to admit sexuality's power over us.

The only way to accomplish emotionless sex is through alcohol. As Peggy Orenstein points out, "Hookups aren't just lubricated by drinking; they are dependent on it."[33] It turns out that when it comes to sex, it's really hard to make it not matter without some help. In the words of one female college freshman, "Being sober makes it seem like you want to be in a relationship. It's really uncomfortable."[34]

Lisa Wade asked a group of freshmen to keep a journal of their experience of hookup culture for her research. To her surprise, some shared accounts of sober sex. And it was completely different. "They talked about having sex while sober in these reverent tones like it was an amazing unicorn: it was meaningful in a way that drunk sex is not."[35]

Reverence and meaning arose from doing one simple thing: feeling. Blessing the body and its sensuality. The cardinal sin of hookup culture is not the sexual desire itself but how it's joined to utter heartlessness. Why is hookup culture terrified of having feelings associated with sex? Why is falling for someone and having heartfelt, sensual sex the worst possible outcome? I think hookup culture gives us a picture of what we all become terrified to do with sex. Feel it. Risk it. Reverence it.

Authentic sexuality requires a connection to your body and self so that you can tune into your partner. Without sensuality, sexuality does not work. Everything goes wrong. The mechanics require the proper poetics. It becomes about getting an orgasm. I'd venture to say that sexual sin is not about too much desire but rather too little sensuality. Or, as I said in the introduction, too little heart.

The Bravery of Sexual Aliveness in a Numb World

Dan Allender once said, "Innocence is the ability to be in awe."[36] When I heard him say this in a lecture, I thought about my ache for my own sexual innocence and my heart just about burst. I almost got up right there and ran out into the world to shout it from the rooftops: "Someone knows how to get our innocence back!" Yes, if we can recover a sense of awe, we get our innocence back. That is staggeringly good news.

Everything I've talked about so far in this chapter—being moved by beauty, being alive to the world with our senses, and the specific way we feel that sexually—all of this comes back to your innocence.

We may confuse innocence with naivety, assuming that when you grow up and learn things about life, you stop being so innocent. This misperception is especially powerful in the realm of sexuality. Our sexual innocence seems to be lost with all that we've seen or done (or had done to us). How could we possibly get it back? After all, we know things now. We've experienced things. How can we unsee what we've seen? Or unknow what we know? I've had clients laugh at the idea of regaining sexual innocence. It seems ridiculous to them, not to mention too good to be true.

The term "innocence" also holds the connotation of being without fault. But what if we are at fault in some area of our sexuality? In the moral sense, innocence seems lost in the heart of any sinner. We've *done* wrong and we *feel* wrong for having done it. We feel pinned to the ground by our guilt, no matter how much we may ache to get our sexual innocence back. It feels hopeless. How could anyone be made innocent again?

God seems to hold a different definition of innocence. At one point, Jesus' disciples chased off some children like vermin for getting too close to him. Jesus stopped the whole scene and brought a child right into their midst. "Unless you receive the kingdom of God like this child, you won't get in" (paraphrase of Mark 10:15). That doesn't leave much room for confusion. Because how do children receive anything if not with awe and wonder and exuberant excitement? In a word, they receive things with innocence.

Somewhere along the way we started to think of innocence as childish and something we need to outgrow. You know, it's that cute thing kids do when they greet the world. It's sweet in a child but cringey in an adult. So we found a way to look down on it. We somehow believe that becoming unflappable is a sign of maturity, that excitement should happen only when we're kids. Somehow we should no longer be moved by life when we grow up.

This goes back to that vision of manhood that seeks to make men unmovable. Men are the rocks, the stable ones, the steady ground under everyone else's feet. We think that we are most fully men when we are unemotional, which furthers this awful sense that it's childish to be so awed by life.

Yet Jesus makes clear that childlike wonder is the way he wants us to receive everything in life. Innocence has never been about a lack of knowledge of the world. Innocence is the ability to receive the world with wonder and awe. To be curious about life and explore, experience, and be moved by it. That is the innocence we're talking about here, the type of innocence that God calls us to. Innocence does not come or go with being faultless. Think of the Pharisees. They could lay claim to being faultless in the eyes of the law, yet they had lost so much heart. They had lost their sense of reverence or worship.

We all face the same temptation to forsake our innocence.

What have you done with the lover within you? What have you done with his innocence, his sensuality, and his capacity to be awed at beauty? There's a good chance you've disowned him, exiling him to the shadows of your being. I bet you don't see him as your greatest strength or guard him as your very heartbeat.

In the eleventh hour, when I showed up to finally ask Amanda out, it called something out that was so unformed in my lover heart. And despite the fact that two years later we did get married, there was still so much of me that remained uninitiated and stuck in the shadows. My sexual story still lived buried inside of me for the most part. I had not entered the dark cave of my shame and all I'd forsaken there.

It's taken twenty years to really know how to show up well in sex and romance—as the lover, virile and vulnerable.

If you are ever to have an alive and full sexuality—indeed, even a full life—you must fight to get the lover back. And if you're going to accomplish that, you need to know where you lost him in the first place. We must become the revolutionaries of a more human masculinity, one that shakes off the counterfeit masculinity of immovable bravado and puts our relatedness and aliveness at the center. As James K. A. Smith writes, "To be human is to be a lover." We need to humanize our sexuality.

Unfortunately, instead of sensuality and aliveness, many of us have settled for so much less. If you grew up in the church, there's a good chance you've been told purity is the goal of your sexuality. Purity culture, the Christian reaction to the sexual revolution, intended to instill a sexual ethic in young people. It may have started with a desire to hold the church to a standard of sexual holiness; purity culture is at least loosely connected with the biblical idea of pursuing holiness. But it failed miserably in practice. In reality, it damaged or destroyed the sensuality within so many men and women. We need to dismantle that once and for all.

Let me tell you about a place where awe can take you that purity alone never can.

TWO

God Most Wants Your Awe (Not Your Purity)

Yet we've so narrowly missed being gods,
bright with Eden's dawn light.
—PSALM 8:5 (MSG)

There is a way of beholding that is a form of prayer.
—DIANE ACKERMAN

"Come on. Let me show you something."

Kyle and his friend, Tommy, had been playing video games all Saturday morning up in Tommy's bedroom. The virtual adventure of the game was fun, but Tommy had a real-life adventure in mind. He led Kyle down the hall ever so quietly to his parents' bedroom. Kyle followed across the threshold with absolute hush. Parents' bedrooms are not usually permitted places of play. This felt daring.

Once inside, Tommy unearthed a magazine from his father's

nightstand drawer and sat on the bed flipping through the pages. Kyle moved close enough to get a look. His heart began to race. A naked woman peered back at him with her glistening body on full display. He had never seen anything like this.

Suddenly, Tommy's mother called his name from downstairs. Tommy shoved the magazine back in his dad's nightstand. And with all the speed the two boys could muster, they raced out of the room and dove onto the floor of his bedroom, back to the video game they had been playing all morning.

Later that night at home, Kyle could still recall the warmth he felt inside his body. It stayed with him all day long. A new world opened up to him, and with it came an unbelievable excitement. As he lay in his bed staring wide-eyed at the ceiling, he prayed with pure innocence, "God, thank you for naked women."

———

This story is complex, like almost all our stories of sexuality. I imagine you felt the danger as much as anything else. This is a story of many things, including an evil assault against Kyle's heart. This father's use of porn is devastating in itself, and the impact on both boys is a story of sexual violation. There is so much broken here.

But it's also the story of Kyle's innocent heart bearing witness to beauty. And with it, the natural, pure desire to say, "Thank you."

The Goal of Your Sexuality

If you grew up around the church, you probably absorbed the idea that the most important aim of your sexuality is purity. But that leads into all kinds of difficult struggles with desire that look more like repression than transformation. And if you grew up guided by the broader culture outside the church, permissiveness masquerading as empowerment or blessing (limited only by the principle of consent) was probably the implied message related to sexuality.

Both messages seem so lacking to me. Neither purity nor permissiveness can bless pleasure or speak to all the ways the body integrates with the heart.

So we need to step back and ask, What is the goal of sexuality? What does a man's sexuality move him to do? Where does his sexual energy take him?

Eugene Peterson writes, "The sheer wonder of life, of creation, of this place where we find ourselves alive at this moment, requires a response, a thank you . . . Gratitude is our spontaneous response to all this: to life. Something wells up within us: Thank you!"[1] An innocent heart, when confronted with beauty and stirred by wonder, will want to say, "Wow . . . thank you!" That's the goal of all this being moved by God's good world: that your heart would overflow with gratitude for the fact that you were created to be moved. This, I believe, is the goal of your sexuality as well; that out of your sexual experience you'd say, "Wow . . . thank you!"

Your sexuality as a man was meant to drive you to awe and gratitude. As it turns out, science backs up Peterson's insight. Researchers have recently taken an interest in the little-understood emotion of awe. To study it, one research group put people in beautiful places—a grove of trees, a breathtaking overlook, or an art installation—all to evoke awe and allow the researchers to measure the impact. They discovered that awe offers a staggering amount of prosocial benefits. People who experienced more awe in their lives were happier, more generous, more helpful, more cooperative, more ethical, and more humble.[2] So powerful is the impact of awe that even a single minute of standing in a grove of towering trees led people to become measurably more helpful and ethical.[3]

This led the researchers to wonder what was provoking these responses. They concluded, "Awe imbues people with a different sense of themselves, one that is small, more humble and part of something larger."[4] Awe by nature calls us *up* and *out of* ourselves, encouraging us to be available for the world around us. It does this by making us feel that we're a part of life's grandeur. Not lost or small, but belonging to something beautiful and good in the world. After experiencing awe, people had some sense of their personal concerns being smaller and less important. They were naturally moved to want to be connected to the greater good of life. It produced both reverence and belonging. Not surprising, these same researchers concluded that most people live awe deprived.[5] With busier lives often spent indoors, we rarely get lost in the wider wonderful world.

Could it be that our encounter with beauty is truly the place where all spiritual belief begins? Maybe awe is the beginning of all real belief.

What Is Awe?

So what is awe? We all know the sensation it gives us. The big eyes, the gasp of air, the full-body *wow* that washes over us. We shiver with goose bumps (small muscle contractions in our hair follicles called piloerection, your *other* erection).[6] But still . . . what *is* it?

The word "awe" derives from the Old Norse word *agi* meaning "fright."[7] Yes, fear is certainly a part of it. Awe invokes some sense of reverence for the power of what is before us. As I said in the previous chapter, there is a power to every beautiful thing—not necessarily that the beautiful thing is physically big but that there is a gravitas to its beauty. The researchers from the study described above concluded with poetic simplicity that awe was an experience "in the upper reaches of pleasure and on the boundary of fear."[8] That may sound very odd for those two sensations to even come near to each other. We typically don't associate fear and pleasure.

Is such a tension possible? Terrifying goodness sounds oxymoronic, like dry rain or giant ants, ideas that might work for a fairy tale but not in real life. We have trouble categorizing it. When we experience awe, we are overcome with something we cannot look away from. In the words of Dan Allender, awe is "being afraid of something that we are simultaneously drawn to."[9] That is a wild experience, one to which we have very little to compare. Unless, perhaps, you're a parent who has ever taken a child anywhere near a mascot.

I remember the first time my oldest son, Brandt, encountered a mascot. We were at the zoo for a kids' craft hour, and they had someone in a big blue teddy-bear suit milling about, high-fiving children and generally being soft and teddy-bear good. Brandt sat in my lap, staring wide-eyed with concern yet unable to look away. Somehow the mascot spotted him and bobbled over, believing he or she could alleviate this fear. That did not happen. My son, alert to the impending encounter, shrilly screamed, "*Go!*" I responded quickly to the command and retreated us to an acceptable distance, shielding his view with my turned body. Brandt snuggled up close to my chest but gazed just over my shoulder. He still could not look away.

My children have repeated this reaction often—be it with Santa or clowns or even the animals at the zoo. When the lion roared his guttural roar or the orangutan swung himself across his cage to smack the glass inches from our awestruck faces, my children stood frozen in that vortex of terror and intrigue. Slowly, over years, they have built the courage to stand closer and revel more in the magic of these moments.

Does God Want to Scare Us?

Nearly every person in the Bible who encountered God or an angel fell down in terror. No wonder every heavenly messenger first had to comfort his audience with the words, "Do not be afraid." Jacob actually called God "the Fear" (Genesis 31:42), which is not any sort of affection I know about. But it seems to bear affection, a wink to God. Jacob was no stranger to fear and spent much of his life fueled by the stuff—fear of his brother, his uncle, the king whose son raped Jacob's daughter. Jacob never saw a fight he didn't feel the need to run from.

As Jacob fled his brother, Esau, after cheating him out of his birthright, he stopped for the night to sleep. It was there that God met him in a dream. Jacob saw a vision of angels coming and going between heaven and earth. And he heard the voice of God, comforting him and reassuring him that he would always be with him.

This was not immediately comforting: "Jacob woke up from his sleep. He said, 'GOD is in this place—truly. And I didn't even know it!' He was terrified. He whispered in awe, 'Incredible. Wonderful. Holy. This is God's House. This is the Gate of Heaven'" (Genesis 28:16–17 MSG). After the wave of terror passed, Jacob whispered in awe, "Incredible. Wonderful!" It seems it was here he formed his affection for the trembling, moving presence of God.

The writers in the Bible called this awe-filled experience the "fear of the Lord." I did not grow up understanding this to be an enjoyable experience. To my Sunday school–formed heart, fear of the Lord meant that we needed to be afraid of God. And this is precisely the reason we will not want to sin anymore: because God is scary. We feared him like we feared every mean adult who wanted us to behave.

My grade school principal, a towering, sour-faced old man, always came outside to the playground just as the recess bell rang to snarl, "Letsgo! Letsgo!"—apparently because terrified children run faster back to class. I always felt so *caught* playing and having fun. That's the God I pictured. Enjoying him, reveling in him, was never something I considered. He was never described to me as awe-inspiring goodness. Powerful, yes; but wonderful? Not so much.

Many of us have had this same fear tactic used to scare us to pursue sexual purity. We live with the fear that God will roar in anger at us if we mess up sexually. I know men who shake in terror when something goes wrong in their life, fearing God is punishing them for masturbating or looking at a woman lustfully.

But I believe this gets the heart of God wrong. God wants to awe us, not terrify us, into relationship. He does not want us to simply behave ourselves like scolded children. He wants to *move* us. And the only way for this to be true is for him to be truly good.

Yes, God is powerful. God thunders and booms. God flashes and flames and glows hot with glory. His presence disrupts. People fall flat on their faces because of a bodily fear reaction so primal that it could hardly be called reverent or even spiritual. It triggers the brain's autonomic danger system, the amygdala, the part of our brain that constantly sifts our sensed experience for danger. Before we are even consciously aware of what we're seeing, our amygdala is processing preconscious feelings about it, sensing the level of safety.[10] The amygdala is what enables us to jump before even fully registering the presence of a snake in front of us.

But God always invokes more than simple terror. People don't just run. They stick around, held by something more. Though fear may also be an ingredient, there's something else going on with awe that keeps us from outright fleeing the scene. I believe that urge, the thing about awe that makes us stay, is also rooted in the body. Awe definitely begins as a response to the presence of power—our body's reaction to what Eugene Peterson called the "More and Other."[11] But then it becomes a real embodied *pleasure*—the delight of being in the presence of pure, distilled goodness.

But awe for God doesn't stop here at mere pleasure either. The waves keep coming. It draws out something even deeper in those who experience it. It lays open maybe our deepest desire: to become "more and other" ourselves. As the psalmist exclaimed of his experience of awe, "Deep calls to deep" (Psalm 42:7). Real calls to real. It's as if the presence of God can shine right through us, exposing all that's true of us. It prompts our deepest vulnerability, disarms our most stringent defensive impulses, and reveals our shortcomings. God's presence reckons with us, causing us to confront our deepest longing to be more than what we are right now.

Maybe the prophet Isaiah put it best after seeing an awe-inspiring vision of the throne room of God when he cried, "Woe is me! for I am undone; because I am a man of unclean lips" (Isaiah 6:5 KJV).

This is the power of awe. It moves us from fear to pleasure to longing.

I can remember one time while driving when I crested a hill and met a stunning sunset. Its piercing rays wowed my heart and instantly made me feel convicted for my impatience a few minutes earlier while trying to get my sons in the car. After we oohed and aahed together at the sunset, I felt compelled to apologize to them.

God wants to awe us into holiness. He wants to move us from fear to pleasure to longing, to be good and to be "more and other" like him. This is never more true than in our sexuality. The goal of your sexuality is this awe. God wants all that moves in you sexually—all your arousal and sexual desire—to lead you to awe and gratitude for him. Our sexuality asks us to humble ourselves in its presence, to reverence it. But if we brave the tremble, we find something more waiting for us.

United with the Beauty

Last summer, our family took a trip to Telluride, a mountain town known as Colorado's little Switzerland. We met a local family one evening that told us of a beautiful waterfall located just a short but rather steep hike off a side street. The next morning we set out to find this glorious waterfall.

The hike proved to be every bit as steep as they claimed. With three boys in tow, I wondered what we'd gotten ourselves into. I prayed under my breath the whole time for mercy for my utter foolishness. I had to sherpa each of my boys past sections where we could have very easily tumbled twenty feet down into the river. And then, as quickly as it rose, the ground leveled off and we emerged at the base of a thundering waterfall. This was a mountain stream, not a full river. But water falling one hundred feet still rumbles. The spray and wind from the cascade pressed against us.

It was stunning in its power. And for a minute we all simply sat, catching our breath, wowing and guffawing out loud. But the more I settled into the experience, the more another urge washed over me. There was a little pool at the bottom of the falls located just before where the stream meandered its way farther down the mountain. I wanted to get in it. Without a change of clothes, I settled for wading in the water sans footwear. With the cold water gripping my feet and the pulsing waves of spray scattering across my vision, the sensation of awe was gloriously magnified. My whole body felt it now.

But I kept thinking of what it might feel like to be drenched in this water. Deep was calling to deep. Ah yes, I wanted even more. I wanted to be taken into the water, into the mountain. And I wanted to take the whole scene into me. It was a sensation that existed almost wordless in my body. And it's a sensation I have often experienced in the presence of beauty. It almost feels scandalous to admit. I wanted to be drawn into the beauty of the waterfall, to be overpowered and remade with the waterfall in me somehow.

C. S. Lewis gave me the words for this desire years ago: "We do not want merely to see beauty, though, God knows, even that is bounty enough. We want something else which can hardly be put into words—to be united with the beauty we see, to pass into it, to receive it into ourselves, to bathe in it, to become part of it."[12]

Do you know this sensation? When I see a mountain, I instantly wonder what it would be like to climb it or bike it. I want to engage it, play on it, reckon with it. I find a similar urge with everything beautiful I experience. I want to find its source, meet the one who made it, and be made like it. All beauty gives us this chance to turn toward God in greater union.

Sex gives us a living picture of this. Your sexuality was made to mirror the same heart longing. It is the beautiful otherness of lovers that draws them toward union with each other, compelling them to commit their lives to one another.

God's Purpose in Awe

Remember that research on awe I mentioned earlier in this chapter? Remember what they concluded actually goes on in the human heart to lead to such profound change? It turns out that awe actually makes people feel small. That sense of smallness produces humility. Humility makes people feel like they belong to a much bigger, more beautiful world than they previously realized. And when people feel connected to something bigger than themselves, it makes their own concerns and troubles seem small. They are drawn to embody the good before them. They become more like the thing they experienced.

It's not just perspective; it's *connection*. We don't often think of feeling small as a gift. But when it's experienced in beauty, in awe, in transcendence, in the presence of something good, it makes us feel like we belong to something much bigger than ourselves. In the end, it's not simply that God wants to leave us trembling with slack-jawed awe at a distance. He intends for awe to lead to something: "The fear of the LORD is the beginning . . ." (Proverbs 9:10). But it is only that: a beginning. When God stokes up all this wonder and awe, he intends for it to go somewhere. He's not simply leading us on.

God knows the tension in us. He knows that we are terrified when we are exposed by his absolute goodness, but that we also long so deeply to join him, to belong to the beautiful. Remember that the prophet Isaiah, whose vision we talked about earlier, was not left in the agony of his woe. An angel came toward him in the room with a burning coal and touched his lips, consecrating his words and encouraging him in the midst of his fear. Think of the angels bringing good news of great joy to the shepherds. Or God showing up to tackle Jacob and free him from his fear. Time and time again, God comforts and encourages the people who are terrified at the display of his power, beauty, or goodness. God means to give us his goodness, not terrify us. He is always the one crossing the divide.

God is romancing us. He doesn't want us far off. He intends to draw us toward himself. He wants lovers, not simply admirers. God has been romancing you your whole life with every sunset, wildflower, or elk in rut. When you felt your heart rise in your throat at seeing your first child, or when you first heard a cello, or when you saw your first butterfly emerge from a cocoon, God was drawing you to himself. Every time you've experienced awe in the face of beauty, God was calling you. He is after your heart.

Human Glory Invokes Awe

You don't need an angel to freak you out in the night or a waterfall rushing past your face to experience awe. As I said in the last chapter, researcher Dacher Keltner discovered that the thing that invokes the greatest awe in us is other humans. And in particular, it's humans who embody moral beauty—what I called the beauty of presence, not simply appearance. Things like courage, kindness, and humility.

I think the story of Jesus' transfiguration in Matthew 17 holds a picture of this awe for another human. The story goes that Jesus invited his three best friends to spend a night with him in the mountains. ("Oh, they're camping," said my sons when I read them this story. Yeah, that's probably right.) Just when his buddies turned in for the night and were sacked out, they were jolted awake. Jesus, who just moments before had been praying, was now *glowing*, his face and clothes ablaze like the sun. The disciples were terrified. The scene was so wild they couldn't even process what they were seeing. *Are we in danger? And why is Jesus glowing?* But then the wild got straight wacky. A cloud descended around Jesus and a booming voice spoke words of blessing over him. The text says, "They fell facedown to the ground, terrified" (Matthew 17:6). And then they felt Jesus touch them. And as quickly as it began, it was over.

The transfiguration is a theologically rich story, but at least a part of what's going on is that, for a moment, the veil over Jesus was lifted and the fullness of his true identity became visible to the disciples, overwhelming them with beauty and power.

The Old Testament authors described moments like this with one word: "glory." It's a vibrant word in itself. The Hebrew word *kabod*, which we translate as "glory," conveys both heaviness and brightness at the same time. It describes something with weight, gravity, substance, such as the thick clouds of divine presence in Exodus 19:16. But it also refers to light, radiance, majesty, as symbolized in fire (Exodus 24:17). Both ideas convey majesty or authority. The transfiguration is a scene of the overpowering glory of Jesus, his literal lightness but also the gravity of his presence.

God is not the only one who bears this glory. Humans are created in his image (Genesis 1:26). We are image bearers. And Scripture is full of accounts of people who, much like Jesus on the Mount of Transfiguration, reflected divine glory in dramatic ways.

Think of Stephen in Acts 6–7. Right before he confronted the religious leaders and gave his thunderous account of the story of Jesus, his face started glowing like an angel's (Acts 6:15). The gravity of his speech bowled over the religious leaders, and his glory boiled their fury. Refusing to be moved by Stephen's presence toward the truth, they killed him. It was all a tragic refusal to be awed.

Or take Moses after he communed with God on Mount Sinai and received the Ten Commandments. In another bizarre scene of human bioluminescence, after Moses came down to the people, his face glowed. The people were terrified of him. Again, fear in the presence of glory. To ease their fear, Moses began to veil his glowing face after communing with God (Exodus 24:29–35).

And it doesn't stop there.

Paul said that you and I and anyone who communes with God

will glow. "And we all, who with unveiled faces reflect the Lord's glory, are being transformed into his image with ever-increasing glory, which comes from the Lord, who is the Spirit" (2 Corinthians 3:18). This is a staggering reality.

I've never seen someone actually glow. But we carry this idea in our everyday language. After a stage performance, we may tell someone they were *glowing*. We may tell a beautiful woman that she looks *radiant*. We might see someone smiling in pure joy or happiness and say they are *beaming*. Tell a child you have a present for him and his face will *light up*. I just read an ESPN social media post that mentioned an athlete who *shined* in a game. We may even tell an athlete, "You were *on fire* out there." It's the language of glory.

We have this in our theology too. No matter what condition we're in now, we have all been made in his image. We still bear the glory of God and shine his image in the world. David put it in scandalous terms: "What are mere mortals that you should think of them, human beings that you should care for them? Yet you made them only a little lower than God and crowned them with glory and honor" (Psalm 8:4–5 NLT). Or, in Eugene Peterson's paraphrase, "Yet we've so narrowly missed being gods, bright with Eden's dawn light" (MSG).

That is so scandalous. God has laid the glory on so thick that we are all nearly gods and goddesses ourselves. We shine divine presence in the world. No wonder we are so moved by each other.

C. S. Lewis bids us all wrestle deeply with this reality:

It is a serious thing to live in a society of possible gods and goddesses, to remember that the dullest most uninteresting person you can talk to may one day be a creature which, if you saw it now, you would be strongly tempted to worship, or else a horror and a corruption such as you now meet, if at all, only in a nightmare. All day long we

44

are, in some degree, helping each other to one or the other of these destinations. It is in the light of these overwhelming possibilities, it is with the awe and the circumspection proper to them, that we should conduct all of our dealings with one another, all friendships, all loves, all play, all politics. There are no ordinary people. You have never talked to a mere mortal. Nations, cultures, arts, civilizations— these are mortal, and their life is to ours as the life of a gnat. But it is immortals whom we joke with, work with, marry, snub, and exploit—immortal horrors or everlasting splendors.[13]

Yes, we are flesh and bone, but you have never met a mere mortal. Everyone has been bestowed a glory to steward. Which means no one is ugly or boring or revolting. And if they seem otherwise, they are either hiding or rejecting the glory God made them with—or you just didn't look close enough, curious enough, or with the right eyes and heart.

A Theology of Clothing

Which brings us to a necessary discussion on bodies and clothing. We are the only species that wears clothing. (Don't say hermit crab, because he is wearing a whole house, not a shell shirt.)

I once heard a version of clothing theology that went like this: After Adam and Eve fell into sin, they hid in shame. God gave them animal skins as a mercy, a covering for their shame. And this sacrifice of an animal for covering foreshadowed the Jewish sacrificial system and the death of Jesus for our sin. I think some version of this is true. But it holds an implication that is dangerously wrong. It implies that bodies are shameful and must be covered up. It says that clothing hides our guilty bodies, which we should be embarrassed for exposing. (And every pastor preaching modesty just said, "Amen!") But if our bodies are the artwork of God, the display of his glory, then something about this perspective is wrong.

I do believe clothing is a gift this side of Eden. As a resident of Colorado, I appreciate that clothing gives us protection from the elements. I love flannel season as much as the next bearded mountain man. And as a Dutch, pasty-skinned white person, I thank God that sun shirts are cool on beaches. Clothes are protection. And clothes can be a wonderful source of self-expression too.

But more importantly, there is a hidden gift in clothing. Far from the safety of sinless Eden, bearing the weight of glory is no easy task. To be naked is a weighty thing, a reverent unveiling of our body's full glory. Clothing gives us shelter and comfort but also a choice in the matter of who we disrobe for and transfigure in front of. It soothes our nervous systems. This is probably more true for women, who suffer the impact of beauty culture and the judgment of the male gaze. But what man wouldn't shrivel and shrink at the thought of being in the buff in public.

What I'm driving at is this: Clothing serves less to cover our shame and more to veil our glory. In this broken world clothing is not a statement of the shamefulness of our bodies, but rather a recognition that most of us are not able to appropriately receive the body's full glory. Think of all the glorious things in the Bible that get covered. After Genesis 3, one of the next biblical mentions of animal skins is their use as a covering of the tabernacle and its poles (Exodus 26). The tabernacle was basically a giant portable tent the Israelites used as their sacred place of worship—sacred because God met his people there. And the tabernacle's most sacred relic, the ark of the covenant, was housed behind a curtain in the holy of holies and had to be veiled from sight whenever it was transported. Later the permanent temple also had a giant, extravagantly designed curtain to veil the holy of holies (2 Chronicles 3:14).

Can you hear the theme? Glorious things are veiled. Clothes are a literal and symbolic veil of glory. We still practice this today at weddings, where a bride often veils her face. Far from being a covering for shame, like Moses she is muting her radiance so the crowd, and especially her groom, can handle her stunning presence without passing out. It foreshadows the unveiling of bodies to come. Tremper Longman notes that in Song of Songs, the lovers actually use temple elements in their descriptions of one another's naked bodies, making a connection between these sacred things.[14]

Reflecting on his first year of marriage in his book *The Mystery of Marriage*, author Mike Mason describes his experience of beholding his wife's nakedness:

> I still haven't gotten used to seeing my own wife naked. It's almost as if her body is shining with a bright light, too bright for me to look at very long. . . . My wife's body is brighter and more fascinating than a flower, shyer than any animal, and more breathtaking than a thousand sunsets. To me her body is the most awesome thing in all creation. Trying to look at her, just trying to take in her wild, glorious beauty, so free and primal, so utterly unchanged since the beginning of time . . . I catch a glimpse of what it means that men and women have been made in the image of God.[15]

Before nearly losing himself in the tractor beam of the memory of his wife, he turns back to you and me.

That shy but driving curiosity we have for other peoples' bodies will be with us our whole lives. There's a Peeping Tom in all of us, for we can never see enough, never drink our fill. The truth of this is grossly mirrored in the man who is a slave to lust, for whom one stripper or one glossy photograph is never enough. But such lust of the eyes of the flesh is only the perversion of a perfectly natural and healthy curiosity, healthy because it is the Lord himself who made us curious, who has caused us to be fascinated with one another's flesh. God has given the naked body its shining glory and has done so for the sole purpose of making it a marvelous harbinger of his own infinitely more illustrious glory.[16]

No, this does not sanction lust, watching porn, or undressing others with your eyes. Mason is blessing *curiosity*, the draw to glory. In many ways, as he says, a consumption of naked bodies as a practice is lust, the abuse of our curiosity and awe. Lust is not too much desire but too little; there's so much to arousal beyond sexual gratification. You were made to be moved *to worship God* through the glory of other people. All genuine awe leads us to God. You were made to take in and awe at the full presence of another. You are walking among near gods and goddesses.

Saint John Climacus, a seventh-century Christian monk, shared this anecdote about chastity:

> Someone, I was told, at the sight of a very beautiful person felt impelled to glorify the Creator. The sight of them increased his love for God to the point of tears. Anyone who entertains such feelings in such circumstances is already risen before the general resurrection.[17]

That is not a given for any of us. Anyone could be driven mad with lust rather than let his or her heart turn to worship God. We may want to take for ourselves a person's body, to have it, to covet it, to consume it. But if we let ourselves be truly moved by another, we can indeed be moved to worship God—to say with Kyle from the beginning of this chapter, "Thank you!"

Sex as Embodied Awe

What does any of this have to do with sex? Well, in a word, everything. Awe was the world that sexuality was meant to live in. "The fear of the LORD is the beginning of wisdom," said the writer of Proverbs 9. I say it's the beginning of everything. All of life is meant to grow from and culminate in this slack-jawed wonder. This awe *is* life. As Proverbs says later, "Fear-of-God is life itself" (19:23 MSG).

So yes, awe is absolutely meant to be the beginning of your sexuality. From curiosity to arousal, from the play of sex to orgasm, postcoital embrace, and everything in between—it was all meant to live in the realm of wonder and leave you searching for someone to thank.

The very first words uttered by a human in the Bible come as a response to sexual awe and arousal. Adam broke into spoken-word poetry when he beheld Eve's naked body. And it's her body that he praised. In his poem "When God Dreamed Eve Through Adam," poet Richard Chess imagines this genesis of human sexual experience, this moment where Adam awoke from sleep and met Eve. He ends the poem with this refrain:

> When he stood back from her
> suddenly he understood the world
> would never culminate nor close with him
> And he was frightened, the first, the original
> terror which he couldn't tell from wonder
> as he stood there regarding what was made.[18]

Terror which he couldn't tell from wonder. We don't know for sure what this moment was actually like for Adam, but we do know that something led Adam to speak in lyric as he beheld someone so like him and yet so utterly other. *More and other*, in her own way. You may not break into song or drum up poetic verse every time you're aroused. That might result in a lot of poems. But the awe will be there if you want it, a poetic sentiment, a desire to reverence the beautiful.

Arousal is born from awe and enlivens your body so that you begin and end in gratitude. We were made to experience sex as a full-body arousal, as an experience of transcendence, as an experience of awe. Orgasm was meant to be the crescendo of awe.

Melanie Robson, a psychologist and sexologist, puts it this way: "An orgasm creates intense delight but I think also plunges us into a small state of fear. You lose yourself when you orgasm. You become intensely vulnerable, intensely open, intensely big and small at the same time. You become everything and nothing. It asks you to risk deep connection—to yourself and/or to another person. It's easy to see how frightening this state of being can be."[19]

In the harrowing wildlands east of Eden, we rarely experience our sexuality as simple wonder, awe, and gratitude. We know so many other, darker feelings there—pain, shame, guilt, embarrassment, heartbreak. And tragically, when we hear that awe and gratitude are the places where our sexuality is meant to flourish, it seems laughable or even repugnant to our jaded and broken hearts.

The Lie of Purity Culture

Before ending this chapter, we need to finish a conversation that was only hinted at earlier. Many of us were taught in church that what

God wants most for our sexuality is purity. We built entire youth group movements on this very premise. An entire industry got in on it, encouraging kids to wear purity rings and sign contracts and go to purity rallies (as I did), all with the goal of abstaining from premarital sex. At a youth rally, with every eye closed and every head bowed, I was asked to give my life to Jesus and then to contractually commit to stay sexually pure. I did, with a sincere, vulnerable desire to honor God.

Purity culture sure made it seem that purity was the entire goal of sexuality. Sexual desire was something to contain and corral and cage. Our best hope was *not* to feel wonder and awe by suppressing them. I certainly don't remember any message that blessed sexual desire or arousal or invited us to be grateful to God for it. It treated all sexual arousal, experiences, or awakenings with immense fear. Never anticipation.

I know a man who announced to his wife that he had conquered lust. He claimed he was so pure he was no longer moved by beautiful women. Didn't even notice them, he said. His wife sat across from him at a Starbucks, aghast in disbelief when he told her this. About that time an attractive woman walked past their table. His wife asked, "So you don't even notice her?" "No," he said. Something in her heart dropped. She realized that if this was true, he could not behold her beauty either.

Something in this man had died on his path to purity. This is the fruit of the church's obsession with sexual purity. We teach women that their bodies are scandalous and that men's desire must die. It kills something off in a man. It emasculates him, neutering him of all that rightly moves him. It traumatizes men by leading them to believe that any sexual arousal or experience is terrifyingly close to sin, if not over the brink of ruin itself. Teaching a man that purity is the sum total of his sexual ethic will lead him to kill off something good within him. That's not what God wants.

Purity in the Bible is never an end in itself. Purity is always preparation for worship, for meeting with God, for being moved by and united with him. That was the goal. Union and worship with God. Purity served to prepare the heart for this experience, that as lovers of God we would be wholehearted in our love.

Making purity the goal of your sexuality is a really bad idea. Purity that is not in service to awe bludgeons a person's body and being. So many men and women in church were traumatized by purity culture, which I believe is inherently abusive. It violates the very glory of God within us, that our beings are made to be moved, aroused, and awed. And it dissociates people from their bodies, setting them up for further sexual abuse and violation, because they no longer know their bodies.

I read a story once from a mom who had this to say about her son:

> Yes, I knew men and boys were visual—but I didn't really grasp just how visual until my son was thunderstruck by the pictures in the Victoria's Secret shop window at the age of 4. "I like those ladies," he said, in an awed tone of voice, suddenly and completely oblivious to everything else around him. "Their bare tummies make my tummy feel good." The male brain is the male brain from the earliest age, that means we moms need to know how to help those little eyes be careful what they see from the earliest ages.[20]

What a heavy burden to put on a young boy. She heard lust in the heart of a four-year-old's simple awe for the beauty of bodies. A boy this age is not even sexually awakened. This suspicion for all that moves in the masculine heart, even at such a young age, is the same heavy burden that encumbers so many men.

Whether said or implied, purity culture equated almost any

experience of sexual arousal or desire, or any expression of sexuality, with being sinful, impure, or dirty. Instead of the biblical idea of purity as fidelity to God, we heard a more literal definition of purity: that we need to be "free of contamination." "Contaminated" is exactly the word so many of my clients use to describe their sexual shame.

And once you're contaminated, how do you ever become uncontaminated? We equated virginity with purity, and losing one's virginity was often described as irreparable damage. That is a devastatingly destructive message.

So let me be clear: sexual arousal is not lust. It does not make you impure. Sexual activity does not fundamentally ruin your body or your sexuality. It does not make you dirty. Nor are virginity and purity the same. Yes, there are sexual ethics and morals, of course. But it's always about the heart. We *are* called to purity of heart, to fidelity to God. That kind of purity *does* matter, and it does affect our entire being, including our sexuality.

But the real danger here is when we actually repent of our sexual desire, fearing that our sexuality is inherently dirty and broken. I believe David's words in Psalm 139:14 must become our words for our sexuality, that it is "fearfully and wonderfully made." We must begin and end with this reverence for our design.

Purity is the gift we get on the path of awe. Take one of the most popular verses on sexual purity: "Since we have these promises, beloved, let us cleanse ourselves from every defilement of body and spirit, bringing holiness to completion in the fear of God" (2 Corinthians 7:1 ESV). Can you hear it? The whole goal is the fear of the Lord. Awe. And purity is only the preparation for it. Let me give you my paraphrase of that verse: "God makes good on his promises, friends, so open your heart to God and he will make it whole and free, so that your jaw will drop even more at his goodness and holy fire."

Author Winn Collier, when asked to define the holiness of God, said,

I think of fire that burns so hot you crave to be near it—but you tremble too at its ferocity. I think of those stunning moments (at the edge of the Grand Canyon, at the birth of your child, in the terrible reckoning with how the pain you carry—and the pain you inflict—reveals wounded love) pierces you so profoundly that you know something deeper than you have ever known it before. And you have no words. But somehow in that strange, unspoken knowing, healing happens. I think of becoming truly human, more alive as the fire burns, the piercing cuts, the balm heals. And God is the fire, the piercing, and the balm.[21]

That's the work of God, to give you back your heart and sexuality, whole and healed. And the path to it is not purity, but awe.

THREE

What Is Sex?

Life must be lived as play.
—PLATO, *LAWS* 7.803C

The beauty of the human form in motion reaches its zenith in play.
—JOHAN HUIZINGA

Trevor still remembers the day his dad took him to Sonic for a slushy and the sex talk. The invite itself surprised him. They did not hang out or talk much. His dad's anger always left Trevor looking to preserve as much distance as possible between them. But with his crushed ice in hand, his dad gave him the anatomy-lesson version of the sex talk—how tab A fits into slot A and sperm meets egg. Trevor remembers very little of what he said. To go from talking almost never to *this* talk felt awful. He pushed himself up against the passenger-side door and waited for it to be over.

I suppose now he knew about sex. But did he? Sure, he knew how the parts fit together. But mostly his body remembered the feeling of being trapped in a car in a vulnerable conversation with a father who never made it feel safe. Body parts and a shutdown heart.

Is this what sex is?

If we received a sex talk as a kid, there's a good chance it was this one: you learned how the anatomy fits together and how the sperm and egg meet. And that is really helpful to know. But it's rudimentary. The anatomy lesson is often shoddy and reductionistic. A woman's parts were probably called a vagina, not a vulva, which completely leaves out the clitoris and a woman's pleasure. Rarely are the different arousal cycles explained, much less masturbation or wet dreams or the difference between arousal and desire. It assumes the plumbing kind of just works. And notice how everything past the genitals gets left out. There is no description of how the whole person participates in sex—including the heart and mind.

But sure, I guess we know that tab A goes into slot A.

You can have a functional understanding of sex and still not understand sex.

Sex Was Intended to Be Play

Would you guess that Hugh Hefner actually got something right on this one? He got it right *and* horribly wrong. But let's start with what he got right. After quitting his job as a copywriter for *Esquire* magazine because he couldn't get a raise, he decided to start a magazine himself. So with $8,000 pulled together from investors, including his mom, he started a magazine for young bachelors. He wrestled with the title right up to the end, when his friend's mom suggested *Playboy* based on a startup car company she worked for.

It stuck and became the icon that it is today.

But why did the title stick? Of course, the photos helped, including the ones of Marilyn Monroe in the first issue, which were used without her permission. Was that it? Or did something else resonate about it?

If we simply pick apart the title and its connection to sex, we get pretty close to the answer. When the magazine launched in 1953, a lot of men had returned from the brutality of World War II to settle back into civilian and domestic life. Opportunity burgeoned before them. The 1950s erupted with economic and social growth.

But all this progress and affluence was a thin veneer over the massive trauma held in these men's hearts. And to those that had suffered and lost so much to the toll of war, what could be more compelling than the invitation to be a boy at play? *Playboy* magazine offered a promise of innocence. It was all manipulation, of course, but it struck a chord.

Somehow Hefner made a connection between sex and play. And he got it spot-on. Everything else he did was a horror story. He created an empire of misogyny that objectified women. Far from recovering anything innocent, it kept men immature, self-absorbed, and lustful. Everything he did made sex into something shallow and violating. There was nothing truly playful about his vision for sexuality. Yet he stumbled onto a glimpse of the original goodness of sex, only to abuse it for his own ends.

Sex, at its most basic level, is play. Play is its *essence*. It's not simply that sex can be playful. All sex was meant to be play. Even when it skews serious or mundane, it still follows the fundamentals of play and cannot diverge too far from it without becoming something else. Everything that goes wrong with sex goes wrong because it violates the nature of play.

We carry this knowledge in our language, even if we don't often notice it. There's a reason we call the buildup in sex "foreplay." It's the "beginning play" because it's only where the play starts, not where it ends. The whole experience of sex is play.

If romance is the adventure of love, then sex is love at play. It's not the only place our love plays. But it's a big one. My wife and I love to hike, discuss books, dream up adventures for our family. We play card games and have even done couples yoga. And we make love too.

Sex is play in the fullest sense. It mirrors everything we love about games of sport, though it's not played to score or win; the goal of sex is far more mutual, like a dance. We don't play as opposing teams, though the *separateness* and *otherness* of lovers is very important in fueling the desire that drives the play. But like all good athletics, sex requires focused physicality.

Sex is also play in the theater or stage sense. Sex always follows a script, a plot. Sex is never simply a bodily function like sneezing or breathing or getting thirsty. It's *storied* with meaning every single time. There is no such thing as storyless sex. Even if it's a bad story, sex is always a passion play. The story nature of sex is even wired into our bodies. Notice how our bodies' sexual arousal cycle (desire, excitement, plateau, orgasm, resolution) parallels exactly a story arc (inciting incident, rising action, climax, resolution).

Couples will sometimes complain about sex becoming too routine, following the same old script. Sex was made to thrive in romance, and it's vital that couples learn how to write a better sex story, one that increases connection and passion. Emily Nagoski calls this "adding more to the plot."[1]

Because sex is play, everything else we get is its fruit, not its essence. We may love the physical release, the euphoria, the deep pleasure of touch, or the cuddling, closeness, or connection. We may be trying to get pregnant. Maybe it's a way to blow off steam, get exercise, make up after a fight, or just have some fun. But I believe all of these are the *fruit* of sex and not the essence of the act itself.

Listen to Diane Ackerman's definition of play from her book *Deep Play* and see if you hear the play of sex within it:

> Deep play arises in such moments of intense enjoyment, focus, control, creativity, timelessness, confidence, volition, lack of self-awareness (hence transcendence), while doing things intrinsically worthwhile, rewarding for their own sake, following certain rules (they may include the rules of gravity and balance), on a limited playing field. Deep play requires one's full attention. It feels cleansing because, when acting and thinking become one, there is no room left for other thoughts. Life's usual choices and relationships are suspended. The past never happened and the future won't arise. One is suspended between tick and tock.[2]

Did you hear it? Intense enjoyment. Timelessness. Transcendence. Full attention. Feels cleansing. Acting and thinking become one. She is talking about play in general. But she could be talking about sex too.

Johan Huizinga wrote an entire book on play called *Homo Ludens* (which translates as "man who plays"), in which he studied how play shows up throughout life and forms whole cultures. Here is his working definition of play:

> Play is an activity which proceeds within certain limits of time and space, in a visible order, according to rules freely accepted, and outside the sphere of necessity or material utility. The play-mood is one of rapture and enthusiasm, and is sacred or festive in accordance with the occasion. A feeling of exaltation and tension accompanies the action, mirth and relaxation follow.[3]

Again, Huizinga is describing play in general. But he could very well be describing sex. Take that last sentence—can't you just picture lovers lying with bodies entwined in postcoital repose, smiling and giggling?

Genesis 26 records a really interesting story about Isaac and Rebekah. A famine plagued the land and forced Isaac and his family to find respite in the land of the Philistines. It wasn't the safest place or situation for them. But God promised protection. Isaac feared for his life anyway, thinking the men would kill him for one simple fact: his wife was beautiful and they would want her. So he cooked up a lie for the king of the land, Abimelech, by saying Rebekah was actually his sister. It was a coward's move. And, laughably, it was a lie he couldn't keep up anyway. One day the king looked out a window and saw the two of them doing *something* together—something that instantly let him know Isaac lied to him. In a rage he summoned Isaac and confronted him: "She is your wife!"

What did the king see them doing? Whatever it was left him with absolutely no question about Isaac's deception. It must have been sexually explicit; this was not a simple hug. The Hebrew word *metsakheq* used in Genesis 26:8 to describe what they did gets translated as *caressing* in the New International Version, and most other translations follow suit. But the actual Hebrew word means "to laugh or play." The Hebrew literally says Isaac and Rebekah were playing together. The King James Version even translates it as "sporting together" (which is a hilarious description). We can put it together, can't we? They were caught in the play of sex.

Why Our View of Sex Changes Everything

Thinking about sex as play may be a fun mental exercise, but why does it matter for your life or mine?

We so often reduce sex down to simple intercourse (vaginal penetration), which is largely male-pleasure centered. While over 90 percent of men orgasm through intercourse alone, only about 25 percent of women do.[4] To truly be a lover, then, we must expand our view of sex as more than intercourse, and foreplay as more than a forgettable afterthought.

I believe, too, that recovering the awareness of sex as play can help us recover the heart of sex and return it to its proper place in our lives. It can help us recover both the gravity and levity of it all. If we don't know the essence of sex, we will get it all wrong from there.

But resurrecting sex as play will be difficult.

We have a billion bad associations between sex and play, which brings us to everything Hugh Hefner and *Playboy* got wrong. His version of sex had very little to do with true play. It brought pornography into the homes of millions of Americans, causing secondary sexual harm to so many unassuming children. It made *playmates* into glossy images of women that got men off but required no actual pursuit—or play—from them. Hefner's entire empire focused on male gratification at the expense of women. He inhibited millions of men from developing into truehearted lovers who knew how to play well at sex.

And there are so many other bad connotations with the word "play." We talk about "getting played" when a person tricks or deceives someone romantically, leading them on in order to use them sexually. When someone has an affair, we rightly say they "cheated," language we use for those that violate the rules of a game. Often guys describe "scoring" with women. We call these men "players," those who make a habit of using people sexually or romantically. We talk of being "toyed with" to describe the moment amorous love is not playful, where someone is manipulating or treating too lightly a person's heart. And lest we forget that most awkward of such phrases, "playing with yourself." It brings immense shame and degradation to the act of masturbation by comparing it to a lonely game of one.

These are more than simple wordplays gone wrong. The realities behind them are deeply painful. The realm of evil has ruined sex as play for a very long time. So many have felt violated and harmed any time play mixes with sex. A broken heart. The mockery of being toyed with. The manipulation and glee of an abuser in the harm of sexual abuse. And the shame so many carry for their masturbation. Yes, evil has owned the language of play and sex.

The irony here is that evil cannot actually play. Evil always twists and breaks the rules to bring violation to sex. Think of evil's introduction in the story of Adam and Eve—as a serpent. Despite the protest of snake fans, those cold reptile eyes have come to symbolize a coldhearted creature intent on devouring its prey. (Research seems inconclusive whether snakes are actually capable of play at all. We certainly know they don't get playful like mammals.) What is absolutely clear is that evil intends only to manipulate, violate, devour.

To understand what evil has twisted, we need to get clear on the question: What actually is true play?

Defining Play

Right away you may say that calling sex an act of play reduces sex to something silly, trivializing its gravity and importance. You know, child's play. A hearty game of tag is fun but hardly sexy.

But this association with childhood games is actually a good one. It calls us to bring our innocent wonder and playfulness back to sex. I fear we feel the pressure to outgrow our playfulness as men, to replace play with more serious endeavors. And sure, we have adult versions of play: a fly-fishing trip or golf league or poker night with our buddies. But so often we see it as something fun to do to entertain ourselves when we're bored. It's something to pass the time, a way to check out, a distraction from the real hardship of life.

We hold play as frivolous. The thing we do after we accomplish the important stuff of life. Work hard, then play hard. But when there's always something that needs to get done, we hardly play. One reason we may have an obsession with sex is that we've lost our permission to play as men.

But even "trivial" games can have great power. One night on a camping trip while our boys were young our family played Frisbee for well over an hour in the fading light. It sounds so trivial, but it became a magical moment we all remember with delight. No one planned it. It just happened. And even now as I remember their faces I'm brought to tears.

Play can be light and, well, playful. But that doesn't make it meaningless.

Play Is Reverent

Play is way more expansive than simple games. So much in life can be play. Fishing. Cooking food. A church service. Woodworking. Playing a musical instrument. Writing poetry. Dancing. Sailing the ocean. Scaling a sheer granite wall thousands of feet up—all of that is play.

As we grow as men, life invites us to greater and more significant forms of play. Diane Ackerman calls this "deep play" because it arises from the depths of us, calls more of us out, invokes a greater risk, and offers a greater reward. Even while laboring in the pursuit of something as weighty as justice, a lawyer in a courtroom plays as he choreographs the evidence and witnesses on the stand. Play is involved in the way you draw out your child's heart in a conversation or pursue true connection with your wife. These are all serious and meaningful activities, yes, but play nonetheless.

This is not to kill off what Johan Huizinga called the "play spirit"—the playfulness and effervescence we love so much about play.[5] Here is the irony: play can be both serious and light. It can hold great meaning and yet stay fully playful. Indeed, it should. Play is not frivolous. It's deeply important to our well-being. C. S. Lewis says, "We must play. But our merriment must be of that kind (and it is, in fact, the merriest kind) which exists between people who have, from the outset, taken each other seriously—no flippancy, no superiority, no presumption."[6]

Catch that last line. Play is a reverent act, and all good play happens when we respect those we play with. That means no arrogance. No presumption of outcome. Professional athletes know this. That's why their entire lives revolve around physical and mental training. They would be fools to not take their competitors seriously. So, football players study video of the other team before their next game to learn strengths and weaknesses. Skiers and bikers ride courses in advance to learn every turn.

Sex as play is a reverent act. It cannot be flippant or born of arrogance. It respects and honors and reveres the other person. This is where a deep knowledge of your partner is so essential. You can hear this in the way the Hebrew writers of the Old Testament described sex as "knowing" each other. "And Adam *knew* Eve his wife; and she conceived" (Genesis 4:1 KJV). This implies an intimacy that is fuller than simply knowing what his wife looked like naked.

Sheila Wray Gregoire has pointed out that this same Hebrew verb "to know" is used by David in Psalm 139,[7] where he described God's knowing of him and exemplified what it means to really know someone:

What Is Sex?

You have searched me, LORD,
    and you know me.
You know when I sit and when I rise;
    you perceive my thoughts from afar.
You discern my going out and my lying down;
    you are familiar with all my ways.
Before a word is on my tongue
    you, LORD, know it completely.

—PSALM 139:1–4

Imagine this as poetry from one lover to another. You've pursued me. You know the terrain of my heart. You know what moves me, drives me. You know my funny quirks and deepest pains. You can even finish my sentences. And all of this knowing informs your love and passion for me.

This kind of deep knowing includes understanding each other's bodies—those places of greatest pleasure for the other and each other's scars and moles and mannerisms. We must study the terrain of each other's hearts *and* bodies.

The erotic love poetry of Song of Songs captures this so well, revealing a deep, patient mutual knowing of every part of the lovers' bodies:

Behold, you are beautiful, my love,
    behold, you are beautiful!
Your eyes are doves
    behind your veil.
Your hair is like a flock of goats
    leaping down the slopes of Gilead.
Your teeth are like a flock of shorn ewes
    that have come up from the washing,

all of which bear twins,
    and not one among them has lost its young.
Your lips are like a scarlet thread,
    and your mouth is lovely.
Your cheeks are like halves of a pomegranate
    behind your veil.
Your neck is like the tower of David,
    built in rows of stone;
on it hang a thousand shields,
    all of them shields of warriors.
Your two breasts are like two fawns,
    twins of a gazelle,
    that graze among the lilies.
Until the day breathes
    and the shadows flee,
I will go away to the mountain of myrrh
    and the hill of frankincense.
You are altogether beautiful, my love;
    there is no flaw in you.

—SONG OF SONGS 4:1–7 ESV

This is what it means to reverence your beloved. Compare that to what one college student had to say about his hookup experience:

The sex can feel like two people having two very distinct experiences. There's not much eye contact. Sometimes you don't even say anything. And it's weird to be so open with a stranger. It's like you're acting vulnerable, but not actually being vulnerable with someone you don't know and don't care very much about. It's not a problem for me. It's just—odd. Odd, and not even really fun.[8]

This is why hookups, affairs, and porn all cheat the *play* of sex. The true *knowing* that is essential to all good play is missing. The heart is not naked with the body. And therefore, there is no intimacy and very little meaningful play. It's frivolous and pointless and unfulfilling.

The play of sex compels us toward this deeper knowing so that we can pursue the greatest pleasure for the other. To know someone is to embrace the patient, slow process of pursuit. It's an endless endeavor of curiosity. This shouldn't be a surprise—as we talked about in the previous chapter, each of us contains a limitless mystery that will never be fully known by another. You can always learn more, study more, be curious about more within your spouse.

Play Is Freely Chosen

"Wanna play?" Thus begins most children's play. My youngest son asks me that question every day. And it highlights an essential aspect of all play: play must be freely chosen. Every person involved in play must have the freedom to choose to play or not. Everyone has to *want* to play. Here is Huizinga again: "First and foremost, then, all play is a voluntary activity. Play to order is no longer play: it could at best be but a forcible imitation."[9]

To say it another way: play requires *consent* to be true play. Without consent there is no play. It's essential to its nature. And consent is not simply *permission*; it's really an act of *invitation*. Asking another person, "Do you want to play?" requires humility, risk, and vulnerability on the part of the asker. And it's a question that honors not only someone's will but their desire too.

This is why consent is essential to sex; it makes it genuine play. We live in a wildly good day in which "yes means yes" is a culturally accepted rule for all things sexual, even if it's not always practiced. We've moved beyond "no means no," which made consent about permission, not invitation. Genuine consent asks us to care about the desires of our partner, not just find the limits of what they're willing to give in to.

This acceptance of consent is fairly new. Marital rape was not fully outlawed in the United States until 1993—though, again, this has not stopped its practice. As a therapist, I've borne witness to the horror stories of sexual coercion and assault in marriage. Some believe that saying "I do" in our vows is all the consent that anyone needs. This is ridiculous. Even children know that play stops and starts and must be invited each time to begin afresh.

Consent is really about desire. Each participant has to want to have sex for it to be true sex. No one should be forced into sex from obligation. Any type of coercion transforms it into something other than sex: namely, rape or sexual assault or abuse.

One partner may have more frequent desire for sex (on average desire is slightly higher in men[10]) while the other wants it less. Some have spontaneous desire that seems to arise out of nowhere, while others' desire is more responsive to the mood and context and tenor of the relationship (sexual desire is generally more context dependent for women due to a lower sexual concordance[11]). Nevertheless, it's our responsibility to ensure that our partner feels free to say no. However, if someone regularly feels no desire, we need to ask curious questions about why sex does not feel playful and fun.

Once both partners feel properly invited and full of desire, then let the play begin!

Play Requires a Playground

All play happens on a playground set apart for a certain time. In other words, it's contained. It doesn't go on everywhere all the time. All of life is not play.

This can be the strict fifteen-minute quarters of a football game or the flow of a tennis match that follows a certain structure not based on time. It can be a concert that carries on through several encores, but it doesn't go on forever. It flows with a beginning, middle, and end. Like a story played out before us.

Sex plays itself out to an end too. Rather than a specific timeframe, it follows a physiological progression through the arousal cycle, as I mentioned above. Researchers William H. Masters and Virginia E. Johnson discovered that men and women all travel through the phases of excitement, plateau, orgasm, and resolution. These are body phases, not simply emotions. And bodies cannot be forced. One person may orgasm in a minute, while another may take an hour or never travel all the way through. It is essential that partners both talk and read each other's bodies to know where the other is on this cycle. That is a big part of what makes you a good lover.

Interestingly, another researcher, Helen Kaplan, later criticized Masters' and Johnson's model for lacking one major component: it never mentions sexual desire.[12] It speaks only of the body-arousal response. Desire and arousal are not the same thing, as I said earlier. Desire was made to begin it all. Consent as invitation is essential to true sex.

But, like any form of play, sex doesn't go on forever. All of life is not sexual. Some people schedule it, others find that it must arise spontaneously. But ironically, as with all play, sex is also a time away from time. People talk about getting lost in the moment of play, experiencing a kind of timelessness. It's one of the greatest gifts of play: to transcend our sense of time and be lost in the moment. As Diane Ackerman says, "One is suspended between tick and tock."[13]

All play also happens in the magical realm called the playground. We aren't just talking about swing sets and slides. It's any consecrated space, secluded from normal life, set apart for play. That could be an auditorium, a soccer field, a courtroom, a chessboard, the keys of a piano, the pages of a book. It can even be sacred, hallowed ground, like a cathedral for worship.

Sex has its sacred domain too: the literal or proverbial bedroom. During weddings, the betrothed are often called to keep the marriage bed pure. It's a funny picture if understood literally as a promise to keep the playground of sex clean. But the phrase honors the sacredness of that space. Of course, sex doesn't have to happen in a bedroom. Lord knows, people have had sex in many, many unusual places, some honoring and some not. The lovers in Song of Songs sneak off to a lot of places, often outside. But still, "Come away with me!" is an invitation to seclusion. Sex is not a spectator sport. The naked vulnerability of its participants can only be honored if they are hidden away together.

Huizinga makes clear that this being set apart also creates a world away from the world.[14] Like a magical realm of sorts. Athletes talk about the feeling of being transformed when they step onto the playing field. The rest of life fades and only the game exists. The stage of a play, with props and sets, truly becomes another world, one where actors and actresses transfigure themselves to become the characters. They leave the humdrum of life backstage to shine their talents.

The bedroom becomes this place of magic too. There can be an ordinariness to the work of life together. Not that we lose moments for awe; indeed, there are many. But in that space away—a bedroom or a tent or the countryside—we transfigure, literally disrobe, and become embodied. Whereas before we may have been buried in the busyness of planning life, here and now we are lovers yet again.

How we set up this playground of love matters. We have friends who used to have sex in the back of their camper van on dates when their children were infants and toddlers because their small townhome felt so consumed with "baby world." They found a set-apart place that better helped transport them into the world of their romance.

If the space for play isn't set up right, it can rob the dignity of the moment. I can still recall the time in high school when my friends and I met up at a restaurant only to find that the people in the car next to us were having sex. It was 8 p.m. in a busy parking lot under fluorescent lights. We all howled with laughter as we threw pebbles at the window to try to get them to realize they were being watched. No luck. Nothing about that situation felt sacred.

All of this is to say that the stage matters, the playground matters. It sets the tone and creates a place where play can happen freely—whether it's the iconic rose petals on the bed or simply putting sex on the calendar.

Play Has Rules

You won't get very far into any game without learning one of the most important aspects of all play: the rules. Nothing can rouse an entire stadium of spectators to their feet more than a bad call from a referee. The rules really matter. Entire athletic careers have toppled when someone failed to follow the rules. Lance Armstrong could tell you about this. Tom Brady's "Deflategate" low-pressure footballs almost got him there. Nothing violates the essence of play more than someone cheating. No one tolerates people who play dirty. Nor should we. There is no glory to the game if someone manipulates the play to his advantage. So too with sex.

But rules and sex can admittedly get pretty tricky and messy.

Our culture holds only one absolute sexual rule: consent. It's a good one for sure. But then what? Author Abigail Favale says, "Consent should be the starting point rather than the end of the discussion about sexual morality. It's not enough to say that the best we can expect from sex, morally speaking, is that it's not rape."[15]

We've lost the rest of the rules.

Purity culture was the church's attempt at expressing a set of rules. It failed miserably, as discussed in the previous chapter. The rules largely shut down sexual desire and offered no meaningful sex education or sexual blessing. Recently, a client in the beginning of a dating relationship said, "Purity culture gave me so many rules that I'm lost. I don't know how to navigate." The rules drowned out his own intuition and killed the play of romance.

What if we just didn't have any rules around sex? Hookup culture comes the closest to rule-free sex in our day, although as I said earlier, it does have one very big rule: it must be meaningless. But that's not working out very well. One in three college students reports that their hookups were traumatic or difficult to handle.[16] What college campus isn't struggling with the collision of student alcohol abuse and under-reported sexual assault? It's rampant. No rules is no solution.

In play, the entire point of rules is to enhance the glory of the game and allow the greatest thriving of its players. We could hold each such rule against two questions: Does it protect and support the players? And does the game go better with such rules in place? Hookup culture offers a negative answer to both questions—and so does purity culture.

We understand that God made sex to be more than a simple bodily function. We aren't mere animals. Something far more sacred happens in the commingling of human persons. Paul even spoke of it as mysterious (Ephesians 5:32). And as such, the exclusivity of this sacred union is something God seems very interested in protecting. Fidelity gets highlighted a lot. Lust violates the boundaries of exclusivity and fidelity. So does adultery or fornication. But beyond this, the rules of sex have almost no overt playbook.

God's goal with every human, as expressed in the Bible, is that we would come to not need stated rules anymore. Rather, he wants the rules "written on our hearts" (Jeremiah 31:33). At one point in the New Testament, a religious leader came to Jesus and asked him for the most important command from God, to which Jesus answered, "Love God and love others. That's the summary of the whole rule book" (Matthew 22:36–37, my paraphrase). In other words, love is the rule. Everything must be done in love. Sex was made to be driven by love.

Rules may be helpful for a time. But "do this, don't do that" can get us only so far. God's hope is that you don't need to live by a strict set of external rules. For the best players, the rules become second nature. They become virtues or habits, like a jazz musician who just feels his way around the musical scales. God wants your heart to be driven by a love *instinct*, we could say—a love that's become second nature. "What is the most loving way to have sex?" should be the question we ask ourselves and our partner. The path of love may feel clear as mud at times, but that's where you must learn to walk it out with God.

Play also follows the basic laws of the universe. Music exists within the mathematics of sound waves, which can be bent only so far before descending into cacophony. Gymnasts may push the bounds of gravity but learn really fast they must submit to its rule.

Play is known in neuroscientific terms as a mixed state. It blends sympathetic activation with parasympathetic soothing—a rare combination. We feel vigilance and alertness but also comfort and safety. It's exciting and soothing all at the same time. It's safe enough that we don't topple into the overwhelming fear (i.e., fight or flight). But it also draws us to the edge of our vulnerability and risk, bidding us to step into the unknown of the moment, to let go and take a risk. Sounds familiar doesn't it—a lot like our definition of awe? "In the upper reaches of pleasure and on the boundary of fear."[17]

The play of sex dances in this mixed state of excitation and soothing, tension and relaxation—drawing us through our body's unique arousal structure, which is why we must always be attuned to the pleasure and discomfort thresholds of our partner. Again the goal of all rules is to ensure the safety of the players and the most glorious play.

All of this gives play a sense of intention. It's not chaotic or cacophonous. We should have a general sense of its flow and movement. In fact, it's this ordered flow and movement that gives play its aesthetic quality. Play is beautiful to experience. As Johan Huizinga says, "In play the beauty of the human body in motion reaches its zenith."[18] Oh, how true this is in sex. The primal capacity of the naked body in sex to arouse and reach pleasure is truly awesome.

Play Is Not Just a Means to an End

I have a friend who absolutely loves mountain biking. He feels a deep, compelling drive within him to ride and ride. He even says he *has* to bike for his well-being. "Ride or Die" stickers were created for this man. But we all know his life doesn't actually hang in the balance. He just really, really likes it. He needs food, water, air to breathe, and shelter. But no matter how gripping the desire, he doesn't *need* to ride his bike.

Even though there may be lots of things we get from play, play itself is not borne of necessity in the sense of bare survival. Even when we live to play, we don't play to live. Yes, play absolutely makes life more livable. But nothing kills true play more than making it an obligation, a necessity, something essential to life or death.

In the same way, as we said earlier, sex is not a need. It's a desire. No matter how deeply you want or pine for sex, you don't need it. People don't die without sex like they die without water.

There's a way of approaching sex, especially for men, that makes it seem like a need, a bodily urge that you must relieve. But this is just not true, as we discussed previously. There is no scientific basis for the idea that anyone needs sex. On a macrolevel, we as a species need to perpetuate our existence through "being fruitful." But within your body, it's not a biological need. Semen is recycled by the body just fine. Epididymal hypertension—colloquially called "blue balls," where blood builds up in the testicles and causes painful swelling—is a real thing. But even this is not deadly. It sucks but it won't kill you.

You may feel the growing tension of desire and arousal in your body, the synergy between your hormones and biology and heart. And research shows men's bodies respond (with increased testosterone) to women's ovulation cycles.[19] But again, while all of this is a complex journey with your body, it does not mean you need sex to live.

I met with a woman for counseling whose husband had convinced her that he needed sex, that all men needed sex. She believed him and did her best to honor his supposed need whenever he asked, which was nearly every day. Beyond his never considering her desire, there were times during sex when it was too painful and she asked to stop. He claimed he could not stop until he finished. When I told her this was all a lie and complete nonsense, she struggled to believe me. But this man was making it all up. A man can stop anytime he wants to stop.

We may seek sex for a lot of reasons: to find comfort or closeness, to experience a release or rush, to respond to our spouse's desire, to have kids, to get rid of a bodily urge, to manage our anxiety, to express our overflow of love for our spouse, to avoid something within, to connect with something within. A lot can lead us to want sex.

Nothing kills the play mood more than making it a means to an end. Psychologist and author David Schnarch says, "We don't realize that seeing sex as a 'drive' makes us focus on relieving sexual tensions rather than wanting our partner."[20] Whatever leads us to sex, we must always embrace the desire nature of it. We want it. We don't need it. We must create an environment of desire. That's the most inviting thing we can offer ourselves and our partner. Need demands. Desire invites.

Play Has an Objective

If soccer players sprint their hearts out to score goals, fly fishermen work those perfect casts to land beautiful trout, and musicians practice to master the music, what are we playing for in sex? Simply put, we play for the pleasure, the fun of it. And we do this not just for our own pleasure but for the pleasure of our spouse as well. This indeed is the essence of true lovemaking. As Dan Allender has said, "Love is the giving and receiving of pleasure to the glory of God."[21] Love pursues the greatest flourishing, the truest pleasure, for the other. And love receives this pursuit as well. And therefore we play for the intimacy and bond that mutual pleasure creates.

Some have argued that sex is first and foremost procreational. We were certainly called to be fruitful and multiply. I do believe all sex was meant to be generative and creative. But we call it "making love" to honor that its procreative quality extends beyond simply producing children. Philosopher Friedrich Schiller believed that all good play produces some form of beauty.[22] We see that in the glorious children born of sex. But again the beauty born of sex is more than children. If we follow the story arc of sex, the climax within the arousal script puts pleasure and love unavoidably at the apex. Of course, one could read too much into that. Children are a fruit of this joy, too, but they are not the sole point of sex.

When my wife and I endured the agony of multiple miscarriages, we felt absorbed in a hyper focus on trying to get pregnant. All that pressure and fear made sex difficult. I felt like a stud horse that had to deliver on command to catch that magic ovulation window. It robbed sex of its normal pleasure, of connecting and playing and enjoying one another.

Of course, the greater joy of parenting invited us back to each other. But when pleasure and intimacy weren't first and foremost, we struggled.

This is written into our anatomy. I said before that our genitalia are wired with eight to ten thousand nerve endings in the glans penis and glans clitoris. This is lavishly unnecessary—unless God really cares about our pleasure. By the way, the clitoris as an organ has no other function except pure pleasure. And this does not account for the topography of all the other sensually alive skin on our bodies. Your body is made to give you a hormone dump of pleasure at the simplest of touches. All of this screams God's intent for pleasure to be a major aim of sex. You were literally made for pleasure.

This mutual giving and receiving of pleasure is in crisis. Researchers have discovered something they call the "orgasm gap" to describe the significant pleasure inequality between men and women in the way some couples have sex. In a survey conducted by Sheila Wray Gregoire, Rebecca Gregoire Lindenbach, and Joanna Sawatsky, 95 percent of Christian men reported experiencing an orgasm always or almost always during sex compared to only 48 percent of women.[23] That 47 percent difference is a big problem. Lisa Wade reported similar findings for the population at large.[24] If a man is the only one getting pleasure out of sex, that makes for bad sex. It is not truly making love unless the pleasure is received *and* given.

"The orgasm gap is not a biological fact; it's a social one," says Lisa Wade.[25] In other words, it's not that women can't orgasm as often. It's just that how certain couples are having sex does not prioritize *mutual* pleasure, in this case the pleasure of the woman. Yes, men may orgasm more quickly on average, but when we learn our partner, stay patient with her, value her pleasure, and ask what pleases her, this orgasm gap tends to disappear. To be a good lover is to care about and prioritize your wife's pleasure. That's how we make love.

What does it mean to do this to the glory of God? Good sex doesn't need some special consecration or a sprinkling of holy water to bring God glory. Sex played well is a thing of beauty in itself. Recall again Johan Huizinga's observation: "In play, the beauty of the human body in motion reaches its zenith." Sex in its playful essence radiates the beauty of the human body and therefore the glory of God. Sex is beautiful in itself.

Of course, God's glory requires we honor his design, from the biological realities of our bodies to the marriage context he's established. But just following the rules does not automatically make sex honoring. The heart is required too.

Somewhere inside we must say, "Thank you!" The physical pleasure must reverberate through the whole person to stir our spirits to worship. Dacher Keltner in his research has discovered that humans actually sync up when they experience mutual awe together. Literally, cortisol levels match and heart rates begin to beat in unison.[26] It happens for crowds at sporting events, backpackers on trips, or churchgoers in worship. Anytime people move in unison to the rhythms of awe, they experience what he calls "collective effervescence." I love that term. It's the union of mutual pleasure and transcendence. And not surprisingly, it also happens when long-term lovers unite in sex.[27] Sex is collective effervescence.

Play Creates Lasting Bonds

Johan Huizinga put beautiful words to the bonding nature of all play.

A play community generally tends to become permanent even after the game is over. . . . The feeling of being "apart together" in an exceptional situation, of sharing something important, of mutually withdrawing from the rest of the world and rejecting the usual norms, retains its magic beyond the duration of the individual game.[28]

Biologists believe that all mammals play in part for precisely this reason: it creates social connection and attachment. This may be the most obvious element of play present in sex. We know the deep bond sex creates between lovers. As Emily Nagoski puts it, fundamentally, "sex is an attachment behavior."[29] And it's true that during sex the hormone oxytocin gets released in enormous quantities. It's called the cuddle hormone, and it's the same one released in mothers and infants during breastfeeding.

Research seems to indicate the closer the emotional connection to your partner, the greater the amount of oxytocin released and the better the orgasm.[30] Sex is not the only thing that bonds us. Attachment involves care and connection in myriad ways throughout life together. But sex is a place our attachment truly plays. Nagoski says, "In the best romances, the sex advances the plot, carrying the hero and heroine, against all odds and in the face of many obstacles, through one of the behavioral markers of attachment."[31]

Can you see why an anonymous hookup or pornography confuse the body and heart? There is no lasting bond to keep.

What Sex Asks of You

To be a true player of sex is to become a lover. We must learn the ways of lovemaking and practice love so it becomes second nature, like a dancer's cha-cha on the dance floor or Roger Federer's forehand tennis swing. We need to learn the ways of love like a Jedi learning the Force.

Sex as an icon, as an artistic witness of the heart of God in the world, invites us all to make a true passion play of our love—love in *all* its expressions, not just sexual love. All of love must be play. It cannot be only duty and tasks and hard work. I think that's one reason God put Song of Songs in the Bible. It should stir us all to be more passionate in every expression of love.

Risk

First and foremost, lovers risk. As a therapist, I'm given a front-row seat to the lives of couples, including the inner workings and struggles of their sex lives. It's always amazing to me to hear how scary it can be to risk desire, especially sexual desire, even in a long-term marriage relationship. Some couples simply stop risking at all and become sexless. Desire is a risk. Always. Some may not feel this risk strongly, but others know it deeply.

I wonder if this is why some couples have code words or gestures to initiate sex. "Do you want to go . . . you know . . . snuggle?" or "Can we . . . spend some time together tonight?" One man simply puts on sweatpants and his wife knows that this is her cue. Make of that what you will. This can be fun and playful or necessary with little children around. But it highlights that asking is always vulnerable—as it should be. I admire the lovers in Song of Songs for this reason. "Come away with me, my love!" It's a full-hearted and forward invitation.

Will you humble yourself to the invitation of desire and not manipulate sex by making it an obligation, a need, a duty for your partner? Consent must be invitation, an expression of desire and not just permission. Amid jobs and children and school and sports and the stuff of life, no one is handing me and my wife time for romance. To keep sex from becoming a chore, we have to labor to cultivate the adventure of our love and our sex life. But fighting for it has been rewarding and meaningful to us both, asking us to risk desire with each other and bringing new passion between us.

To risk is to be fully present, to be vulnerable. As Brené Brown has said so well, "Vulnerability is our most accurate measure of courage."[32] Vulnerability is being open to the moment without a sense of control or demand but also without withdrawing, to let it unfold and keep your heart open to it. Mike Mason notes, "If the heart is not naked with the body, the whole action becomes a lie and a mockery."[33]

There are ways of having sex that reward you with very little. Hookups, often fueled by liquid courage, ask very little of you—and reward you with little. Pornography is the same: there's no risk and no real play. We've domesticated our play and lost its deepest expression. The best play puts something on the line.

As quoted earlier in this chapter, I think Johan Huizinga said it best when he said, "The play-mood is one of rapture and enthusiasm." His word "rapture" means to be "seized" or "carried away." "Rapture" is derived from the same Latin root as our word "raptor," as in birds of prey. The word has a sense of being willing to be overpowered by the moment and responsive to your partner's presence. Dan Allender has said the degree to which you risk is the degree to which you will experience rapture.[34] If there is not risk, our play and our sex become more an act of distraction than a true moment of engagement.

Be Humble

In this sense, lovers come at the play of sex with humility. This is not a world to conquer. It's a place to be undone. You must always be open to learning and finding your way. As I stated before, those among us with the most humility experience the most awe. And those who open themselves to awe in turn grow more humble.

A humble lover comes to serve, to learn, to listen, to receive, to hold his desire in tension with the greater moment. Hear these words from Paul: "Do nothing out of selfish ambition or vain conceit. Rather, in humility value others above yourselves, not looking to your own interests but each of you to the interests of the others" (Philippians 2:3–4). Reading this in the context of sex, our exclusive pleasure is never the most important thing.

If you focus solely on your own pleasure, you will miss out on all the nourishing beauty of the moment. Having said this, it's also true that humility is not humiliation. We do not engage in sex to abase ourselves or disown our desire. Mutual pleasure requires holding both lovers' desires in tension.

Be Innocent

Lovers bring their innocence. We end where we begin. Jesus said that the very basis of our life in the kingdom of God is this childlike posture (Mark 10:15). That could mean so much, I know. But children know how to play with exuberance, joy, rapture, and enthusiasm. They know how to bring their innocence to play.

You haven't lost that innocence, not entirely. This may be the hardest part of the play of sex, though: to have innocent sincerity. Lately God has given back to me the ability to laugh after sex. It feels very vulnerable in the moment with my wife to be brought to laughter after orgasm. But it's a place in which I am rediscovering my innocence.

Tension to Resolution

I love how Johan Huizinga ends his description of play: "A feeling of exaltation and tension accompanies the action, mirth and relaxation follow."[35] Tension to resolution. There is not much in life that gets resolved. So many plots seem to languish in perpetual, unresolved tension. *Will our kids turn out well? Will that person ever change? Will everything be okay?* We are always coping with ongoing tension. Life will always hold tension until the day Jesus brings his kingdom to earth. But the play of sex and the bodily resolution of orgasm can be one place where we let our bodies experience tension that leads to resolution.

There's an archaic French phrase for orgasm, *la petite mort*, which means a mini death.[36] This phrase describes the momentary near lapse of consciousness in an orgasm, an almost death-to-life journey. What a wild place to find a picture of death and resurrection. Could sex be a place we practice resurrection, to borrow a phrase from Eugene Peterson?[37] Meaning, can the pursuit of healthy sexuality actually be a foretaste of what's to come when Jesus brings his kingdom to earth? Can orgasms actually help grow us spiritually to anticipate this day? Can true pleasure do this?

I believe wholeheartedly that the answer is yes. All true play changes us. All true sex changes us too. Recovering the playfulness of our sexuality plunders back from the realm of evil the true nature of sex, letting us rediscover that sex is love at play, a place where our playful innocence can show up—a place where our pleasure brings glory to God and transforms us into something more than we used to be. A place we meet God.

But here and now, evil is not so easily outsmarted. If the play of sex can be *this* powerful for good, evil knows it must go after our childlike innocence as early as possible.

FOUR

Your Real Sex Education

From the beginning it has been God's purpose for
this world to be one of emerging goodness, beauty,
and joy. Evil has wielded shame as a primary
weapon to see to it that that world never happens.
—CURT THOMPSON

D o you remember your sex education?

Mine came in fourth grade. One fall day after lunch, our teachers split the boys and girls into separate classrooms. Thank the Lord we had a male teacher, Mr. B, to lead us boys into the forbidden world of sex. To hear one of the women teachers, who felt like grandmothers, talking about penises and vaginas would have turned our faces a billion shades of red. Mr. B put us at ease. He was a really funny man who animated his eyebrows to rouse laughter between riffs of endless dry humor. I felt that we would be okay.

We filed into the room full of giggles and raced each other toward the desks farthest from the front of the room. I didn't have the greatest success and ended up in the middle somewhere. The TV sat on a cart in the front, a portal from which we could never again return. The secret knowledge would forever be ours. Mr. B furrowed his usually playful eyebrows and scowled his face. "Boys, boys, you need to knock it off." My chest tightened. *What was this stern tone?* He tried to discipline the nervous laughter out of us. But the best we could manage was to hide our faces in our arms crossed on our desks.

He dimmed the lights and our education began. It felt forbidden to talk so openly about boys' and girls' anatomy, let alone how these biological puzzle pieces fit together. At one point I literally went and sharpened my pencil just to have a minute to catch my breath. I'm serious. I sharpened my pencil, which I was not using at all. I just needed a chance to look away and let my insides catch up with everything I was hearing.

And two videos later, it was all over. Mr. B returned to the front of the room. "Any questions?" he asked. As if anyone had any ability to talk. Nor had his eyebrows returned to their usual playfulness. And then we were dismissed. I guess I was *edu-ma-cated* about the birds and the bees.

But really it all started on the playground a few days before.

A permission slip had gone home to parents about these videos a week prior, and someone in my grade caught wind of what was coming and leaked it to the rest of us. We were getting the private parts talk. Well, that set it off. For a whole week, conversation between boys and girls shut down. Okay, maybe a few of us whispered in corners on the playground; the hushed tones and giggles always gave it away.

One day, near the tire swing with no girls around, my friend Adam asked, "Do you know what sex is?" I dropped my head and confessed I didn't know. This seemed to be exactly what he hoped to hear. Seizing the opportunity, he announced with pride in his voice, "Well, I already know. Want me to tell you?" A change at a foretaste of this secret knowledge seemed irresistible to me. "Sure," I said. Sex, he informed me, begins when a man and woman wrestle naked together. At some point the woman scares the man. And he gets so startled, he starts to pee. The woman quickly catches his pee in her private area. "And that," he said with gusto, "is how babies are made."

I stood blank faced, my mind looping the vivid scene he'd just narrated. Could *this* be true? *This* is sex? My heart dropped; my belly churned. It fascinated me and yet it all seemed so gymnastically impossible. How could that work every time? Wouldn't the guy catch on and not get scared anymore? And isn't the whole pee thing a little gross? Now decades later, I wonder where Adam got his information. It sure sounds like a child's interpretation of porn. But in that moment as a boy, I was thinking only of my own shock.

That day after school, I must have told my mom, but I don't remember much of that conversation. I do remember a few days later while at her friend's house, she called me in from playing to the kitchen where they sat and prompted me, "Tell Miss Joan what you learned on the playground." It confused me but I complied. I told them what my friend had told me about sex. And they burst into laughter.

I get it now, just how funny this description is. Even then, I wanted so badly to laugh with them. But I didn't get the punch line. Instead, I burst into tears and tried to run out of the room. My mother, realizing her mistake, hugged and comforted me. But it did little to take away the confusion and hurt. I now know enough of my mother's story to recognize the great fear that probably lay behind her laughter. But in the moment, I knew nothing.

My first lesson on sex ended where I believe evil hopes all our stories of sexuality end: in shame.

Your Sexuality Is Storied

Our sexuality does not come to us neatly packaged in a box with a label and instructions. Nor does it stay in the controlled confines of a classroom or the safe space of a sex talk. It is never simply a bunch of information we learn and tuck away in the recesses of our brain for future reference, like how to change a car tire.

Sexuality comes to us all as a mysterious force that one day just shows up, a surprise character in the story. We were just going about our little lives when suddenly, there it was. Maybe someone introduced it to us, or we felt it stirring in our bodies. Either way, it found its way into the plots of our lives without preamble. One moment we don't know and the next we do. And not just once but again and again it finds its way into our world and our bodies. Our sexuality is awakened and roused from its slumbering presence within us.

Sex education is always an embodied experience.

Your sex education is far more than the moments you learned (or didn't learn) about the birds and the bees. It's *all* the ways sexuality began to make its presence known in the plot of your life in all its innocent, awkward, embarrassing, beautiful, funny, weird moments. And, sadly, in all the shameful, abusive, or violating ways too. Your sex education is your collection of all these stories.

More than simply an orientation, your sexuality is *storied*. And those stories formed you and became your real education. They also became the template for your arousal, the scripts of the sexual play you live out. Remember, all sex follows a story arc. And here is where it gets written.

Do you know those stories? They can be anything from the beautiful to the seemingly mundane to the terrible. They could include the euphoria of first falling in love or the innocent discovery of your own genitalia. Maybe it was a short conversation on the playground, like me, or the laughter of a family member. And yes, it might be the horror of sexual abuse or the broken heart of a romantic betrayal.

All these stories are your sex education. Or better said, they are your sexual *formation*.

More than simply giving you data, these stories set a mood and formed your imagination for sex. They gave your body and being a felt sense of what sex is about.

Maybe more than any other topic, learning and talking about sexuality takes us into our bodies. Maybe we can talk about rock strata or the migration patterns of Canadian geese without much emotional presence in our bodies. But sexuality is not learned abstractly. It's never simply taught. It's imagined, felt, experienced. We aren't simply *informed* but are rather *formed* in our imagination, our relationship to our bodies, and our view of others. A mood is set.

Sexual formation happened for me with Mr. B's serious face and on the playground and in the kitchen at my mother's friend's house. And when my seventh-grade crush turned the corner of the junior high hallway while I stood by my locker, I met my sexuality in a new way there, too, as a force awakened within. I knew puberty was coming thanks to those videos in fourth grade and hearing my older brother's voice drop, watching his body grow big, and seeing him shave. But no one prepared me for what sexuality would feel like in my body. When my crush walked by, my heart beat fast and the very center of my chest felt floaty like I had just inhaled a whole balloon of helium. My voice probably cracked like I'd inhaled helium, too, when I mustered the courage to say hi to her.

Another chapter in my storied sex education was written when my friends and I were buying fireworks at the local convenience store in eighth grade when I noticed the pornography magazines on the back wall. Curious, I pulled one down. Nothing could have prepared me for the feelings that washed over my body in beholding a naked woman for the first time.

We have a strange sense that sexuality exists completely hardwired in our DNA and therefore beyond the impact of storied experience. We act as if it clicks on at puberty and sort of runs itself as a predetermined bodily function. We treat it like pure instinct. No one taught us to sneeze or how to breathe. We think sex is something like that. It just works, and reveals itself to us fully formed. We think it functions beyond the veil of experience, that what we do or what we learn or what happens to us doesn't affect our sexual desire.

Yet studies have concluded that early childhood trauma, like sexual abuse or even physical abuse, can invoke an earlier onset of puberty.[1] That is staggering to me and clear evidence that our stories show up in our sexuality. Like being roused from hibernation too early in the bitter cold of winter, our trauma can awaken our sexuality before its time. Our sexuality lives our story right along with us.

The Haunting of Shame

We all know that our stories are not simply beautiful plots of innocence with our sexuality unfolding alive and well. We all experience things that feel confusing or downright haunting in their memory. How do we start to unpack *these* stories? We must honor the reality that sexuality in all its beautiful, innocent goodness is not the only mysterious presence that shows up in these stories. There are many characters. We are somewhere in the plot. Our sexuality is there. And other people are there too. But one mysterious presence haunts it all.

Adam and Eve met this presence, arriving unbidden in their midst.

You'll remember that Adam's "sex talk" was not all talk. Genesis 2 describes how God walked Adam through the animal kingdom where each had a partner of its own kind, almost as if he was trying to give Adam hints and provoke his loneliness for companionship. After a night of fever dreams, Adam awakened to God, who was ready to introduce him to someone unlike any other creature he'd yet encountered. Man met woman. And man broke into poetic verse.

Here, as the light faded on the two new lovers, the narrator notes, "*This* is the reason that a man leaves his father and mother and embraces his wife" (Genesis 2:24 CEB). What reason? In a scene of immense relief, Adam's loneliness dissipates in the overflowing joy of meeting his person, his flesh and blood, his partner. He has found belonging. And so has Eve. The scene drips with erotic energy as they behold each other's naked glory. It's the stuff of romance—connection and deep relationship, companionship, and the beauty of sexual play. And it's exploding in Eden for the very first time.

The curtains close as the writer says, "Adam and his wife were both naked, and they felt no shame" (Genesis 2:25). What pure, unadulterated goodness! Sexuality as it was truly meant to be. Body and heart joined together so completely that nothing stood between their intimacy. No baggage, no insecurities, no body struggles, no trauma or wounds. We are witnessing a world where everything was as it should be.

In our English translations, the chapter ends here. But remember, the original text did not have chapter divisions. I appreciate how chapters and verses help us navigate Scripture—but you've got to be careful. Those artificial breaks can give us such a false sense of separation. Sure, we may need a breath after that last scene, a psalmist's *selah*. But the original writer did not give us one. He did not want us to close our eyes for a second. He wanted us alert to what came next. Here's how it reads without the chapter break: "Adam and his wife were both naked, and they felt no shame. Now the serpent was more crafty than any of the wild animals the LORD God had made" (Genesis 2:25–3:1).

In an instant another presence made itself known in the story. In the very first sexual moment, with devastating swiftness, evil came to haunt the naked innocence of Eden. What a heartbreaking head spin! I want to scream, "*No!*" at my Bible, "Not now, not this scene!"

What follows does not at first seem like an act of war. The serpent just asked a question. This is no big siege tower; but oh the hidden knife of it. The serpent directed his question at Eve, though Adam seemed to be right there with them. The serpent's question was intended to sow doubt about God's heart. And when that door was opened, the serpent accused God of withholding something good from Adam and Eve. The serpent set them up to believe they could be like God, "knowing good and evil."

The deep irony here is that Adam and Eve were already made "like God." It's repeated three times in Genesis 1:26–27 to make it loud and clear. Evil offered them the very thing they already had. And they already knew good, since creation itself was called "good" repeatedly by God. The good was their playground. The only real offer in the serpent's words was to know evil, to no longer be naïve, as it seems. He tempted them with so-called freedom from their innocence.

And they took the deal. They ate the fruit. They got the new eyes, and for the first time innocence was lost. They surrendered their freedom and aliveness in exchange for the burden of knowing evil and betraying the God of life. Sin entered the world and its first fruit was *fear*. It was not a fear of something outside themselves, like a bear or a flash flood. No, it was a fear of their own skin, their own naked bodies, and each other. They suddenly felt so exposed. The moment they heard God walking in the garden, they ran and hid.

That fear is called shame. Yes, shame is a form of fear. Research shows that shame releases stress hormones in the body, signaling a threat like any other danger. Emily Nagoski writes, "Your body reacts to negative self-evaluations as if you're under attack."[2] Except in this case, *we* are the lion we fear. And the fight-or-flight instinct kicks in, which is exactly why Adam and Eve ran to hide.

Evil reveled in its victory. There is more to the story, of course. God did not leave them hidden in the bushes, frozen in shame. But for the moment, we watch as the ripples of sin and shame undo the pure, arousing goodness of the world.

Adam and Eve's story of sexuality very quickly descended into a place we are all familiar with: shame.

Evil's Goal for Your Sexuality

And on and on it goes. Evil's greatest hope, to this day, is for *all* our stories of sexuality to end in shame. Remember, I said that sexuality always lives in a story. Evil wants to write the scripts of your arousal. The realm of darkness wants your sexuality to be tethered and bound to fear and shame so that you don't have any knowledge of sexuality without shame or any experience of arousal without fear.

Yes, I believe in an actual realm of evil spirits, fallen angels who seek to bring harm to the glory of God and his people. I find it hard to explain away the worst of our world and the harm in people's stories any other way. Mental health or accidents or simple conditioning don't capture the haunting horror and trauma present in the evils of, say, sexual abuse.

Let's make this very clear: evil hates your sexuality. Evil does not want you to be free and sexually alive. Why? Because first of all, sexuality is the creation of God. It stands as a witness to his heart for his creatures to experience pleasure and joy, desire and intimacy, union and ecstasy and romance. *That's* our God. The one who invented the wild pleasure of sex. Evil is hell-bent on warping and twisting the goodness and beauty of God's great design for human sexuality.

Why is evil so focused on ruining sexuality of all things? Because your sexuality is directly connected to the lover within you, that part of you most susceptible to being moved and undone by God's goodness, the beautiful world he created, his glory in another human, and the joy of sexual play too. Evil knows that our identity as lovers is what enables us to become worshipers. If your heart and body are aroused, you will be moved to want to thank someone. Again, in Eugene Peterson's words, "Gratitude is our spontaneous response to all this: to life. Something wells up within us: Thank you!"[3] Our hearts will want to find the one to thank: God himself. We will want to find the one that every sunset hints at, to find the artist behind the art, to know the God who made orgasms and ripe peaches and first kisses and the sound of summer nights. We will want the very source of it all.

Evil does not want you aroused by the world, because once you're aroused, you'll go looking for the one whom you can thank. You will want God. And that is the very thing evil wants to keep you from. Because sexuality is so powerful and universal, it's an easy target to undermine our identity and our chance at communion with God. It's a place where fear and shame can all too easily replace awe and worship. If you live in fear and shame, you will shut down and hide your sexual self, your lover. You will stop being moved. You will stop looking for and worshiping God.

When shame and fear attack the lover within each of us, we become numb, unable to love anyone well, blind to the beautiful, the true, and the good. We become disconnected and unwilling to risk for the sake of meaningful relationships. You might still be functioning biologically, but you're not really *living*.

The war against your lover heart has been raging since Eden. Yes, we *all* fell from glory in Adam. Yes, all of us are born with a fallen heart. But *total* depravity is not *utter* depravity. You are not entirely abandoned to sin. God's original blessing remains on you, and yes, on your sexuality. But evil never stops trying to tighten the bonds of shame and fear, hoping to drag you into perpetual and final defeat.

Let's try a little exercise. Take those lines from the biblical text and put your name in it. "Sam was naked and without shame. Now the serpent was crafty. . . ." That's your story of sexuality and mine. Maybe you've never envisioned your sexuality this way, but true freedom must start here, with recognition of the source of our brokenness.

Can you begin to see where shame was woven into your story?

The story of your loss of innocence might start with a massive moment of obvious harm, or you might need to trace it back to nearly forgettable, mundane events. It's not about the intensity of the facts on paper. It's about the experience you felt in your body and the meaning that experience made for your heart.

Nick leaned forward from the backseat of the pickup truck. He was not going to miss a single word of the conversation between his father and his uncle, Phil. It was summer and Nick had been invited along on his first fly-fishing trip with them—an absolute rite of passage. It would be just him, his father, and his uncle for a week.

This was the stuff of a fourteen-year-old boy's dreams. His heart burned with the joy of getting a pickup truck seat in the world of men. And his heart soaked in every bit of blessing. He hoped this might be the trip he was finally trusted with a fly rod as a full-fledged man.

Earlier that day, Nick had helped his father load the fishing raft on the trailer and fill the truck with all the gear. Now, as they drove, his dad and uncle traded stories of life and boyhood. There was the time they raced down the big hill on bikes, pretending to be fighter jets in formation. Except Phil missed the turn at the bottom of the hill where the road split and crashed headfirst into a tree. They talked of life as men. Phil shared the latest stresses in his job as a commercial contractor. This ritual of men talking warmed Nick's heart.

They stopped for gas often. Such was the way with a truck that drank gas like cheap beer on a hot day. As they all piled out at one stop, Phil walked to get more road snacks. Nick's dad turned to Nick and called out, "Fill 'er up!" Nick felt the gesture of blessing. He unscrewed the gas cap, pulled the pump handle out, and on his way to inserting it managed to spray gas all down the side of the truck.

His father huffed in anger as he grabbed the handle from Nick. He jammed it in and said, "You're nothing but a wet dream!"

The words landed like a fist punch square in Nick's chest. His dad just dismissed his masculinity, his entire presence, as the messy disappointment of a nocturnal emission. And it left him feeling every bit of the sexual violation. He felt castrated. His heart shut down for the rest of the trip, and his father never noticed.

In the very place where Nick's heart hungered for a rite of passage as he came of age, he got a gut full of shame. By way of his father, evil landed an arrow.

The Dark Magic of Shame

Here's the deal: you think it's just you. You think it's just that you're messed up or broken or sinful. You think you did something to bring on all this shame. That you are just a horrible monster and deserve it. You think something is fundamentally wrong with your sexuality. That you are deviant or a pervert or a monster. And that everything in your story happened because of you. You may hear these very whispers. That's the wild spell of shame.

So what is this dark magic called shame?

From my front-row seat as a therapist, I've heard it described a lot of ways. Most say they just feel bad or awful or guilty. Others say they feel gross or disgusted with themselves. They often get sick to their stomachs. Shame can feel like being dirty or slimed, like your insides are covered in black tar you can't wash off. Shame can look like depression in some people. Others feel it as an anxiety attack that ripples through their being, screaming, *What did I just do?*

As we said, shame at its heart is a form of fear. This is certainly how Adam and Eve experienced it. The instant they knew shame, they felt terrified. And again, it's not so much the fear of an outside threat, but more that something inside us is dangerous. We begin to fear our own vulnerability. Brené Brown describes shame as a "vulnerability hangover."[4] And yes, sometimes the fear stays as a kind of nausea. Other times it is full-fledged panic.

I think Dan Allender put it best when he described shame as the fear of exposure.[5] In this sense, it's really a fear of eyes.[6] In shame, we become terrified of being seen, that people will discover something awful or hideous about us. We feel caught not so much in our guilt but, far worse, in our vulnerability, gripped with our greatest fear: that we are deserving of rejection. We fear our nakedness, literally or figuratively. We feel weak, inadequate, foolish, or even outright evil.

What is the universal sign of shame? You'll know it as soon as I say it, because you intuitively notice it all the time. Dropping the eyes. Looking down or away. Doing anything to avoid eye contact with another person. My CrossFit coach even said it to our class the other day. We all had our heads down looking at the floor while we lifted some heavy weights, and he belted out, "Heads up! We are proud of ourselves, people. Not ashamed of ourselves." He knew the sign.

I had one of those dreams once—the "being naked in front of people" dream. This was back when I worked at a megachurch. I dreamed that I was at the staff Christmas party. Everybody mingled in the church foyer, sipping hot drinks, snug in their sweaters as a jazz band played in the corner. And I was standing stark naked right in the middle of everyone. The dream literally started this way, in pure panic.

I crawled and hid behind any meager plant or oblivious person or edge of a tablecloth I could find, trying to make it to a door that was open. But they were all locked. I woke up in a sweat, still shaking an imaginary door handle, desperate to escape and hide. The feeling still grips my body as I write.

That dream held so much meaning for me at the time. I got hired on as a young twentysomething with no real experience in ministry. I was handed a list of tasks and ministries to oversee and told to get to work. I often shut my office door, just to keep people from noticing I actually worked there. I daily feared that someone would barge in and say, "How did *you* get hired?" and escort me out the door. This was a shame dream. My nakedness represented the deep exposure I felt in that new role. Being caught naked may be the universal experience of shame. We even say, "I felt so naked" regarding such experiences. It captures the fear that the worst of us is on display for everyone to see.

No one can stay in shame very long. It's too deadly. It feels like living death. No wonder people who feel ashamed say things like, "I was mortified" (which literally means "put to death") or "I felt so embarrassed I just wanted to die." The threat of utter rejection feels like we're facing certain annihilation. And so, like Adam and Eve, we run and hide. It's our way of escaping the penetrating feeling of having eyes on us. We need to get away from those eyes.

Oh, we hide a billion different ways. Most often it's simply to shut down the part of us that we think got us in trouble. After that day in the kitchen in the wake of my mother's laughter, I buried my sexual curiosity so deep. I stopped asking questions. Something about my sexuality felt wrong or broken, and I didn't want anyone to see it.

Shame can trigger immense self-hatred. Cussing ourselves out, calling ourselves names. The self-hatred can even tempt toward self-harm as retaliation against the self. I know many clients who, in the thick of recalling past sexual harm, have punched themselves in the face or whipped themselves or done angry workouts as payback to the parts they think are weak within them. Indeed, some people despair of life and want to die.

But most often we simply bury our sexuality or disown it and abandon it to roam the wilds of our being. That's when the lover within retreats to the shadow self. As we have said, sexuality is not simply the act of having sex. It's the lover heart within you. It's the innocent awe you bring to the whole world. And shame is the lover's mortal enemy.

The Lover's Buried Story

When I say that a story ends in shame, what I mean is that right in the midst of a story where our curiosity or arousal or lover self is present and alive, something in the story turns bad and shame immediately shows up. Psychologist Curt Thompson puts it this way: "It often occurs when we are moving in a direction of creative exploration, minding our own business, when an unexpected force of nature enters and brutally throws us off course."[7]

Creative exploration is a beautiful picture of the posture God designed us to have with his good world. We were made for this posture in the realm of our sexuality too. This is the heart of the lover at play.

Shame traumatizes our curiosity. A truism of neuroscience is that "what fires together wires together." When we experience two things at the same time, our brains make neural connections between the experiences. This can be positive, like the way I associate the smell of smoke coming from my neighbor's house with the taste of his delicious smoked ribs. It can also be a negative association, like the pain of sunburn I associate with the beach. And the brain works to remember positive associations and bury the bad ones as deep as possible.

So literally, these stories of your lover in his "creative exploration" of the world get wired to shame in your brain. And that negative experience tells your brain to bury these stories deep down. Our brains work to bury our shame in silence and secrets. We suppress it. We think that if we don't acknowledge it or talk about it, we won't have to feel it. But that's not how this works. It's not that we don't still feel shame. We absolutely do, despite our best efforts to avoid it.

Let me say with full confidence that you have sexual shame. It's not just you. Really. It's not just you.

Oh, how evil hates your sexuality. Evil wants you to do more than just sin with your sexuality. It wants you to disown it or hide it or bury it in shame. If it can accomplish this, evil will seem to have won.

Evil knows God wants lovers most of all. Not robots, not duty-bound children, but deep-hearted, fully alive lovers of God and his world. Your lover was meant to be the very center of your being.

Life without your lover heart is a miserable life.

So what's your story? Do you know your sexual formation? Your lover self has a story. Evil wants to write the scripts of your arousal. And evil came early for you, long before you hit puberty and got your man-size body. Let's go tell that story.

FIVE

The Wounded Lover

There is no greater agony than bearing
an untold story inside of you.
—MAYA ANGELOU

Reentering terrain we have fenced off as forbidden
is an act of profound courage. It requires learning to
read our story with eyes that see as God sees.
—DAN ALLENDER

A lmost no one comes to my counseling office saying, "I'd like to talk about my story of sexual harm." Very rarely are these stories sitting on the surface of anyone's life, because evil does terribly effective work. I hate that sentence, but evil has a knack for getting people to bury their stories of sexual harm. Indeed, it plays on the design of our brain's wiring, that tendency we talked about in the previous chapter to bury that which feels too overwhelming, especially the pain of shame.

Men come to counseling most often with something on fire in their lives or with their sexuality in some sort of wreck. That's where we start. And then we slowly unwind the story and break the spell of shame little by little "with backward mutters of dissevering power," in the words of John Milton.[1] Our stories don't come to us prepackaged and obvious. They bubble up in the present day as the hidden subtext of the moment. Stories are acted out unaware. And it takes a while to untangle those plot lines.

Most often men carry stories of sexual harm as "the weird thing that happened that one time." "Weird" seems to be the code word, probably because they did not know what else to call it when it happened. "Weird" conveys both the shock of the event and the shame it left them with. Often as the stories start to reveal themselves, men will say something like, "I haven't thought about this for a long time," or "I thought this was my fault," or "I swore I would never tell anyone this," or even "I planned to take this to my grave." Indeed, these stories can become a living grave.

As my friend Jan Proett says, we don't go digging for stories. This is not about digging into the past. That never does anything good. We are simply going to be curious about your life and your sexuality. We need to make room in you for these stories to come back to you, because when you make room, they *will* come back. And when they come walking through the doors of your conscious memory, we need to teach you how to face them and even welcome them. These stories are not your enemies. Though buried in pain and fear, uncertainty and shame, these memories are parts of you wanting to come home.

I want to help you walk through your sexual development, to consider where harm and shame began to enter in, so you can stop living under their power and get your whole lover heart back. How does the lover develop within each of us? And where does he take his core wounds? Those are the questions we will pursue in this chapter.

Your relationship to the lover within began well before your sexuality awakened. You've been a lover since the moment your life began. By now you know that your sexuality is about so much more than simply having sex. It's an invitation to the whole world of your lover self.

A good lover must be alive in three areas: embodiment, attachment, and sexuality. You need to be able to live well in your body, to know how to connect and bond emotionally with someone else, and to be present and kind to your body's sexual arousal.

Your Embodiment Story

You were born in a body. And that body is your presence in the world. In other words, you don't just have a body, you *are* a body. It's not all of you, of course. You also have an immaterial aspect, which includes your soul, spirit, mind, and heart. But your body is as much you as anything else. Some like to say that the body is simply the container for the soul. But Jesus' resurrection in an actual body should put an end to that misperception. You exist as a body now, and you will exist as a resurrected body for eternity. God made your body, and it still carries that original blessing.

Your body is made to help you experience and explore the world. When God dropped Adam and Eve in Eden and told them to be fruitful and multiply (Genesis 1:28), he gave us the world as our playground. You are invited by God, as Frederick Buechner said, to "touch, taste, smell your way to the holy and hidden heart of it."[2] Go and explore, enjoy, try it out, be curious! Our bodies were created to encounter others and indeed to meet God in his good world.

Your body is born sexed, by which I mean children are born male or female with the kit to match. Already with this one sentence, I may be touching a tender area for you. There is a world waiting to size you up and influence your relationship to your body and your penis, from the doctors in the delivery room to the middle school locker room and beyond. Some of us come to feel like a foreigner in our own body, as if it has betrayed us or doesn't feel like a place we belong. Many things can rob us of the freedom and innocent joy of feeling alive in our bodies.

Some men get labeled as intersex for having genitalia that appear ambiguous or unusually formed in some way. They can suffer unnecessary surgery against their will as children to make them look "normal."[3] For those with chromosomal abnormalities leading to ambiguity in the external presentation of their genitals and other sex-related features, sometimes a sex is assigned to them (including attempts to surgically remove any ambiguity) before the person gets to participate in the decision with full self-awareness. But even the intersex community does not typically advocate for a third or fluid gender.[4] The most challenging cases of intersexuality still bear witness to the sexual binary created by God. Befriending our sexed bodies is difficult work.

Some men simply feel their bodies do not mirror the truth of their essence, that they got the wrong body for their gender. The agony of this must not be underestimated. To feel so at war with your biological sex is to live a divided life.

Sensual, Not Sexual

Children are born sexed but not sexually awakened. That happens later at puberty during what Michael Gurian called our second birth, when a boy is born into a man.[5] While children may not be sexually awakened, they are wildly sensual. As discussed in the previous chapters, although we often equate the two, sexuality and sensuality are not the same thing. Children taste, touch, smell, hear, and see their way into the world with gusto.

Children bang pots on the floor to hear the sound. They stick their hands right in the thickest mud just to feel the texture and pleasure of goopy earth. What baby does not put nearly everything it can find instantly in its mouth? I once found a dead fly in my son's mouth in his journey to taste the world. Indeed, our bodies become one giant instrument of sensual adventure. Children even talk this way: "I'm cold . . . That's loud . . . This tastes funny." A sensual play-by-play of how life is going.

But our bodies are not simply sensory instruments for receiving data and learning the world. We are made to push against the world, to run and jump and climb and figure out where we end and where the world begins. I loved riding my bike as a kid, and I learned the limits of my balance by crashing more times than I can count. I remember the feeling of my T-shirt flapping behind me in the wind as I rode my Schwinn Sting-Ray down the hill by my house. I think being given the freedom to go fast made me brave. I also reveled in climbing trees. The taller, the better. That feeling of hovering over the earth, of knowing the power of wind on tree limbs and the limits of my fear. I swayed in the arms of a thousand trees.

Such is how we come to learn our bodies. Neuroscientists call it "proprioception" or "kinesthesia"—our ability to sense our body's movements and positions, tensions and strength. There is an actual neural network in our muscles that connects with our central nervous system. Some have called this our sixth sense, because it helps us locate our bodies in the world and sense what is going on there.

We learn how to animate our bodies, to exert force when we need to jump off a rock, or to remain still and subtle enough to hold a butterfly or sneak up on a snake. This exploration and adventure is essential to learning our bodies. Unsurprisingly, almost all of this happens in play. Play commingles body movement, delight, and relationship. The activity of embodied play is how we come to fall in love with the world. The lover comes alive in play.

How did your play go as a boy? Were you blessed in your play? Was there freedom to explore the world?

Nothing brought Ryan more joy than moving his body. No matter the sport, he always seemed to be the fastest and most capable kid on the field. His athletic prowess made him king of his neighborhood. Everyone wanted him on their team—because he was good but also because he made play so fun.

School told a different story, though, with teachers treating his active body as a challenge to be overcome rather than a gift to enjoy. But then came field day in third grade. Of all days, Ryan thought that surely field day would bring a break from the constant instructions to slow down, settle down, and sit down. Plus, he would see Ann, his crush from a different classroom, the one he'd been writing notes to all year. She always brightened his day.

Field day started great. Ryan raced the fifty-yard dash and advanced all the way to the finals. Everyone in his class knew he would win. He was just that fast. With a photo of the finish to prove it, he took first place. But when it came time to receive his prize, the teacher handed it to the second-place finisher. Ryan stood baffled and speechless. None of this made sense. The teacher who was handing out prizes was Ann's mom. How could she do this to him? *It must be the notes I wrote to Ann*, he thought.

Whether that was true or not, something inside Ryan began to die that day. He became convinced he needed to stop showing up so fully. Not only did his active body feel like a problem but so did the early, innocent attractions of his lover heart.

This story became a theme that played itself out time and again throughout high school and college, with many football and basketball coaches shaming him for being too proud or arrogant for his athletic ability. And he started to believe the lie. That once-playful, openhearted boy learned that neither his capable body nor his passionate heart was welcome. What should have been sources of confidence and joy became areas of uncertainty and shame.

———

Engagement with our bodies helps us listen to and befriend them, a process called interoception. "I'm tired" or "I'm hungry" or "Will you hold me?"—these comments arise from listening to our bodies. And the more our caregivers respond to these requests, the more we live empowered in our body connection. If we are held when we cry, fed when hungry, comforted when we ask, we will pay more attention to our body's voice.

As children, we also befriend our bodies by exploring them. We stick our fingers in our noses or belly buttons. We tug on our ears. We may even get a toe or two in our mouth. We learn what our bodies feel like, what they do, and what the parts are called. That includes our beloved penis. It's so out there, waiting to be discovered. And it's your body, so of course you get to touch it and learn how your plumbing works.

"What are these little balls under my penis called, Dad?" This is for sure a question I got asked as a father of three sons. Oh, the joys of making ritual connection to our penis, the exclamation mark that we are *boy*. What fun we have in learning to pee outside or "sword fight" with yellow "lightsabers" in the toilet. I remember with delight the freedom of peeing behind the garage so that I didn't have to come in from playing. Your body is yours as a gift of existence and no part is shameful. We get to study and explore every part.

It's not uncommon for children to discover masturbation in this exploration. Even babies in utero have been known to discover it.[6] Again, it's not yet sexual, but it's certainly sensual. It's not in any way sinful, for it is neither lustful nor fantasy driven. It's just sensual exploration, which often falls in the category of self-soothing, much like thumb-sucking. We will talk more about the complex (and sometimes fraught) link between sexuality and self-soothing in a later chapter.

All of this to say, the importance of embodiment cannot be overstated. Embodiment is absolutely fundamental to healthy sexuality. Sexuality, as I've said, is built on sensuality, on our capacity to give and receive pleasure through the senses.

Where Shame Creeps In

Evil does not want you living well in your good body, your physical presence in the world. It will find ways to pry you away from a connection to your body and sabotage your friendship with it.

———

Michael loved wrestling with his young son and could tell these times fed his son's heart. Michael felt the nourishment of it, too, the depth of their father-son bond. It gave Michael a big smile whenever his son ran or jumped or explored the world. But when his son started asking questions about where babies come from and his own body, something shut down inside of Michael. He shared, "I just can't say 'penis' without feeling shame. My parents never used the actual word. We weren't allowed to say 'penis.' It was like a swear word. I get so jealous of my son's freedom. He can say it with empowerment, but I still can't say it without flinching in shame."

I have heard many versions of this same story, where "penis," "vulva," and "vagina" are seen as taboo and not given their real names. What drives this hesitancy?

Giving something a name is a way of blessing it. In Eden, God's relationship with Adam centered on the ritual of naming. On their daily walks, Adam named the things he encountered, the gifts God had given (Genesis 2:20). Naming our body parts carries the same sacred blessing. So what does it say to a child when everything on our body gets a name *except* one part—and we act as if saying that name is like swearing? A ritual of blessing becomes twisted into a curse. We cannot love that which we don't talk about.

———

Chris remembers bath time well. Most children delight in the endless entrancing ways that water can be poured, sprayed, splashed, and launched across a room. Surely Chris had those moments too. But he most vividly remembers when his mother made him wash his "private parts." She seemed to think he never got his penis clean enough. And often she took it on herself to take over the scrubbing, sometimes to the point of pain. An obsession with cleanliness became a script for harm on his body and his sexuality. Chris's body still held the visceral tendency to flinch when he would recall this story. He felt like his very maleness was hated and harmed.

To have the way you move your body or the parts of your body made into an enemy is to violate something God made good in you. Yes, there are ways we can use our bodies for harm, even as kids. But healthy and whole sexuality begins with a love for our bodies and a connection of care for them. We need to be able to be present in our bodies to be a good lover.

Your Attachment Story

The way we give and receive love on a daily basis with the people most important to us is called attachment. Despite what the name implies, attachment is not constant connection like being attached at the hip, as they say. Attachment is the carried feeling of love—a feeling of love that gets in and sticks with you. It's the rhythm of connecting in close proximity and then adventuring out into life apart from each other, all while carrying each other's love in our hearts. It's how our relationships breathe.

Inhale, connect.

Exhale, adventure apart.

We all want connection; we all want space. Even infants need moments of looking away from their mother's gaze (about every eight seconds) before looking back into her loving eyes.[7] Being able to connect with an open heart *and* to take time apart while keeping the other in your heart—that is attachment at its most secure state. Can you separate and return to each other well? Of course, no one can do that flawlessly. Attachment requires we learn to repair connection when we hurt or disappoint or miss each other. This bond lets us walk through conflict without overreacting or withdrawing

Our ability to connect emotionally is essential to the act of sex precisely because the heart is always present in sex. *Always*. Even when you think sex is just an act of the body, it's not. Sex is never just about sex, because we are not merely animals. Again, as Emily Nagoski makes clear, "Sex is an attachment behavior."[8] Sex is built on the bedrock of emotional connection. And the fruit of sex is a deeper emotional bond.

To bring your heart to your beloved is to risk opening up and sharing what's going on inside—and to make space for your partner to do the same. We talk not simply about the facts of our lives but our felt *experience* of those events. Emotional connection goes hand in hand with physical affection. It's the experience of nonsexual acts of touch—kissing, hugging, and holding hands—that mirrors the emotional connection.

Every man must learn to navigate well these roads of emotional intimacy and physical affection. We must learn to maintain that close bond over time, to care for it and guard it as if our life depends on it, because it does. Every man I have ever met needs to feel emotionally connected, heard, safe, comforted in his closest relationships. Life will try to beat the heart out of you. But I find most men actually know they need close connection to survive, even if our masculine culture doesn't make it easy for us to admit.

This is not rocket science, really. But though attachment is not that difficult to understand in theory, it can be difficult to navigate in practice. We don't teach these skills in the standard-issue masculinity often promoted by our culture. I had to learn it in the backroads of the masculine journey, in therapists' offices and men's retreats and friendships with risk-taking, vulnerable men. Attachment is also difficult because we all bring to love our history of being loved. How we bond arises from our history of bonding. Our early attachments to our parents and caregivers shape our rhythms of love. And that can make it feel very complex and hard to traverse.

Yes, how you were held and loved and cared for as a child impacts the future of your sex life. As therapist Sue Johnson points out,

> Males may be particularly vulnerable to touch hunger. . . . [F]rom birth, boys are held for shorter periods and caressed less often than are girls. As adults, men seem to be less responsive to tender touch than are women, but in the men I see, they crave it just as much as do the women. Men do not ask to be held, either because of cultural conditioning (real men don't hug) or lack of skill (they don't know how to ask). I think of this whenever my female clients complain that men are obsessed with sex. I would be, too, I say, if sex were the only place apart from the football field where I ever got touched or held.[9]

Were you given affection and care? Was love available to you when you needed it? Did your caregivers tune into you and pay attention to your feelings? Could you get your parents' attention, their gaze?

Could you climb in the arms of your parents and feel safe and secure? Did they give you calm presence? And did they let you set the rhythm of care? Were you held and comforted when you needed it? And were you equally celebrated or tickled when life called for that too?

Was there a safety and a strength afforded you? Could you get affection without being smothered by it? Could you begin or end a hug when you wanted?

Were you blessed to explore the world beyond your parents and return with celebration and affection? And did they let you go? Did they empower you to explore the world? Of course not. No boy got all of that, or certainly not all the time. No one gets the perfect parents with perfect care. Outside of Eden we all suffer wounds in these areas.

Ranch life in rural Nebraska kept Greg's father almost always occupied. Cattle rearing demanded long, grueling hours. But every night, his father finally came in for dinner. And while he showered off, Greg and his brother waited just outside the bathroom, nearly giddy with the craving they had for time with their father. These boys were alive to their wildly good attachment hunger for a father who had been off adventuring at work.

But what could and should have been a ritual of attachment and bonding never really happened. Instead, their father emerged naked from the bathroom, ignored them, and walked across the small ranch house to his bedroom, giving them only a disinterested glance. Greg remembers marveling at his dad's strong, lean body—and the size of his father's penis, which, to a boy, was spellbinding. *Will I ever get that big?* Greg remembers wondering. But this nightly walk of his father from the shower, past his boys, and to his room became a ritual not of blessing but of neglect and sadness. All that flesh and skin made Greg ache for his father's hugs and play and touch all the more. Yet the message was clear. You can look, but you will not be touched or hugged or loved.

And worse, now a man, Greg can recognize that his father seemed physically aroused by this parade. His big penis was often in some state of erection. This was his father's runway, and he made his sons his audience. "It feels like my father sexualized our hunger for him," Greg said as he processed these memories. "And that has really messed with my sexuality. We were just two eager boys looking for love. He made us his voyeurs. That really makes me angry." This became a subtle but powerful form of sexual harm in Greg's life.

Eric's mother always had the pantry stocked with snacks for him and his friends. To a teenage young man, food is a powerful form of kindness and affection. But there was a catch: when she offered snacks no one could say no. Literally, she would not take no for an answer. Everyone had to take something. It stole the kindness out of the offer. Eric and his friends knew she needed them to take snacks so she could feel better about herself, and they begrudgingly obliged her.

"The hard part for me is that she demanded hugs the same way," Eric said. "She seemed to offer them as a gift, but I could never say no. They were more for her needs than mine. I learned to numb out when she hugged me." In attachment terms, there was no opportunity to have space or desire of his own. We got to this story in therapy only because Eric's wife had asked for more pursuit, affection, and sex from him. He resisted affection with her, keeping his distance, and did not know why. He was stuck guarding the lover within. He had shut down his attachment needs to prevent further smothering or violation but inadvertently cut himself off from all affection and the safe love he longed for.

———————

As a boy, Mark lived with a true childlike heart. He remembers one Fourth of July standing on the front stoop of his house, waving a little flag and singing the national anthem at the top of his lungs. That boy did not have a care in the world and lived his heart out loud. But when Mark first came to counseling, he hated that boy.

Up until he turned seven, every day ended much the same: after putting on pajamas and brushing his teeth, Mark went to his father in his easy chair and kissed him goodnight. But the night he turned seven, his father refused his kiss and said with a cold, stern face, "It's time to be done with that. You're getting too old."

The rejection crushed Mark's heart. Even worse, it began the complete loss of any affection from his father. Only later would Mark learn that his father was given up to an orphanage by his own mother when he was seven. He had reenacted his own story on his own son. But Mark knew nothing of this story—only the crushing rejection and immense shame of wanting what he was told he shouldn't want.

How did Mark eventually embrace the memory of what he had long tried to forget? He came to counseling for his sexual struggles, not least of which was his many years of sexless marriage. He had stopped pursuing his wife affectionately or sexually because he had felt her rejection of him. And the thought of risking affection again felt terrifying. It froze him. Without recovering the heart of that boy and his brave way with affection, it was impossible for Mark to pursue his wife.

———

Again, we bring our history and past experience of love into our current relationships. But to truly make sex an act of love, we need to recover the freedom to give and receive affection.

Your Sexuality Story

One day as children we awakened to the presence of sexuality in our body. One day it shook off its slumber and we suddenly had hormones rushing through our body. Sex was no longer imagined but within us and around us. Puberty is the God-given announcement of this new horizon.

I can remember as a camp counselor the difference between the elementary school kids, who missed their parents and hovered close to me, and the junior high students, who sometimes missed their parents but had to be guarded from sneaking out at night with the girls.

Sexuality had shaken off its slumber indeed.

Chris remembers the day in fifth grade when he and his friend Joy talked on the playground about sex. They wondered what it would be like, this sex thing, and how certain things might feel. Joy shared more than Chris had ever heard about. Still, this conversation stayed alive and curious and playful. Neither of them made it more than that.

But Mr. Smith, their teacher, overheard them, resulting in a meeting with Chris and his mother. Mr. Smith spit his anger as he reprimanded Chris for his dirty talk and warned him to stay away from Joy and her bad influence. How could Mr. Smith act so aggressively, certain that he was right about what had felt so playful and innocent? None of it made sense.

Chris said nothing but his heart was pummeled, not so much by the anger but by the judgment. It landed on him and his sexual curiosity like a curse. Yet to this day, what brings him the deepest tears in this story is remembering how his mother sat and watched Mr. Smith's whole rant and said nothing. By her silence, she condoned his verbal violence aimed at Chris's sexual innocence.

None of this erased the sweet memory of Joy and their playful conversation about sex. But it was buried in that curse and a well of shame.

One night at dinner when Josh was thirteen, his father looked at him and said, "You stink. You need to shower more." His siblings smirked and laughed. It was true his body had begun to change with puberty. But his father hadn't mentioned it or even seemed to notice until now. Josh sat in the silence of his public humiliation.

A few weeks later, his father came to Josh's room to talk, something he never did. He opened the door and said with the same scowled face, "You need to stop masturbating. We can't keep cleaning these sheets. It's wasting water." Josh again flushed with humiliation. He had discovered masturbation in the sensual exploration of his body. Sheets felt good on his genitals. And when he kept rubbing, he discovered orgasm quite by pleasant accident.

In the name of puberty, Josh's father wanted him to use both *more* and *less* water. Clearly, this was not about water. Something made his father antagonistic toward Josh's growing body. To Josh's thirteen-year-old self, it felt like his dad thought his body and sexuality were disgusting. No one cheered for him or welcomed him into the world of men. His coming of age was not heralded and celebrated and nurtured. Instead, he stepped into manhood in a blast of his father's contempt. Evil had joined disgust to his sexual awakening and growing body. And this was the closest thing to a sex talk he ever got from his father.

———

Trevor got in the car with his mom after loading the groceries into the trunk with her. He tucked the last bag by his feet, hoping she wouldn't spot it under his seat. But no such luck today.

"What's in that?" she asked.

He said nothing.

"Did you buy something?"

He acknowledged he had.

"Well, then show me."

Trevor sighed and pulled out the muscle magazine he'd bought with his own money when his mom was off in the produce section. She saw the guys with their shirts off and screamed. His face got hot with a burning shame. And not another word was spoken between them. Trevor just buried his confusing sexual questions deeper inside.

—————

As I've said, the sex talk is really hundreds of sex, body, and romance talks. Parents need to build with their son an ongoing conversation about his life, his identity, his heart. And within that conversation of life comes the conversation on sexuality. These are usually basic and short when we are young. By older childhood, most kids are ready to know the basics of sex. But of all times to be invited to know your sexuality and your body, puberty provides this rite of passage, marking a moment to get more intentional with these talks.

We need to be introduced to the lover within, to have him welcomed into the world of men. We need to learn about romance, the adventure of love, and how to know a partner as a deep mystery whom we are always discovering.

Our first lesson on romance often comes from our parents, whose displays of love and affection (or lack thereof) formed us. What did your parents' marriage feel like to be around? What was the mood? We absorb the feel of romance long before we even have the ability to name it. I can remember several moments when my wife and I made up after a fight and hugged out our reconciliation in the kitchen. Our sons would run from the other room and hug our legs as we hugged. I marveled at how they could sense what was going on. It was instinctive. All was well again in their world. The tide of love had returned to the home, and they couldn't help but splash in its waters.

Every romance ebbs and flows with the waters of passion. How did your parents enact passion? How did they live it out? Passion can pour out as affectionate love or flare up as anger. Some of you had parents that never hugged or touched. Others had parents who couldn't keep their hands off each other. Some witnessed open rage or the horror of domestic violence. Some saw deep affection and laughter. Others felt the icy coldness of a passionless love or the covert contempt of a civil war.

You may be readily aware of how your parents' relationship calibrated your view of passion, romance, and sexuality. Even as I write these words, I can recall the exact feeling of my parents' romance. It would be decades until I had the words to untangle all that they played out before me. But it often begins to show itself when we engage in romance for ourselves.

Eventually we get our own history of romance, of love, of crushes, and yes, of rejections or "never beens." I remember falling in love in eighth grade. At my crush's end-of-the-school-year pool party, when word got to me that she liked me, I dug deep into my middle school heart and asked her out.

We went to the mall. We went to movies. Sometimes I hung out at her house and we used her hot tub. She had a big screen TV where we watched movies. We snuggled and held hands, but I never kissed her. I still remember standing by the vending machine at school one day when an upperclassman asked me, "So did you get some?" I had nothing to say. And in that moment, I felt so inadequate as a barely young man. Here was the test, I guess, of manhood. How much had I consumed this girl?

The truth is I really did feel the desire to kiss her. But more because I liked her a lot. We wrote letters back and forth even though we saw each other every day. I kept ChapStick in my pocket to bolster my courage. But I did not know the first thing about kissing a girl.

My father built our family house that same summer. With my new man-size body, I reveled in the chance to be with him doing man's work. I was his right-hand man. I slid him shingles as he nailed them down and hauled lumber when he needed it. We developed an intuition between us, a way of communicating the project's need of the moment with few words.

One day while working together, I went for a walk on our new plot of land up the long and winding driveway. I thumbed the cap of my ChapStick, really hoping my father would notice I was gone and come find me. My young lover heart wanted to know how to kiss a girl. I needed to know that falling in love was about knowing and enjoying someone. I needed my father to lead me past the macho masculinity that told me to get some.

He never did come find me. And I don't fault him for that moment. He was building a house, after all. But the conversation never came that day or any other. He initiated me into working as a man—but not into knowing how to love as a man.

The Many Facets of Sexual Abuse

Our sexuality is meant to be experienced as an awakening. It's designed to rouse itself in its own time, at the pace of our bodies and hearts, through innocence and curiosity and love. "As it so desires," says the poet in Song of Songs 8:4. Sexuality is made to be felt in our bodies as a form of adventurous curiosity, full of discovery and intrigue. You were meant to be able to ask all the questions in the world, to be moved and aroused in such a way that your heart and sexual desire could grow up together.

But as I said before, evil wants to derail our sexuality early and narrate the story. And nothing has a more profound and swift negative impact on our sexuality than sexual abuse.

A widely accepted estimate says that one in six men has been sexually abused compared with one in four women.[10] But these numbers are almost certainly lower than the reality for both genders, given the phenomenon of underreporting and that the numbers only cover abuse involving overt physical molestation. Research says that men are far less likely to report their abuse than women. In one study of adults with *documented* cases of childhood sexual abuse, only 16 percent of men affirmed that the abuse happened, compared to 64 percent of women.[11] Abuse is underreported and underacknowledged across the board, but especially for men.

Something keeps men silent. Many men carry the shrapnel of sexual harm within their bodies and hearts. Though the method of abuse is sexual, its impact is myriad, affecting physical health, emotional well-being, relationships, our nervous system, our spirituality—nearly every part of our lives.

Anytime anyone uses their power or position to gain sexual gratification from another without that person's full consent, that is abuse. Remember that all play must be free to qualify as genuine play, and therefore all sex must allow for full consent. A child cannot consent, full stop. Children simply don't know what's being asked of them. Even if a child says yes, they don't know what they're consenting to. Children simply cannot know. Consent requires freedom, which in turn requires maturity and deep clarity about what is being asked. Any relationship where power is being abused collapses the possibility of freedom and negates the possibility of consent.

We usually suppose that abuse is violent and forceful—a creepy stranger who assaults from behind a bush with swift action. That does happen, but it's not typical. Most abuse (up to 90 percent) comes from someone the victim knows, either a family member or acquaintance.[12] And the power used is often not physical restraint but the power of relationship, influence, or authority. Abuse is set up, staged with patience, and manipulated with craft and cunning to leave you thinking it's just you.

And sexual abuse can also be subtle without ever involving touch. So many men's first exposure to pornography is an act of sexual harm. I talk to so many men who discovered porn by finding it lying out on the back of a toilet or on their father's nightstand. Some had an older brother or peer invite them to look at a video. I believe this always involves the selfish gratification of the person doing the inviting. Most victims have no idea what is coming. The offer or invitation is devoid of care for how this will disrupt the victim's sexuality or innocence.

Cory grew up in a small church, where his closest peers were a couple of older boys. He really looked up to these guys and wanted to be their friend. When he was twelve, while at a church gathering at one boy's house, he found them in a basement bedroom huddled together around a porn magazine. "Hey, come look at this," said one boy. In that moment, Cory felt caught. Here was the invitation to be included and accepted—the very thing he'd always wanted. Yet he'd been taught about porn and knew he didn't want to come any closer.

"Nah, I'm good," he said. The boys looked up, and Cory saw they were not going to accept his answer. "No. Look," one said. They all moved his direction and pinned him to the bed and forced the porn in his face. It was only a minute before they let him go and left the room laughing. But that minute felt like a year to his body and heart. He felt like such a coward for not being able to fight it. That scene still haunts him to this day.

These days, porn exposure is most likely to come via unrestricted access to the internet, where parents take no care to guard a child's heart or discuss the dangerous impact of pornography on his growing sexuality. We live in a time of unprecedented access, and the porn industry wants you to find it. The average age for boys to first see pornography is now twelve years and trending younger.[13]

At fourteen, Troy heard his older brothers talk about girls they thought were cute and whom they might ask out. He was deathly afraid to join in because he felt too embarrassed by one thing: he didn't know how to kiss a girl. So he Googled it. When the screen filled with pornography links, his heart raced and his body warmed. Technically, no one was forcing him to stay. But a dizzying world of intrigue opened before him. He hadn't tried to find it and no one had forced him to look. But evil, by way of pornographers who know search engines really well, still assailed him, drawing his heart into a crazy-making world of arousal and shame. But since it seemed like all his fault, he waited a year until he told anyone about his porn use.

Can you see the assault on his lover heart? Nothing could be more innocent than just wanting to know how to kiss a girl. Google does not make for a good surrogate father or mother. Yet if you fully blamed this young man, you're likely to miss your own assault.

The Abuse Cycle

Abusers read their victims very well. Especially in the early stages of abuse (grooming), it can feel as if the abuser is simply offering compassion, help, or care. Sexual abuse victims describe feeling really seen, sometimes for the first time in their lives. It can feel amazing. And in many ways, there is no difference early on in abuse between care and grooming, except of course for the intentions behind the abuser's actions. Many abusers work with profound patience, intuiting their victim's needs and attending to the hunger they eventually manipulate.

The abuser's goal is to make the abuse feel like it's simply a natural outflow of the relationship. The sexual harm is often scripted as an act of gratitude for the care the victim received in the relationship, a kind of reciprocal gift. Oh, but there is always a hidden knife, a threat of loss, harm, punishment, or exposure if the victim does not comply. However it's scripted or manipulated, the abuse presents an impossible bind for the victim: follow through or face further harm or lose the relationship all together.

Again, the trap is rarely physical and most often relational. By the time the abused person might be able to scream, fight, or run, the emotional snare has already snapped shut. Their bodies keep moving but their hearts shut down or dissociate until it's over. Some criticize victims for not screaming or fighting back; such criticisms fail to understand the complex maze of emotions and manipulation at play in such situations.

As I said, abuse can be more than molestation or genital touch leading to sexual release. It can also involve the pleasure of voyeurism (even emotional voyeurism), watching a victim aroused or shocked. It could be the thievery of touch that's not overtly sexual, a hug or some other form of affection that crosses boundaries in subtle, ambiguous ways. It could be the relational trap of a special connection, making the abused into an emotional lover, leaving them vaguely aware that an emotional boundary has been violated though it's scripted as a privilege.

Sometimes an abuser's greatest goal is the pleasure of power, to experience dominance, a kind of sexualized ego stroke. Lost is the mutual respect and humble awe and reverence for the other. This is not innocent play. This is harm.

———

At youth camp over the summer, Chris and his buddies lucked out on having the coolest youth intern for their cabin counselor. They felt so chosen. One day, Chris walked into their cabin only to find his counselor with his pants pulled down. He flashed his penis and then laughed. "Oh, it's just a joke," he said. Chris laughed, too, but felt horrified on the inside. This act felt so foreign and out of place at a church camp from a Christian counselor, but he assumed he must be wrong for taking it so seriously. It was over in a matter of seconds, but it froze him inside, making him scared that he invited it somehow. Decades later, the pain still in his body, he wept in my office when he could finally name it as violating.

———

Wyatt and his neighborhood friend had played together all summer afternoon, as Wyatt did most days to escape his parents' anger. The day naturally ended in Wyatt's basement for a sleepover. Their sleeping bags side by side on his floor, his friend exposed himself to Wyatt. "How about you touch me?" he said. Shocked, Wyatt refused. "Fine, then I'm going home. And I won't be your friend anymore." Wyatt thought of all the bike riding and fort building they'd done, and how good it felt to have a friend. He couldn't imagine having nowhere to go when his parents exploded in anger. How could he choose? It was an impossible bind.

The Well-Laid Trap of Abuse

Sexual abuse harms in a million ways. But maybe its greatest harm is the assault on innocence. As I said in an earlier chapter, sexual trauma can actually awaken a child's sexuality before they are ready, an intrusion rather than an invitation. Instead of being awash in curiosity and innocence, the body and the heart awaken to sexuality abruptly, often awash in pain and shame. As the poet of Song of Songs wrote, "Do not arouse or awaken love until it so desires" (8:4). I believe we can also take this as a warning to protect children against abuse. It happened then. It happens now.

Nearly every man I talk with who has survived sexual abuse has battled feeling both weak and foolish. "I feel so pathetic. Who gets abused and can't stop it?" The voice of shame comes quickly to turn victims against themselves. Being abused can create feelings of powerlessness because trauma in the body creates shutdown, even a freeze state. It has nothing to do with the raw strength of a person. And again, abuse is almost never about sheer physical power alone; it usually proceeds via manipulation and betrayal from someone trusted. Abusers are skilled at getting away with it, and they hope their victims feel guilty.

The poison of shame plagues victims with the question, Why did I fall for it in the first place? To feel like a fool is to turn against our own innocence. It's important for victims of abuse to learn the truth that abuse is a choreographed event, a trap that's been set with patience. Abusers even craft their own exit strategy, making the abused person feel like a fool to cover their tracks. They are skilled at leaving you holding the bag, making you feel as if you're to blame for what happened, maybe even that you wanted it, that you asked for and enjoyed it.

Due to arousal non-concordance, which I mentioned earlier, it's common for abuse victims to experience sexual arousal during abuse. But this is not the same as desire. Remember, desire and arousal (poetics and mechanics) are very different. Your body can complete the arousal cycle without you ever wanting any of it. Abuse victims may even feel betrayed by their own bodies for this. But abusers play on this fact and accuse you for your body's response.

All of that is nonsense. But so many men feel dirty or twisted, broken or perverted for being abused. I started this chapter by saying that so many stories of abuse are described as "that weird thing that happened." It's often that sense of culpability that keeps us mute about the abuse we've experienced.

You have a story. There is always, always some assault in a man's life on his sexual innocence. Your story lives in your neurology as much as in your heart. I can talk to you about how much evil hates your arousal and has tried to join shame to your arousal through harm. But that's only a map, and a map alone can't help you know a place. You must walk the terrain.

It is not helpful to talk about shame in general. You can't get rid of shame in a general way. We must know the particulars of our own story to engage shame.[14] We must know the words or actions of others that brought the piercing stab of accusation.

Did you hear your story in these pages? My friend, there is always something. I don't know what it is for you. Not everyone has experienced outright sexual abuse. But I know the geography of your life is east of Eden. And so we all experience harm to our sexuality. And these stories are part of why you got rid of your innocent awe, why you've disowned and exiled the lover within.

We've started to discover the map to the treasure of your innocence. But at this point it's only a partial map. I've shown you the way to the terrain of your sexual formation, the stage and the actors who played roles—both positive and negative—in that story, and where shame prompted you to bury that story.

But our stories don't stop at shame. Nor do we simply stay stuck in pain. We must also consider the story of how we've responded to all this. What did we do with our sexuality in the aftermath of shame or abuse? How have we handled our innocence? We have a way of turning on our own innocence because we think it's the thing that got us in trouble. That's the story we need to talk about next.

SIX

Killing Our Innocence

How long will you be incapable of innocence?
—HOSEA 8:5 (NLT)

Shamed men do not make good lovers.
—ROBERT MOORE AND DOUGLAS GILLETTE

The year after I finished college, I took a job in construction. Since men work most of the trade jobs these days, it became my baptism into the larger adult world of men. After the tame halls of academia, getting up early and working from the sweat of my brow brought a good shift back into my body. The boss assigned me to a crew replacing the roof on a university building. Every day we climbed high in the air to tackle the massive undertaking.

I swung a hammer next to these men, where joking and hazing came with the territory. As the new guy, boy, did I get it. Some of it felt genuinely playful. Other times, the teasing had a cruel edge.

Midway through my first day, one of the guys stood up and said,

"Here they come, boys!" Like acolytes being summoned to some ancient ritual, everyone laid down his tools and about-face turned. I, the neophyte, stumbled to attention, trying to figure out what this was all about.

University students began filing in and out of buildings, marching to the next class like trails of ants under our magnifying glass. From our perch, the guys began throwing out comments: "Look at those." "That's a nice set." "Look at that body." "Check out that ass." And now the ritual made sense. We were checking out the women. Only these men did not see women. They saw body parts. Somewhere in the recesses of their masculine hearts, this was arousal turned into mutilation.

It might seem at first like the issue here is run-of-the-mill lust. You know, guys with too much sex drive who need to control their eyes. Boys will be boys. We might recommend some accountability and behavioral tips. But that wouldn't get them anywhere. This would be a shallow view of both sin (as if it can be solved via mere behavior modification) and the human heart (as if it's only sin driven). What's going on here is much deeper than that. Though you wouldn't know it from their composure, these men were escaping something. In the very act of gorging their eyes on body parts, they were trying to flee their shame.

Death by Shame

I said before that evil's greatest hope is that all your stories of sexuality would end in shame, that your sexuality itself would become so buried in the stuff that you shut down or disown the lover within. But the reality is that no one can stay in shame very long—probably mere seconds at most. Shame is too deadly, too threatening. And so we find a way to escape it.

When my shame hits, I can be overcome with something that feels like a panic attack. My heart races, my chest gets tight, and I feel like I need to escape. The trigger may vary, but the reaction is always way wilder than the moment calls for. I can see that now after a lot of work. I might forget someone's name, miss an appointment, or make a mistake fixing my car, and, *boom*, my chest blows up with panic. It's the most awful feeling, and it has all the symptoms of a real panic attack—sweating, an inability to control my breathing, a racing heart.

Recent research in neuroscience suggests that physical pain and emotional (or social) pain begin in the same place in the brain and travel along much of the same neural pathway.[1] To the instinctive parts of our brain, physical and emotional pain are not any different. So the sense that shame could kill us is not a metaphor. It's not an overstatement to say we literally feel like we may die.

Shame actually traumatizes us. Research shows it plunges the body into the same state as a traumatic experience.[2] Remember Emily Nagoski's assertion: "Your body reacts to negative self-evaluations as if you're under attack."[3]

When we register a threat of any kind and no one seems available to help us, our body's nervous system kicks in to help get us to safety. Digestion stops to conserve blood flow, our heart rate increases to get ready for action, adrenaline hormones dump into our system, glucose production increases, and our brain stops all complex reasoning to make life really simple: What do we attack or what do we run from? Fight or flight. And if escape seems impossible, we play dead until the threat passes. We freeze by shutting down, numbing, or dissociating. The entire goal of this system is to keep us alive and intact.

But with shame, the threat isn't external. *You* are the threat. How do you run from yourself? Good luck tackling good ol' "me, myself, and I" or getting a running lead on your own shadow. It's an SNL skit waiting to happen. No one can live in a constant state of terror, especially of oneself. No one can bear the raw terror of shame. We must find a way out of it. That is not negotiable. The body is not made to endure pure terror for any length of time. We *will* find escape.

Contempt as Escape

You've got two options in that moment of shame. In the next chapter we'll explore the right option, the life-giving and healing option for overcoming shame's unbearable pressure. But first, we need to spend some time unpacking the easiest option, the one that most of us default to when confronted with the full-blown crisis of shame: we resort to *contempt*.

Contempt goes by many names and takes many forms—several of which we'll be exploring throughout the rest of this chapter. But in the simplest terms, contempt is hatred. We may call it being judgmental or resentful, critical or negative. But at its core, contempt happens when our hearts turn from love to hatred. It takes the human heart out of its open, vulnerable stance to a guarded posture.

Calling this guarded posture a form of hatred may seem too harsh. Most of the time we don't even know we're doing it. It operates below the surface of our mind, stews in the recesses of our being. It's reactive. But even so, the movement toward contempt, regardless of the circumstances, involves shifting away from love and toward hate.

You can aim contempt at yourself, turning on the part of you that you think got you in trouble. Or you can blast other people with it, casting blame. Or you could aim it at a wall by putting your fist through it. But let's be honest, contempt is a fragmentation grenade. No matter where you aim it, everyone in the vicinity takes shrapnel, including you. It always wounds your heart and the hearts of those around you too.

Dan Allender says the goal of contempt is always to get eyes off us, or at least off the parts of us that carry shame.[4] And so we in a sense "gouge out the eyes" of those exposing our shame or evade them by disowning the parts of us that feel shameful.

The word "vulnerable" derives from the Latin *vulnus*, which means "wound." Being vulnerable literally means that you're able to be wounded. What a wild reality: the very language we use to describe opening up and being intimate also describes the inherent risk of intimacy. But that's why we resort to contempt; it feels more powerful, less risky than vulnerability.

The other night, I made burgers on the grill for my family. When they reached that just-right moment, I felt the joy of a job well done. I topped them off with cheese and decided to give them another minute while I made a quick trip inside to make some other preparations. But in that one minute, somehow the grease ignited at the bottom of the grill. It lit like a blowtorch and absolutely charred the bottom of all the burgers.

I saw the billowing smoke and raced outside to rescue dinner (and maybe the whole house, for all I knew). Notice the crisis trigger. But once the fire was out, my body did not calm down . . . because *shame*. Because I had ruined dinner. Shame quickly gave way to self-hatred. *Why hadn't I cleaned the grill or stayed to watch the burgers or not been such an idiot?*

I devised a plan. The charred part went facedown on the plate. Maybe no one would notice. No one ever said contempt was logical. And now I'm Adam hiding in the garden. I served them up, we prayed, and we began eating.

"Yuck! This is all burned on the bottom!" said my six-year-old son. He turned it over to reveal a veritable charcoal briquette.

I huffed. "Can't you just eat it, buddy? Here, put some ketchup on it." I literally thought ketchup would solve it. I was mad and turned my contempt on his taste buds.

"It's too gross!" he protested.

"Fine," I said and grabbed the damn burger. The frag bomb of contempt had gone off. I walked to the counter and picked up a steak knife (because a dangerous weapon is a *great* thing to operate while in a state of contempt). I was determined to save face. I started sawing off the charred bottom but was working too hastily (self-contempt). And yep, I cut my finger. It came to blood.

If we trust the voice of shame and join the emergency, we will always resort to contempt. We will turn on ourselves in an attempt to disown the part we think got us in trouble. Or we will turn on those around us, preemptively striking out before they have a chance to reject us. It's an attempt at escape (a flight response) by turning off our hearts, relying on self-protection to survive the moment (contempt).

When we are fueled by contempt, in Dan Allender's words, "all compulsions, no matter how bizarre or destructive, provide a context to find relief and work out revenge."[5] Contempt is always one part relief and one part revenge. It's never all sin, and it's never simply a stress response. Yet all of this happens so fast; we can barely see where mere human frailty gives way to actual sin. It's a messy mix of humanness and fallenness.

Contempt-Driven Sexuality

You met Mark in the last chapter at the moment he turned seven and his father stopped all physical touch with him, stabbing him with the words, "You're too old for that now." Shame. So much shame. That boy became a man and found love again. And love became a wedding and the promise of lifelong belonging and affection together.

Waves thundered against the rocks outside their honeymoon suite in Hawaii. And Mark braved his desire for affection by asking his new bride to make love. She sighed with exhaustion. "I'm too tired right now." Navigating a wedding ceremony and reception and another day full of travel had caught up to her.

But shame struck Mark square in the chest. *Who gets rejected on their honeymoon?* he said to himself. Though it had nothing to do with him, it all felt so personal. Who was narrating to his heart?

Hello, evil.

He told himself he needed to stop putting his heart out there so much. This was not the last time he took such a risk, but as they rounded the bend of their twentieth wedding anniversary, the reality was that most of those years had been sexless. His wife protested this at times, most often when she would discover his ongoing use of porn. But for Mark, the passion of a fight felt safer than making love to her. And the women in his porn wouldn't ever reject him.

We can all see that Mark is responsible for his choice to withdraw his sexuality from his wife and take it to women in porn. But can you also see with me that his experience on the honeymoon was probably 90 percent a stress reaction? His sin *began* as a fight-or-flight escape from the memory of traumatic shame that galvanized into a withdrawn heart.

I am convinced every sexual sin a man struggles with always involves some form of anxious soothing. We call sexual sin "carnal" or "of the flesh," but we fail to consider the actual flesh-and-blood body that factors into it. There is some form of fight, flight, or freeze in every sexual sin we commit. And I believe all of these are a form of sexualized anger and contempt, too, a revenge on something or someone. And if we don't address this mad search for relief and revenge, and the shame that provokes it, we won't ever make sense of our sexual struggles. We end up repenting of having a body outright rather than forsaking our contempt to find healing for our trauma and shame.

We mistakenly think a man turns to lust or porn because he's overflowing with sexual desire. And then, in a moment of weakness or temptation, he gives in. We think his so-called sex drive led him to lust. But we rarely stop to think about what preceded the arousal in his body. I believe nearly every pornography and masturbation ritual is, first and foremost, an attempt at soothing a dysregulated, anxious nervous system. One study discovered that men with compulsive sexual behavior developed sexual urges in places in the brain other than the pleasure center.[6] These men craved release without even liking pornography. The urge was driven by something other than pleasure.

During orgasm, our bodies release a cocktail of hormones and neurotransmitters, including dopamine, serotonin, and oxytocin. All of these have wildly positive impacts on the body. Let's stay with just oxytocin for a minute. I mentioned in chapter 3 that it's known as the cuddle hormone because it promotes a feeling of closeness. Oxytocin also buffers the body against the stress hormone cortisol.[7] And cortisol is the hormone that triggers fight-or-flight responses. I probably do not need to tell you that sex relieves stress and anxiety.

God clearly wired our bodies for orgasm to give us comfort. That's a good thing, and masturbation can be a healthy form of sensual exploration (even into adulthood) as a way to sensually connect with your own body, as we also talked about before. The problem arises concerning what we ritualize in our sex or masturbation. What story is animating it? Remember, there is no such thing as storyless sex. Sex is not simply a bodily function like using the bathroom or breathing. Our sexual rituals and rhythms always follow arousal scripts. And evil would like them to be scripts that further our shame and harm.

For example, take the literal act of masturbation as a script. All that self-touch and viewing of skin through porn can easily be a man's attempt at *self-soothing* and feeling comfort (a broken attachment script). Or by literally giving himself strokes and rousing his penis, the symbol of his manhood, it could be his attempt at *self-empowerment* and feeling affirmed as a man (a broken masculine initiation script). But masturbation doesn't address the boy and his pain directly and often just ends in more shame.

Traumatic Reenactment

It's common in sex addiction recovery language to talk about "acting out." That language captures the way our addictions become a release for some internal struggle. But it's fitting language for another reason. We become actors stuck in a story we are trying to escape.

This phenomenon is called trauma reenactment, and it's rooted in the way our brains predict future pain based on our past pain. When something triggers old wounds (stress, fear, anger, guilt, relational conflict, body sensations, etc.), we feel like our worst fear is happening again. And our bodies react by working to escape what we couldn't before. But when our stories have been buried in silent shame, as evil hopes to accomplish, our trauma comes back to us not as pain but as shame. Rather than driving us to seek comfort and care for our wounds, we feel awash in exposure, convinced our trauma is a story of shame. We did something wrong—maybe *we* are wrong—and need to prevent being exposed again.

This could never be truer than in our sexuality and lover self. We aren't simply escaping shame. We are trying to escape our *stories* of shame around these core places, the ones we fear are repeating. And it always ends in harm to our sexuality or lover self.

Remember Greg from the last chapter? After high school he left home and the ranch life as far behind as possible. University life rewarded his energetic intensity and agile mind. Undergrad became med school, which became a career as an ER doctor. He succeeded and thrived, even getting married when he graduated. But the accolades Greg found in his career were not the father's affection he'd always craved, and they did not free him from the shame of that childhood rejection.

The stressful demands of emergency medicine pushed him to seek relief. He found that outlet in anonymous sex with men in gay bathhouses or truck-stop hookups, most often where he was the one giving the oral sex to the other man. (Be curious about this script.) Beyond stress relief, Greg found the sex temporarily eased a pain inside, though he had no idea how he'd ended up with this struggle or what he was acting out.

It was only years later, in therapy, that he began to connect the feeling of seeing another man naked to seeing his father naked during his daily shower ritual. Long after leaving home, Greg was still trying to find the delight of a father in the pleasured face of another man.

But is this true relief? Did his nervous system, traumatized as he was by his father, find real soothing and comfort for his father wound? The scene screams that there is more going on here. There is the obvious betrayal to his wife, of course. But maybe less obvious is the revenge he is taking on that child part of him. Remember the script. To always be the one pleasuring, and sometimes on the dirty floor of a truck stop bathroom, Greg realized he was punishing that boy for being abused and rejected by his father.

Choosing Our Path

Like Greg, we do not choose our path of contempt at random. Like a sniper, we target very specifically the thing we think exposed us to shame. It may be instinctive in the moment, and it's almost always subconscious, but it's the quick reflexes of an assassin. We are that good. We are that cunning. Our contempt is as storied as our sexuality. It always arises from our buried stories of harm, the ones we're too afraid to face, the ones we keep in shame. We are trying to get relief for and take revenge on these places within us.

This is the revenge.

I have said I believe we all have stories of sexual harm and shame. And therefore, it's true that we all will struggle in some way with contempt around our sexuality or lover self. We want eyes off our sexuality. No, we want eyes off the lover within us. He has so little place in this world. He has suffered so much in trying to be alive in us. That is to say, we think the lover is our shame, our weak spot. We think living with innocent wonder got us in trouble. So we aim our harm at him.

I know you don't think that consciously or say it out loud. None of this happens in the aware mind. But when the voices of shame haunt us with what feels like an authoritative voice, we pick up our contempt to fight back.

All this talk of contempt is heavy. I daresay no one chooses contempt with the full awareness of what they are choosing. But somewhere along the way, we move from automatic response to willful participation. We escape the threat of exposure, if even for a minute, and our agony dissipates. Our nervous system no longer feels so spiked. And we feel the pleasure of empowerment in whatever form of contempt we used.

We travel through this process every time we feel shame. If we listen to the shame, we will resort to contempt. This process is especially true when it comes to our sexuality, which is one of the most vulnerable parts of us.

Rituals of Contempt for Others

I stood on that university roof surrounded by men who mutilated women with their eyes. They saw body parts. And it felt every bit like hatred. These were not men admiring beauty in the women before them. I have no clue what shame these men were managing. It was probably embodied shame from a moment long gone.

Our contempt reactions can become rituals. They become a way of life, a habit, a part of us almost like a personality trait. I don't believe this was simply the design of these men's hearts. Somewhere they turned from the terror of shame to the self-protection of sexualized contempt.

Again, lust is not simply an attempt to slake our sexual thirst. Lust is a form of contempt, driven by anger as much as anything else. It's a way to get power where we feel powerless. That part often sits unnoticed, subconsciously lingering within our bodies and hearts.

Some might say, "Oh, but all men struggle with lust. This is just a bad habit." Again, as Sheila Wray Gregoire has shown in her research, lust is not simply every man's battle. And remember also the research that shows that men are not inherently more visually stimulated than women.[8] Further, lust of the eyes is not too much sexual desire—it's too little reverence, too little awe.

The innocent wonder these men were made for, the holy awe, had been withdrawn. Eyes that could have blessed with an appreciation and reverence for beauty instead functioned as weapons of harm and objectification.

A woman once told me in counseling, "Oh, I see men noticing me in the grocery store checkout line all the time. And I'm always flattered by it." Her smile slowly faded and her voice dropped. "But then there are *those* looks, the creepy ones. Certain men stare in a way that feels horrible." This woman's body could *feel* the difference between openhearted awe for her beauty and the closed-hearted consumption of her beauty.

Once we kill off our innocent openness to beauty, we're left with something that feels heartless. Because it is. Again, as I have been saying from the beginning of this book, it's not too much arousal or desire that's the problem but too little. The issue is not too much sexuality but too little heart. We withdraw the part of us most capable of awe.

And when that is withdrawn, everything starts to feel heartless.

There are a million ways to turn from the terror of shame to the counterfeit power of contempt. I am going to name a few, but you need to listen to the same theme over and over again. When a man turns to contempt, especially around his sexuality, he moves from the pleasure of awe and the courage of his lover self to the fleeting pleasure of power.

He kills his innocence.

He forsakes the humility of awe, the undoing of awe, the openheartedness of truly being moved by another person and replaces it with the indulgent feeling of exercising power over another. This is the opposite of what I think Paul spoke of in Philippians 2:3, which in my paraphrase goes like this: "In humility, be wowed by others. Let the glory of others move you, undo you, overpower you." That is the lover heart in every man. If you forsake that, you retreat into the empty pleasure of power.

Rape

Lust requires an act of the will. Even where it is habit, there is participation in the choice to join contempt to relieve shame somewhere. It's angry as much as it's sexual. It could be understood as sexualized anger.

Nothing makes this clearer than the experience of rape. Rape is about power. Sexualized power, yes, but power nonetheless.

In his book *Missoula*, John Krakauer documented the campus rape culture of Montana State University. He shared the story of a woman who met a guy in a bar on a Thursday night. She really enjoyed him. And the magnetism seemed mutual. They were inseparable the whole night, talking and flirting. They even kissed a few times.

At the end of the night, they walked back toward their apartments. When they got to his place, he invited her to come inside. She told him point blank, "I'm not sleeping with you. If that's what you're expecting, I'll just go home." He reassured her that he did not intend that. So she followed him in.

"He seemed trustworthy," she said.

They hung out in his room so as not to wake his roommates. They talked about some abstract artwork of his. And then the conversation melded into kissing on his bed, which was fully enjoyed by both. But when he attempted to make moves for more, she shut it down and reiterated her boundary. No sex. He acknowledged her boundary again.

Because it was late, she decided to stay the night and avoid the danger of walking back home alone. Before they fell asleep, he again reassured her that she was safe and he would not go any further.

But not thirty minutes later, she awoke to him attempting to rape her.

She fled his apartment. He terrified her, and his betrayal crushed her. She woke her roommates and wept with them. And later that day, she pressed charges. And yet, in the midst of it all, she said, "I remember thinking, *Yes, what he did was wrong. But he seemed like such a nice guy. Maybe it was just a misunderstanding.*" But when she recalled his profound flip from kindness and playfulness to assault, she realized it was no accident. He knew what he was doing the whole time.

My heart felt wrecked for this woman. Here was the story of two people caught up in the play of attraction, the fun of intrigue, and the possibility of romance. Who talks about art late into the night? Lovers do! But he betrayed all of this. She got away and escaped the physical harm of assault. But her wounds were still oh so real. She'd met a good lover in him. But he flipped that. He withdrew that. He betrayed his own heart, turning it cold, and in so doing became a savage.

Notice that in war, it's savage men who resort to the murder of men and the raping of women. Why is it not simply murder of everyone? Why rape? Well, it's not out of loneliness for home. It's about power. These are not lonely men at war, but savages looking for power trips and ego strokes.

Sex as Power

You know the type all too well because they make the news a lot— the men who fuel their masculinity with abuses of power, especially sexual conquest, often in the form of sexual violation. Think of the latest politician or pastor, business CEO or billionaire. There is an endless stream of these men. And these are just the ones that make the headlines. They put the exclamation point on the fact that lust is more about power than sex. These are men who prop up egos by making sex a means of control or domination. They join sex and violation.

Normal sexuality requires intimacy, vulnerability, and a mutuality in which both give and receive.

One man spoke the quiet part out loud in his now infamous interview. He spoke for all the arrogant men who view sex as an entitlement: "You know I'm automatically attracted to beautiful—I just start kissing them. It's like a magnet. Just kiss. I don't even wait. And when you're a star they let you do it. . . . Grab them by the pussy. You can do anything."[9]

I grieve for the women who know him. And I grieve for him, too, because he begins where we all begin, with being moved by the beauty of another person. But to what end? To reverence or to harm? Notice he does not see a whole woman, a person to be moved by. He sees body parts to grab.

He claimed this was locker-room talk, implying, I guess, that he was just showing off to the interviewer, or worse, that all men talk like this. He was relying on male culture to come to his aid here, believing men would get his back and excuse this as "boys will be boys."

I hope you see by now that beauty is made to move us. And in this it has immeasurable power. *Power.* That's not cute language. It's the deprived man who has never been leveled by a sunset while he's out doing the mundane. Or unexpectedly encountered a beautiful moment in a movie that cuts to the heart. Or indeed, been undone by the presence of another person—a talented performer, or a child at play, or, yes, the beauty of a woman.

But some men don't take well to others having power over them. Remember, the greater our humility, the greater our capacity to experience awe. Some men just don't want anyone or anything having power over them, even the power of beauty. The shame of appearing weak or undone is too much for them. And they literally refuse to be moved.

"Bravado tends to drown out the sound of wonder," says author

Cole Arthur Riley. "Perhaps you've known that person who devours beauty, as if it belongs to them. It's a possessive wonder. It eats not to delight but to collect, trade, and boast. It consumes beauty to grow in ego, not in love."[10]

Remember the story of Amnon and Tamar in the Bible told in 2 Samuel 13? Both were children of David   half-siblings. The story begins with beauty—of course it does. Tamar moved Amnon with her beauty. This could and should have stirred respect and brotherly love in Amnon, an affectionate honoring of his sister. This did not have to be sexual or deviant.

But Amnon couldn't handle the power of Tamar's beauty over him. It made him sick and, no, this is not simply a thirsty man desperate with passion. We learn real quick that he was sick for some other reason; he obsessed over her. That's our first clue that this is not reverence. He lost himself in her beauty. He couldn't find himself and thought it was *her* fault.

With the help of his devious advisor, Amnon plotted his revenge. He must have her (read: have *power* over her). Can you hear the sense of a man marking his territory? He couldn't be secure until his ego felt more powerful than her beauty.

Together Amnon and his advisor set up a trap for Tamar. Amnon faked being sick and sent for Tamar to care for him. Once they were inside his bedroom alone, he barred the door. Realizing his intent, Tamar pled with him and begged him to see her humanity. He refused and raped her. And we all see the horror of his true heart: "No sooner had Amnon raped her than he hated her—an immense hatred. The hatred that he felt for her was greater than the love he'd had for her" (2 Samuel 13:15 MSG).

Next to the description of the crucifixion, this may be the hardest story to read in the Bible. Amnon could not be okay without assaulting

Tamar for the power of her presence. The hatred was the pleasure. The obsession turned to denigration—the antithesis to reverence or awe for another person.

Beauty threatens the ego. And the egoist faced with beauty chooses domination rather than risking being undone. And so they take revenge on that which moves them. And that's what you need to hear in Amnon's actions. The ego-driven person seeks to undo before he is undone. Sexual abuse of a child obviously falls under this same category of abusing power. Sexual abuse assaults not simply the power of beauty but the power of innocence too. The innocence of children and their openhearted hunger and wonder and play within the world holds a similar awe-inspiring power. An abuser seeks to cannibalize it and take revenge on it, whether he knows it or not. That is its darkness.

You don't have to be guilty of outright rape or abuse to be guilty of using your sexuality for power or ego strokes. There's also contempt in the act of seduction.

We've all met men whose whole act is bravado and swagger. It wafts in with them like overapplied cologne. "You will see me and respect me," demands their presence. It's arrogance, yes, but sexualized. We see this in men who get off on their own awesomeness (even when they are far from awesome). Their own reflection seems to arouse them. Some men use sexual conquest as the mirror in which to catch the gleam of their own reflection. The affirmation of a new fling or hookup feeds their inflated idea of self. The "relationships" they engage in may be consensual on the surface, but they are hardly loving.

Sex paradoxically becomes for these men a way to avoid intimacy, not find it. By getting a lot of sex, some men soothe the fear or insecurity they feel. This is desperate or demanding sex. This is where sex can actually feel like a need—but the real need is to soothe their inner insecurity.

"Hilarious"

Peggy Orenstein noticed a common habit among the young men she interviewed. They used the word "hilarious" a lot in reference to really awful sexual things, from competitions to see who can have sex with the most women to sex jokes in the locker room, the rape of an unconscious drunk woman, or calling women sluts or hoes. All of these were labeled hilarious. If it's just a joke, they seemed to think, it's no big deal. Orenstein summarizes this use of "hilarious":

> "Hilarious" is a safe haven, a default position when something is inappropriate, confusing, upsetting, depressing, unnerving, or horrifying; when something is simultaneously sexually explicit and dehumanizing; when it defies their ethics; when it evokes any of the emotions meant to stay safely behind the wall. "Hilarious" offers distance, allowing them to subvert a more compassionate response that could be read as weak, overly sensitive, or otherwise unmasculine.[11]

Laugh at someone else so you don't get laughed at, the thinking goes. Remember, shame is the terror of being exposed and mocked. And when you're trying to protect yourself from being seen as less than a man, you'll even laugh at utterly violating and heartless acts. That's the spell of macho masculinity—to see compassion as weak. But it actually makes you a coward, the opposite of a man. True courage is about having a heart.

Recently, Tiger Woods made the news for what he later said was all "fun and games." During the Genesis Open tournament, after outdriving fellow player Justin Thomas on the ninth hole, Woods slipped him a tampon. He tried to hide it, but the cameras caught it anyway.[12] You get the punch line, right? Justin hit like a girl. Isn't that just simple fun?

Take a closer look. Tampons help a woman manage her monthly period. Using one to ridicule a man is condescending to the sacred ritual of life and birth that women embody every month as well as the inherent suffering and vulnerability of that cycle. It lowers femininity and female anatomy to no more than an insult, another way of mutilating women into body parts.

I don't know what shame Tiger is managing. This is the same Tiger Woods who confessed on camera that he had cheated on his wife multiple times, even calling it sex addiction. That took humility. He admitted the arrogance of his actions and the damage those actions caused.

But maybe he didn't actually get free of his shame. I don't know his sexual journey, but I wonder if Tiger ever thought he needed more than just to sober up. He needs, like all of us, to get his innocence back.

Porn and Misogyny

Porn use also involves this same pattern of relief and revenge. I said emotional dysregulation and anxiety drive a lot of motivation to look at porn. Porn seems to promise the relief of overwhelm. But it never stays this simple. More is always at stake because, again, you are not simply an animal. You are a complex being.

Porn always tells a story. It always has a script. I listened to a Bible podcast once that asked what the difference was between Song of Songs and porn. The host's conclusion surprised me: the major difference was the storyline driving the lovers.[13]

No matter where pornography begins, it almost always ends in violation and degradation. What a man finds when he first searches is never the only thing he gets. It always ritualizes contempt for someone. Even if it seems nice, it's on the internet for anyone to see, and the internet is not a nice place. Writer Gail Dines points out that a lot of porn bakes misogyny and racism right into it. It focuses almost exclusively on male pleasure and release (the orgasm gap in porn is a whopping 80 percent).[14] She writes, "The story pornography tells about men is . . . as soulless, unfeeling, amoral life-support systems for erect penises who are entitled to use women in any way they want."[15] The soulful, passionate lover of Song of Songs would weep at this. Porn is where the lover goes to die.

You don't even have to watch porn to be impacted by it. The porn industry has begun to *pornify* all beauty standards. We have a whole beauty industry driven to groom men into having contempt for other bodies by foisting impossible standards on everyone, but especially women. Porn wants to destroy any curiosity or appreciation you may have for the literal billions of beautiful ways God has made bodies. It capitalizes on contempt, quite literally. It hopes we see each other, especially women, with critical eyes, sizing them up and judging them. And it hopes women see beauty and body products, surgeries and diets, supplements and weight loss programs as the solution.

A pornified culture enslaves women and leaves men with a very emaciated sense of beauty.

———————

I sat across from Brad, my counselor, and leaned back into the couch, having just opened up about the struggles in my then young marriage. I awaited his response. He looked at me with the calmest, kindest eyes and said, "You are a raging misogynist."

"Misogyny" means the hatred of women. And Brad was telling me my heart was full of the stuff. I couldn't speak for a very long time. He was right. Nothing was *raging* or extreme about my views or behaviors. I was a really nice guy. I looked normal. But he saw the patterns in my young marriage and my sporadic porn struggle. He knew where this all was heading if he didn't intervene.

I tear up thinking about that moment. His comment had the accuracy of a steady-handed surgeon that was coming for the cancer. I needed to let him speak. All my sessions with Brad to that point had left me with no doubt that he cared about me. I knew he meant what he said in love.

He was calling out the ways I had kept control of the power with my wife. In our two-year-young marriage I'd developed this habit of cringing whenever she hugged me or initiated affection. I feared she was trying to take from me; her affection was "needy." So I controlled the affection. If I wanted a hug or a kiss or sex, I initiated. If she wanted it, I bristled and pulled away.

I'd also confessed to Brad my intermittent struggle with pornography, and he got right to the cancer. Whatever else was true of these struggles, I had begun to ritualize my shame and suffering with power over women. Power over my wife, first and foremost, and pornography were grooming me to hold power over women at a broader level. I had no idea the story of sexual harm underpinning all that control. But my contempt was holding the pain at bay.

You can be a nice guy and still hate women. You can hold doors for women and still subconsciously have contempt for them. Contempt for women is as old as the fall of man. When God said to Eve in Genesis 3:16 that "your desire will be for your husband and he will rule over you," he was foreshadowing misogyny. The original goal was not for man to rule over woman, but for co-leadership ("Let *them* have dominion," from Genesis 1:27). A man's desire to rule is part of broken, fallen masculinity. Misogyny disowns the lover within by seeking power over women rather than sharing power with them.

"That dude is such a dick." We all know this phrase's meaning. It's the catch-all phrase for any man who is doing something heartless or contemptuous, whose actions are selfish or disrespectful or just plain rude. But think about it for a minute. We reduce a guy like this down to his genitalia because, symbolically, he regards his own pleasure as the highest priority.

The dominant picture of sexuality in the world is that of the self-absorbed, sex-addicted man driven by his own desires for release and not much else. Sadly, a lot of these guys pass as examples of masculinity.

The writer of Song of Songs made it clear that sexual desire begins in the heart.[16] Not our loins. Hopefully you see that now. But when a man turns his heart cold and bad, reserving it only for himself, he begins to feel *driven* by his animal instinct—because as the heart goes, so goes the person. Maybe this is the clearest picture of other-centered contempt: a guy who's disowned his lover heart becomes such a dick.

But no one is born with an utterly self-absorbed heart, turned off to those around him. Every man is wired to be a poetic lover. Though it's hard to want to extend nearly any compassion to a guy like this, even here we need to be curious at what shame made him disown his heart connection.

Self-Contempt Spurred by Shame

Contempt, as I said, comes in two flavors. Contempt for others is hopefully clearer by now. But we need to discuss self-hatred. Because that fight-or-flight escape from shame can become willful hatred and harm of yourself. We can disown or turn against the parts of us we feel got us in trouble, exposed us to the world, or felt inherently dirty or wrong. This may even seem like the virtuous or moral way out of shame. It may look like an attempt to kill the flesh, to deny ourselves and take up our cross, or to put others above ourselves. Or it may simply look like someone who struggles with insecurity, self-esteem, or self-care.

Those who self-harm deserve compassion, no doubt. But we must recognize the willful act of anger behind it. In simple terms, it's just another form of rejecting ourselves before being rejected. The thinking goes like this: *I will hate the part of me that feels shameful before you reject me for it.* That impulse is still rooted in a desire to escape and self-soothe by splitting your self, isolating and mocking the part that feels wrong or dirty or pathetic. Self-contempt joins the voice of accusation and assaults the very glory of God in us.

Self-Righteousness

The greatest literal example of this came at the hands of Origen of Alexandria, an early church father, theologian, and philosopher. The incident is reported by the church historian Eusebius, though scholars are divided whether it is historical or apocryphal. As his renown as a teacher and theologian grew, it is said that Origen wanted to make sure he avoided sexual wrongdoing, especially because he discipled women. So, after reading Matthew 19:12 about those who became eunuchs by their own hands, Origen castrated himself. No anesthesia. No steady hand of a surgeon. Lopped them right off.[17]

The violence of castrating oneself—taking revenge on one's literal sex organs—stands to me as the ultimate symbol of sexual self-hatred. And yet Origen was not alone in his assault on his own body. Many men now deemed as saints throughout church history have performed similar acts of self-harm. The Latin church father Jerome, after having a dream about dancing women, describes starving himself for weeks (beyond the spiritual discipline of fasting) and fleeing to the desert—"A place of torture for my unhappy flesh"—where he literally bruised his body black and blue against the rocks.[18] There are several paintings of this, depicting him readying a rock to beat his own chest.[19] St. Benedict is said to have done similar by throwing himself into a thorn bush when he felt sexually aroused.[20] The latter has a stained glass window in a cathedral in Nuremberg, Germany, venerating this act as holy.[21]

All these acts of self-mutilation were held as admirable. But in the name of attempting to rid themselves of sin, these men opposed the very design of God within them, shutting down their own arousal and harming their good bodies. And while these may sound like wild tales of self-harm gone mad (or maybe they don't), that spirit lives in the hearts of too many men.

Some of this still gets sanctioned out loud. A man told me about a sex addiction recovery group that had its members pick punishments for themselves when they would "act out." Cold showers. Donating money to an organization they hate. And everyone was encouraged to snap their wrists with rubber bands when they had sexual thoughts.

For some men, this phenomenon manifests as anxiously repenting again and again to God. I know a man who, for ten years, thought of a woman he slept with in college every time he took communion, repenting again and again for this sin. Something initially seems humble and broken about this type of contrition. But without further help geared toward uncovering why he couldn't accept grace, he was really just torturing himself with the aroma of good food rather than eating the lavish meal of God's grace.

Even the message that all men lust can create its own subtle form of self-harm. To believe this is to believe that men are fundamentally programmed to lust. It brings its own shutdown and self-dismissal of your God-designed lover heart. Again, to refer to Sheila Wray Gregoire's study, 76 percent of men believed they had a problem with lust. And yet, when questioned specifically on this, only 33 percent showed any sign of struggling with anything that resembled lust. They were conflating noticing beauty in a woman with lust. Let's call this the self-condemnation gap.

The closest Jesus came to talking about masturbation was in the Sermon on the Mount. Right after blowing his audience's sandals off by saying that lust was just as much an act of adultery as the act itself (Matthew 7:27–28), Jesus said, "If your right eye causes you to stumble, gouge it out, . . . And if your right hand causes you to sin, cut it off. It is better for you to lose one part of your body than for your whole body to go into hell" (5:29–30). What might a man do with his hands while he's lusting with his eyes? We get it, Jesus.

But do we? This is not an invitation to self-mutilation as a cure for masturbating. It's hyperbole. Again, Jesus was inviting his listeners into the world of the heart. If adultery is an act of the heart, cutting off a hand ain't going to help you much. You need to read the heart. It's echoed in Paul's words: "Circumcision is circumcision of the heart, by the Spirit" (Romans 2:29). The kingdom is always about the heart.

Abusing yourself sounds so much like crucifying your flesh (Galatians 5:24) and taking up your cross and following Jesus (Matthew 16:24). But Jesus also commanded you to love your neighbor "as yourself" (Mark 12:31). Jesus assumes self-love. We must be very wary of repenting of having a body with a sexuality when trying to cleanse the heart of sin. You may actually be abusing what God called good in you—namely, your innocent sexual design.

Self-Harm

Of course self-hatred doesn't always take on such a pious tone. Sometimes it's more overt and much less sanctified. I've sat with many men who confess to punching themselves in the face when their sexual shame strikes. It's often scripted with words of self-hatred. "You idiot." "You are so stupid." Some men cut themselves or burn themselves. Some assault their own genitals.

Some do it in more subtle ways, like not eating or overeating. I've certainly done workouts driven by self-hatred where I injure myself. And that's kind of the point. "You wuss," were the words that would echo in my head, my revenge on what I thought was weak about my body.

You met Chris in the last chapter when he was just a boy suffering the sexual abuse of his mother in her act of cleaning his privates too zealously during his baths. Later as a travelling businessman, he found himself regularly away from his family, lonely and bored. Sometimes he would have a meal and retire to his hotel room. Sometimes, when the shame was really bad, he would find a bar and drink himself to oblivion. He sometimes remembered what followed but often didn't.

He definitely remembers the night he got arrested when the police found him in a dark alley engaging in a sex act. That sobered him up a bit. But he was still baffled about the motive. Clearly, this violated his wife and family and God. But we must also see the reckless harm he put himself in, the self-sabotage. This was not a lonely ache for love but flippant revenge on himself. He was living out the dissociative violation of his own body, carelessly putting himself in the same harm.

Self-hatred is not always so demonstrative. It can show up in more passive, subtle ways too. Mark, who you met before in his story of being rejected by his father at age seven, has a habit of forgetting his heart medication. With every physical and new round of blood work, his doctor preaches the same sermon at him. He knows he needs to do it. He knows he needs to exercise. But something simply holds him back—his subconscious self-hatred.

Contempt's False Promise

This brings us full circle. Evil doesn't simply want you stuck in shame. Evil wants your life. And if it can't have that, it wants to kill the lover within you any way it can. It wants to blow up your life, ruin your good name, even take your life. And it hopes to explode shrapnel in as many people around you as possible.

That's the goal of contempt. It seems to promise relief from the terror of shame by offering us something that feels like power. But it's entirely built on one major assumption: that you believe the voice of shame.

Almost none of this is conscious when we're acting out of it. And often the original shame that fuels our acting out cannot even be named. "That's because evil is very efficient," says Dan Allender, "and skilled at what it does."[22] Once we utilize one method of escape, that path gets easier and easier to use. Our shame escape becomes ritualized. What we once experienced as an external temptation becomes an internally motivated habit. We take over for evil, really. Soon, no temptation is really necessary. It all starts to feel normal and familiar, until we don't even think about it.

Did the men on that roof with me all feel simultaneous flinches of shame? I don't think so. I think it was just the ritual. But it was fueled by shame somewhere, sometime in events long disowned. That shame energy still influences today, though the original temptation and ritual are forgotten.

Here's the thing: Not a single act of contempt ever helped anyone escape their shame. Every single story in this chapter depicts men whose contempt left them absolutely stuck in their shame. Not only that, their reliance on contempt actually worsened their situation, because every act of contempt brings even deeper shame than the original act.

It's not just a habit. It's a downward spiral.

Remember Mark? On his honeymoon, he felt like he might finally get the upper hand and reject someone before he got rejected. He would not be that same foolish boy caught off guard by his father's rejection of his affection. So he pulled away from his new bride. It brought relief—for a moment. It felt safer than risking with his wife.

But had he really escaped? The women in his pornography will never reject him. But they also don't actually kiss him goodnight or hug him or give him any real affection. The best he has is his own hand. When he clicks off the internet, he is that same little boy yearning for care and love.

We are never simply reacting or acting out. We are *reenacting*. We end up reliving the very wounding and shame we thought we were escaping.

Radio shock jock Howard Stern, renowned for his interviews with porn stars and intrusive and provocative questions to guests, said this about his own sexual journey:

> After my divorce, I realized, "Oh, wow, I can go have sex." And I
> was running around, picking up women. Then all of a sudden, it

dawned on me that I really didn't need that much sex. I just wanted somebody with me every minute. I was using women as a surrogate mother. When I tapped into that, it suddenly became very childish behavior. And really, was it so great f—ing every night? They're using me for my fame, I'm using them for their beauty, and the whole f—ing thing seemed empty.[23]

Whatever gave Mr. Stern the courage to say this, bless him. He said it for you and for me. I don't know his story with his mom or his divorce, but the man has that same messy mix of wounds and shame as we all do. And he tried to use his power to consume women to soothe an immature ache for attention. And it didn't work. It left him a worse human—messier, more childish, and emptier than ever.

Young and hungry becomes childish and empty in the spiral of contempt and shame. And contempt will never lead us out of this spiral.

This was a very heavy chapter to write and I'm sure to read. You probably feel much of what we all feel when we use contempt to get out of shame—nauseated and despairing. And stuck. There is only one real lasting way out of shame. It's our only hope. Let's discover it together in the next chapter.

SEVEN

The Only Path to Sexual Healing

Then it is only kindness that makes sense anymore . . .
only kindness that raises its head
from the crowd of the world to say
It is I you have been looking for,
and then goes with you everywhere
like a shadow or a friend.
—NAOMI SHIHAB NYE

The television's hum got closer as I descended the basement staircase. The cooler air offered comfort on this muggy summer day. I felt relieved on an otherwise apathetic Saturday afternoon. I turned the corner of the stairs to see my whole family in our "family room." It was a rare occurrence for us all to be together in a room of our house other than the kitchen. The TV kept my brother and father from noticing me. My sister stood helping my mom with our new computer in the corner.

"Sam, do you know what this is about? All these pornographic websites keep popping up and I don't know what's going on." My mother genuinely believed that something was wrong with the computer and innocently wanted my help. I gulped a big breath of air and said, "Yeah, I know. I've been looking at them."

My entire family stared at me with sudden rapt attention. It seemed even the golfer on the television dropped his club and his jaw. I knew it would be a bomb to my family . . . at least I hoped it would be. At nineteen, I was getting scared of my growing use of pornography and really wanted help.

But getting caught like this felt terrible. Excruciating really. I might as well have just walked naked on stage to a gasping and wide-eyed and packed arena. I promptly left the room, double-timed down the hallway to make it to my bedroom, and crashed on my bed trying to get the thumping in my chest to stop.

Now what happens? I thought.

A few minutes later my mom knocked on my door. Um, awkward. I said nothing as she came in. I was still paralyzed by the whole experience. She walked over and sat on the bed. The silence lingered. Then she broke it. "What if I call a counselor for you to meet with?" I nodded, not even looking up, the shame too great to lift my head.

But it was grace. I met with my counselor for two years, and it changed my life. No, it saved my life, rescuing me from an engrossing depression and a very quickly descending darkness called pornography. And it instilled in me a love for counseling that later led me to pursue this craft as a profession. I shudder to think where I might have ended up had I not been caught in my darkness.

There is a gift in getting caught in our sexual shame and path of contempt. Oh, it won't feel like a gift. All those lies and all that hiding will come tumbling down like all kinds of wreckage with a thunderous kaboom. With your shadow self and double life now being so very clear, you will see the hearts of those you love break in front of you. And you will want to run. You will struggle to be honest through and through, trying to hold back the truth of it all even just a little, hoping to ease the pain.

Even if you have to catch *yourself,* getting caught can save your sanity. It can end the double life you've been hiding for so long. Maybe yours is the double life of sexual sin. But there are other subtle ways you can use contempt to manage your buried-lover self. Either way, here's your chance to no longer be a split personality, two people co-existing inside your skin. There will finally be the chance of a true return to peace and wholeness and reality, something never even in the realm of possibility until the truth comes out.

God Refuses to Let Us Hide

God's very first question in the Bible is an act of pursuit. He's trying to find his people. When Adam and Eve partook of the forbidden fruit, life changed instantly. Surely they had experienced so much awe for each other and the good world they inhabited. They knew what it meant to be overpowered with the pleasure of the good. They knew only this full, openhearted, and wildly good way with the world.

But now, for the first time, they knew pure fear with no hint of pleasure. They had never known being overpowered by fear. They felt terror over their own nakedness, their own exposure. So they ran and hid, the reactive response invoked by shame. But in hiding, in listening to the shame, they chose to break relationship with God.

But God does not hide—at least, not to avoid. Instead, he calls out to those that are hiding: "Where are you?"

This is the hide-and-seek I played with my boys when they were little. They hoped in the secret magic most kids believe that, in covering their eyes, they would disappear. God knew full well where Adam and Eve were, but he pursued them to show them one thing. He brings them his heart—front and center.

I can't help but hear in this question his longing to connect with them. We can only imagine what days with God in a perfect world looked like. A life with nothing impeding our connection with him? It's almost too much to imagine. It makes me so homesick. But it's a yearning question from God. He missed them. No, God doesn't need us. But he *wants* us. And he refuses to leave us hidden in shame or stuck in a story of our own making.

Adam and Eve were stuck in a story of fear and hiding. A story that would have gone on ad nauseam if God hadn't found them. God came to disrupt and entice them out again.

Here God displayed the true, wild lover heart—a heart that we are meant to reflect.

This is the deep of God calling to the deep in us all.

So where are *you*? Where is the lover within you? What have you done with your lover heart? Where have you taken your sexuality? And what story are you stuck in like some childhood merry-go-round long after you've screamed to stop?

God refuses to leave you lost in shame. He will not stop trying to find you. There is no such thing as "too far gone" for God. He will disrupt and entice you, even if it takes your whole life.

We aren't made for shame. We don't work well in the stuff. It's not natural to stay hidden or shut down. We are made for relatedness and aliveness, intimacy and adventure, as John Eldredge describes it.[1] Anything less than an alive and related heart just won't ever sit well in us. We will always want intimacy, freedom and wholeness, true virility and aliveness. And even when you cannot or will not want it for yourself, even then God will never stop wanting it for you.

He has a far better story to write for you, one in which his love looks you long in the face with the kindest eyes, hoping you will look back. He wants the real you to be free and alive. He has a story for your sexuality too. He wants you to recover your original blessing, that innocence and wonder and awe he made you with. Your nakedness is not your shame. Your vulnerability is your glory.

God walks the terrain of your life, trying to find you stuck in the story you can't escape.

I heard a story once about a woman who wanted to take her kids to a new park. She Googled it first to get directions and check it out via the satellite images. You know, see the playground equipment and so forth. She pulled up the street view too. As she zoomed in to get a closer look, there sitting on the bench in the official Google photo was her husband. And he was not alone. When she asked him about the picture and the woman sitting next to him, she discovered he was having an affair.

That is a story too wild for coincidence. Caught by Google Maps? I'm left with only one conclusion. God wanted him found.

God wants to find us all. God will go wherever you are to come get you, and he will do what it takes, even catch you in the act. This is the gift in getting caught.

I don't know what you've done to cope with or escape your shame.

It may not be the wilds of sexual indulgence or a park bench date with a mistress. Maybe you just tuck away your passion, keeping your love tame and manageable. Or maybe you have done things you plan to take to the grave.

The wildest part of God's heart is that he is not catching you in the act to rage at you. God is not pursuing you with the goal of exposing you and punishing you. He is pursuing you to bring you out of your sin and shame. He pursues you because he loves you and wants you back.

No matter how much you've given up on yourself, he has not given up on you.

Jesus' Greatest Kindness

I firmly believe that Jesus saved his greatest acts of kindness for the sexually oppressed and broken. He shared his most tender, personal, and heartfelt conversations with them. Take Jesus' interaction with the naked, possessed wild man in Luke 8:26–39 as an iconic example of this very thing.

After a wild night of calming the wind and the Sea of Galilee, Jesus and the disciples arrived in the land of the Gadarenes. And literally the moment Jesus stepped off the boat, a naked wild man ran toward him, screaming at the top of his lungs. This was a man, we later learn, who suffered torment from much evil. Nothing could contain him. People had tried to actually chain him down, but he always broke free. He roamed in the wild of the mountains and even the local graveyards, out of his mind and without a home. His spiritual and mental agony was so bad that he regularly cut his own body in acts of violent self-harm.

We know nothing further of this man's story, nothing of what led to this moment in his life. But read the scene. Human behavior is never random. Nor is the assault of evil. So look with me, as hard as it is. He's naked, exposed in perpetual shame. He has no home, no regular experience of love or care or community. He roams graveyards and wild places, displaying a kindredness with death. And he suffers deep demonic torment. We can only guess the scenes of trauma that led to this depth of oppression. But it must be awful.

Though Luke gave no statement about this and it's obviously my interpretation, my therapist eyes say it has much to do with his body and sexuality. He was a real man after all, with a heart like yours and mine. The demonic presence is myriad; it literally named itself "Legion" (Luke 8:30). In his version of the same story, Matthew actually recorded this as being two possessed men (8:28). This is pure speculation on my part, but I wonder if this is in fact Matthew seeing double because of the man's deep inner split. He literally talked as a "we" under the influence of evil. And no amount of chaining or containing could free or heal him. All of it is so overwhelming and tragic.

As I said, I believe this is a real story about a real man. But I find his plight to be so representative of our own stories. So many of us have banished our sexuality to the wilderness and shadows. As I've mentioned before, we have so few conversations about the lover within us. And he often lives banished to our subconscious, disowned and rejected, roaming the wilds of our being. And to some degree, we all live in the torment of shame. Cursed.

Jesus found nothing repelling about the man. He asked him his name. Oh, the tenderness of Jesus just in that simple act. Jesus was trying to *reach* him. It brings tears to my eyes to think of this fierce kindness. Jesus will not recoil.

The story goes that Jesus confronted the evil oppressing the man and cast it into a herd of pigs, who raced into the water and drowned themselves. What a wild picture of evil's ambition to bring as much death as possible. This caused the herdsmen to scatter in terror. I would too. The herdsmen then told the story to everyone they could and brought the townspeople to see what had happened.

And there they found the man, sitting with Jesus, "clothed and in his right mind" (Luke 8:35). What a truly unbelievable change in this scene. It's calm. The man was well. And he sat talking with Jesus like an old friend. It's so intimate and close. It probably left the herdsmen at a loss concerning how to explain to the townspeople the chaos they had run from earlier.

Why did the Gospel writers mention this man was clothed again? I wonder if the man asked for clothes. Where did he even get these clothes? Maybe Jesus or one of the disciples had an extra tunic in the boat. The clothes signify to me the restoration of this man's dignity. As we mentioned earlier, clothes are a gift of comfort that protect us in the blistering heat and veil our glory from a world that cannot handle it. In being given clothes, this man's authority over his own body was restored.

And what did they talk about as they sat together? This was more than a simple five-minute conversation. I imagine this man had a lot of questions for Jesus, like, *What the hell just happened?* And I can imagine that Jesus offered the man even more healing, unraveling the very story that had brought him to madness in the first place.

Either way, Jesus restored something in this man that left the townsfolk beside themselves. I love Eugene Peterson's paraphrase of this: "It was a holy moment, and for a short time they were more reverent than curious" (Luke 8:36 MSG). No more a pariah of shame and a living terror, his glory restored, the man *moved* people with awe.

The crowd's eyes bounced from this guy to Jesus and back again.

Oh, and the dead herd of pigs. They tried to make it make sense. But it's all too much to take in.

The townspeople asked Jesus to leave. But the man in his right mind begged to follow him. Jesus charged him to go tell his story. And he did. His heart overflowed with gratitude. He had met the kindness of Jesus.

———

Jesus was a wild man unbeholden to the powers of the day. But, again, his wild heart held the most immense kindness for the sexually oppressed and broken, sharing some of his most intimate conversations with them. The naked savage of the Gadarenes received this kindness. But think, too, of the story of the woman caught in adultery told in John 8, an act punishable by stoning under Jewish law (Leviticus 20:10).

According to this story, while Jesus was teaching at the temple gates, the religious leaders dragged her out in the open, right in the middle of the crowd. We should note that they did not bring the involved man there, though by law he too should have been stoned (Deuteronomy 22:24). We can see the sleight of hand that shows their true hearts: their contempt for this woman and her sexuality. In response, Jesus drew in the dirt with his finger. We don't really know what he wrote, but he then verbally called out the bloodlust in these men by inviting the one who was without sin to heave the first rock (John 8:7). Those men may have been gutless, but at least none of them was stupid enough to claim to be sinless. Could it be that they began to see their own contempt?

The power of Jesus' confrontation scattered them until only he and the woman were left. And then Jesus seemed to crack a joke: "So, where is everyone? Is there no one to accuse and shame you?"

(paraphrase of John 8:10). The woman saw his wink and stepped just a little into the play. "No one, my Lord." Oh, the boldness of these words from her very own voice! She was banishing self-condemnation and self-hatred. Jesus turned with what I can only see as the kindest of eyes and said, "Then neither do I. Go and sin no more" (verse 11).

He was wild with kindness.

Or consider the story of the Samaritan woman at the well in John 4. Here again is another story of shame, not least of which is the woman's sexual story. She came at noon to the well—in the heat of the day rather than the cool of the morning with the rest of the women— because that's when no one else would be there. She was managing shame. But God will go where you are to find you. And so Jesus planted himself right there to meet her.

A Jewish man talking with a Samaritan woman crossed so many lines. Jews considered Samaritans to be a stain to the Jewish people since they mixed with Gentiles. And a man addressing a woman alone at this hour would have been seen as scandalous as well. This scenario even shocked the disciples later when they returned from town (John 4:27).

Jesus asked the Samaritan woman for a drink of water. It was a human connection and showed that he did not see her as dirty. She called out the uncouthness of his request, giving him an out if he wanted to save face. But Jesus only took the conversation deeper, playing his cards to get around her shame. He was trying to get to her heart.

Out of curiosity for her thirst, Jesus asked about her husband. She spilled a bit of her story: "I have no husband" (John 4:17). And seeing her vulnerability, Jesus moved toward the most shameful and painful part of her present life. "You have had five husbands, and the man you now have is not your husband" (verse 18). And she played her cards close to keep this about as far from her heart as possible. So she talked theology, making commentary on the prophets and the coming Messiah. Jesus honored the move and went with her conversation. Right when she least expected it, he got vulnerable with his true self: "I who speak to you am he" (verse 26). It was the offer of rescue—love and salvation, not shame and condemnation.

Again, I cannot hear Jesus' words here without seeing the kindness in his eyes. He was not trying to expose her. He met her shame with a bold invitation back to her desire, back to her thirst. And offered himself as her Messiah. Shame blew off her as fast as she could run back to town to tell the people that she had met a man who knew her most terrifying secrets (John 4:29). He was the hero they'd all been waiting for.

Escaping Shame Through Kindness

I said in the last chapter that there are only two ways out of shame. Not much is binary in life, but this one is absolutely blue pill or red pill. The most immediate flinch response we experience in the face of shame is to escape with contempt. Blow up the moment. Run or hit. Stay powered up in a state of defensiveness.

The only other option you have is kindness. We resist the flinch to run even a half second in order to stay in the moment and recognize the shame attack. We pause to breathe and slow down. To take a breath is to give oxygen to your body when it needs it most—our first act of kindness. We work to calm the alarm system of our bodies rather than answer its panic with escape. Tuning into your body rather than shutting down requires getting more vulnerable in the very moment you feel the least safe. It's a brave act.

And then we take the risk to call shame what it is: a damn liar. We turn the tables on shame and question it. That starts with getting curious about what provoked it. Maybe it's lying to you. Maybe love is still available (from yourself, God, or someone else you know who cares about you) and you can recover a sense of safety. Leaning into vulnerability like that takes immense courage.

If you don't want to handle your sexual shame with contempt, you must take a risk on love.

Contempt or kindness. That's it.

The demon-possessed man when he ran toward Jesus risked another round of chains and shunning. The woman caught in adultery, right in the moment she feared for her life, took a risk in trusting that Jesus really didn't want to accuse her. And that Samaritan woman at the well didn't run from an intriguing man at noon but stayed curious about his questions.

Evil wants you to trust the voice of shame, always and forever. Evil hopes you believe that shame is narrating the truth about you and that your only hope is to fight back with contempt. It pronounces, "You can't beat us; you can only join us."

Our God wants to find you. I believe right now he is trying to get to the lover within you. He wants to free your sexuality to be the good thing he created it to be.

But you will have to take a risk on love. You will have to jump.

God knew the risk you'd have to take on him. It's why he's described over and over again as slow to anger and rich in love (Psalm 145:8–9). And as Paul made clear, it's this very kindness he hoped we'd lean into for change: "It is the kindness of God that leads you to repentance" (Romans 2:2). Dare we say, it is *only* through leaning into his kindness that we change?

What Is Kindness?

What is this kindness stuff? Maybe it invokes an eye roll. Kindness feels too close to niceness. "Be nice!" seems akin to the demand to behave. Or worse, niceness sounds like a syrupy sweet, cheap excuse for love. It keeps things looking good on the outside but avoids anything deep or complicated. We're not used to something like kindness having such power. It doesn't seem to feel that way in our world.

But kindness is not niceness. It has more teeth than that. It's brave with the deep things of life. It looks you right in the face and really sees you with no pretense, with no threat of harm. Can you imagine someone who does not flee from you or metaphorically hit you back, who keeps their heart open and available but does not flinch from the truth? That is kindness. Someone who can hold the tension of facing reality but still stays openhearted and kind.

Kindness says *I can handle you. And I can love you.* It's profound.

In this sense, kindness is really an act of presence. It's when someone stays present to us and we stay present to them, even when things get hard or scary or overwhelming. It allows for attachment amid our shame attack. Shame will always tempt us to end connection. Contempt tempts us to break eye contact and get the hell out of there. It ruptures attachment. Kindness beckons us to stay. To risk the moment a little longer than we want.

Kindness is love. It's the experience of compassion that does not fall into pity or resort to condescending rescue. Have you ever felt really seen? Really cared for? That's kindness. And again, according to Paul, it's the very heart of what leads us to repentance. It's the only thing that can change us.

But where does this magical kindness come from? To anyone in the land of the living, God always offers his kindness. There is never a moment he doesn't hold that heart posture for you. When Jesus said he would never snuff out a smoldering wick or crush a bruised reed, he wanted you to hear the utter heart of his mercy. He will care for even the faintest ember of risk and openness in you.

While I was recovering from my own pornography use, I remember my therapist Lottie telling me to start singing, "Jesus loves me, this I know" right after I acted out, before I even closed the browser screen or did anything. I did it. It felt utterly scandalous to invite Jesus into that moment, while I was exposed with the pornography still on the screen. But I didn't invite him. He was already there. She was inviting me to turn my face to his kindness.

Wade sat in my office for many hours before we ever got to talking about his story of sexual abuse. We started with his boss, a man who manipulated him, who lied and asked Wade to cover for him. Wade embodies childlike joy like he's made of the stuff. He could get along with just about anyone. And his pull to go along to get along with his boss was fierce. He knew he was compromising himself to get his boss's favor. It tortured him.

And all the agony of this tension poured out at home on his wife and family. No, not literally in the form of physical violence. But his irritation and anger would come out in moments he least expected. It gutted him to know he hurt them with his sideways contempt. But repenting and apologizing alone was not making it stop. And so he came to me.

As we talked in my office, he found his deep well of anger at being manipulated, and little by little stopped playing along with his boss.

He was being kind to himself. And his growth actually surfaced his memories of sexual abuse, of a cousin and a house in the country in the summertime and a sleepover on the trampoline. Receiving kindness had welcomed back the memories of abuse. He was finally ready to handle them.

We talked for many sessions about this moment of abuse in his life. Especially about the setup. He'd been sent to a sleepover to help comfort an older cousin who'd just suffered the loss of his father. He looked up to this cousin a lot and always appreciated his friendship. And there on the trampoline, his cousin manipulated this comfort into abuse.

"Something died in me that day. I guess I'd call it my innocence," Wade said.

Those words wrecked my heart on his behalf. Wade was childlike innocence embodied. And the fact he thought it was dead grieved me. But he felt convinced it would never again live inside him. A day came when Wade felt a pull to go back home, to revisit his cousin's house and walk the ground he walked that night to the trampoline. The geography of our pain matters. He wanted to say goodbye to his innocence, feeling he needed to give it a proper burial, pay homage to the death of it.

He drove his truck back to his Colorado mountain town for a visit. And while at his aunt's house, he snuck out the door to walk again that march of death to the trampoline, the place he was abused. He stood at the bottom of the hill, like a somber pallbearer turning over his lines of last goodbye to his innocence.

"Can I walk with you?" said a voice.

He looked around. He'd heard that voice before and always took it to be the voice of God. "Sure," he said out loud.

He recounted the story to me like this: "I felt like Jesus walked with me up that hill to where the trampoline once stood. He didn't say much else, though I felt his presence. When we reached the top, I planned to bury the body of the boy I once was. But instead, I felt Jesus say to me, 'He's more alive than you know.'"

Wade wept, hoping beyond hope this might be true. And as we sat together in my office, reveling in this story, he said, "Dare I say, my innocence actually feels resurrected."

Paul described our God as "the God who gives life to the dead and calls into being things that were not" (Romans 4:17). God wants to resurrect you—yes, one day in full, but for now to help you recover your innocence.

Wade lived believing his innocence was as good as dead the day his cousin abused him. He felt convinced that he was a fool for ever trusting his cousin. And worse, he felt perverted for ever enjoying the bond with him. That shame made it difficult to see his boss's manipulation as his *boss's* sin. It felt like something he provoked in people, as if he was responsible for the fact that they were using him. He didn't know where he ended and his boss began.

When he welcomed his innocence back that day, he found a deeper love for the boy in him who cared for his cousin. He saw that boy's goodness—the same goodness that was in the man who had compassion for his boss. It allowed him to see where his boss was using his kind heart. And he was empowered to stop playing along.

That's the story God unwound within Wade. His innocence was not dead at all. It was disowned in the shadows of shame but more alive than he knew.

But it's easy to say this and far harder to experience it. The stories where evil strikes against our innocence and sexuality do not simply exist as lies in our head. Trauma involves so much felt experience, called implicit memory, full of sensations and feelings, sounds and smells, sights and, yes, geography. We are so embodied that we can't simply "speak against the lies" and be free.

Wade was not instantly healed. He walked the ground of his trauma for a long time in therapy by talking out the embodied feeling of his experience. And then he went back to the literal ground of his story. And for whatever reason, in the full sensation of that experience Jesus' voice of kindness healed him.

Unwinding the Story

C. S. Lewis said, "Evil can be undone, but it cannot 'develop' into good. Time does not heal it. The spell must be unwound, bit by bit, 'with backward mutters of dissevering power'—or else not."[2] Ah yes, the spell of evil on you, the shame that entrances you to stay stuck in a story, believing the plot is just you and your bad behavior. That's the spell alright.

And it convinces a lot of men to bury their pain in the hope that it will die. As I shared earlier, one study of documented sexual abuse survivors found that only 16 percent of men admitted to its truth.[3] These boys' abuse had been reported, investigated, and proven true by a social worker, meaning there was no doubt it happened. And yet only 16 percent could acknowledge it. Not everyone has a story of overt sexual abuse. But as I've said, everyone has a story. We all bear the marks of sexual harm and sexual shame. And evil's manipulation of our nervous system keeps us silent.

These stories don't stay buried and inanimate. Evil has been trying to set you up for a long time to keep reenacting your story of brokenness and shame, causing things to happen in your life to get you to believe it's just you, that you keep messing up exclusively out of your own awfulness. It keeps bringing you the same accusations of shame so that you act out in agreement with them. Wade did not plan to work for a boss with a crafty heart who manipulated his kindness for his own pleasure. "Why does this keep happening to me?" he asked, wondering how yet another betrayal of his kindness stacked on top of the rest. "It must be me. I'm the common denominator."

That is the kiss of death in your healing: to believe it's just you and to keep silent. In the words of Dan Allender, "Evil loves silence and secrets."[4]

It's not that evil is responsible for the choices we make. We bear that culpability before God. But the accusations of shame are surely the work of evil. That's the difference. When we agree with the shame, we stay stuck in the cycle of our story, even the cycle of repeating our own sins. This is the traumatic reenactment we named last chapter, and it's often at the root of what we call a shame cycle or even an addiction cycle.

Lewis is right. Time alone is not going to free you from the impact of your sexual story. You have to walk the terrain of the past, maybe literally as Wade did but at least figuratively, uncovering and telling the stories of your sexual formation. I believe this is a part of what it means to "leave your father and mother and hold fast to your wife" (Genesis 2:24 paraphrase). In order to grow up sexually and be a mature lover, we must know the sexual formation of the boy in us and help set him free where he is stuck in stories. We take our sexuality with us when we leave our parents' home.

I find that this is where God uses other people to be the presence of his kindness. A good friend who holds space for you, a therapist who listens, a partner who cares. Look for kind faces. You'll find some. Ask them for help.

The Only Path to Sexual Healing

Soon after my pornography use was discovered that day in my basement, my mother did actually find me a therapist, a man named Peter. I sat in my first appointment like a kid sent to the principal's office, assuming I was here mostly to get scolded out of my porn use and prompted back into behaving. He asked me questions and more questions, about me and my story and life, and I answered them all, still tense for the moment he might turn mean.

But with each passing question, something in me relaxed. And near the end, for the first time in many years, I wept.

"What did you just do?" I asked him as we ended. It felt like some form of magic. I started so frozen and braced for punishment and now sat in tears, really grieving for myself and the pain of my father wound. I see now the curiosity and kindness he used like a scalpel to divide the true me and my story from my self-hatred and growing ritual of contempt. His kindness let me risk on love. That was his magic. But he just answered me with a smile and said, "See you next week."

No, I didn't instantly stop using pornography forever. That took unpacking a few more layers, as I mentioned in a previous chapter. But I took a radical shift that day. The work of forsaking contempt for kindness had started.

A few years later, I sat in a group therapy retreat where I told some of my sexual story. I believed the words I shared would indict me in the deepest way, that these pages told a story that was sure to damn me as being the vilest of deviants. This was the spell of shame. The pages held my fallenness, that was not in question. But did they reveal an inhuman monster, evil to his core? I feared the worst.

As I read page after page with this group, my panicked gaze flitted back and forth about the room. My mind trained on the slightest flinch, sure that someone or everyone might flee at any moment because I was that dirty. But no one left.

And when I finished reading the pages, they all just sat there, relaxed and at rest. A guy across from me looked like he was slumped in a beach chair. The woman to my left may as well have been doing yoga she was so calm. The kindest thing they did for me was just sit there being present and bearing witness. My nervous system began to calm down, and I no longer wanted to bolt. If they weren't scared of me, maybe I wasn't the monster I feared. Their kindness let me relax into my body more. It let me turn the tables on shame and question it. In a word, it let me relax into being curious about my body response. Where did I learn to be so scared of myself?

Curiosity About Sin

One of the wildest gifts the grace of Jesus gives us is the ability to be curious about sin. We don't need to simply repent of sin. We need to be curious about it too—truly intrigued by both our own sin and the failings of others. Beyond simply being shocked or heartbroken, we get to wonder, Why did I do that? Why did *they* do that? This is how we get to the heart of our motives and behaviors. Let it baffle us if we must. But I daresay if you can't be fascinated with your own sin, you can't change.

Curiosity is not meant to excuse away sin but to get to the heart of it. Dan Allender said once in a lecture, "Even in our worst sin, we can't completely eradicate our glory." This means our worst sin is often the place we find hints of our heart's deepest desire. We will always find that many other forces play into the moments of our sin. And often what we thought was our sin wasn't really the heart of what happened.

I thought my struggle with porn was simply a struggle with lust and an undermanaged sex drive. I would have never guessed it was really about control and misogyny and trying to flee a story of pain I could never really escape.

C. S. Lewis said that what we call our sin often involves a mess of circumstances and explanations beyond our control, which can muddle the thing we need to own. "If there are real extenuating circumstances, [God] will overlook them. Often He must know many excuses that we have never thought of."[5] God sees the story that set you up. He knows this. And once we unearth that story, only then can we really see the heart of our sin.

Curiosity is one of the kindest gifts we can give each other. If you think of a fight with a loved one, it's really gracious and humanizing to hear out what may have contributed to why they acted the way they did. The stress, fear, pain, or desire they felt. In other words, at the heart of all sin is the wild tension of the good desires we have brought to really awful places.

———

Here is something that happens often. A man comes into my counseling office, and usually in the course of us talking about how he is doing, he confesses, "I look at porn." It's a worthy and noble confession. I always respect a man who can openly admit it. It's something that takes courage and bravery. Many men never talk about it with anyone in their lives.

Silence follows. We are honoring the ripple effect of his courage, which is a crazy combination of, "I feel more terrible and better all at the same time." But then the question bubbles up: "What do you look at?" Yeah, it's awkward and vulnerable and a step deeper. *You got a license to ask that question?* As a matter of fact, I do sorta have a license to ask that question. Not the point. Calling it porn may help you confess it, but to fully heal it you've got to talk about what you look at, because porn can mean a whole lot of things. It's like having someone ask you what you ate for dinner and telling them, "Food." Right. But like, what food? Saying "porn" tells me almost nothing about what you struggle with. And I get it. What you look at may be what you are trying to forget. It feels shameful or awful, troubling or confusing. And you want to get past it as quickly as you can. If you're going to get to the bottom of your porn use, at some point you'll have to start being curious about exactly what you look at. There is meaning in what you look at. Lots of meaning.

Sexual fantasies are like dreams. They are chock-full of symbolism and subconscious bits of us—a veritable treasure trove of your suppressed stories and desires and aches and longings. Our shadow places can bubble up into our sexual desires and fantasies. Be wildly curious and careful with them. Sure, confess the lust they may provoke, but don't waste them.

This is where we need to bring our greatest curiosity: to the rituals of our relief. In the words of Jay Stringer, we need to listen to our lusts. "If we are willing to listen, our sexual struggles have so much to teach us."[6] This can be our porn use, other unwanted sexual behaviors, or other ways we live out our contempt to protect the lover within. And until we've healed these stories, they get acted out. Remember, all sexuality lives within a story. A passion play. Often our sexual fantasies become the reenacted stories of our pain buried in shame. Not the story of love and romance that sex was meant to be, but the broken fragments and clues of our past pain. Remember, I said at the beginning, our shadow self wants to come back home to us. Our fantasies are often the place this shadow tries to get our attention.

As Richard Rohr says, "If we do not transform our pain, we will most assuredly transmit it—usually to those closest to us: our family, our neighbors, our co-workers, and, invariably, the most vulnerable, our children."[7] And, I would add, even to ourselves, as further self-harm. We follow the smoke of our contempt to find the fires of our shame to redeem the stories of our harm.

Jason sat in my office and spilled the beans on his latest moment of looking at porn. We waited in that awkward silence as he looked at his toes. He broke the silence by saying how crazy it made him feel. It happened after a fight with his wife, which arose because he forgot something at the grocery store. That all seemed so trivial. So I asked, "What did you look at?"

"You really want me to answer that?"

I nodded.

"This feels awkward to talk about." Another pause as he thought and gathered courage. "I guess I was looking for a woman with a really genuine smile."

And just like that we were on very sacred ground, that razor's edge between sin and the image of God in him.

"I guess I wanted to feel liked." And his eyes welled up with tears.

This was not Jason's first day in counseling, mind you. And so where he went next happened because he had begun to welcome back his story. He knew the terrain well enough to let his heart keep talking. And it opened the door to a much deeper conversation.

"I'm thinking of how often I wanted that smile from my mom. It seemed like I only got it when I gave her foot rubs and let her talk."

Turns out Jason's mom regularly asked him to give her foot

massages. It became a ritual where she shared about her heartache with his father, including how few orgasms she ever had from him during sex. Can you hear the script of abuse in his story? The lines between son and confidant were lost altogether. She sexualized this mother-son moment of connection, setting him up to feel his ache for a mother's smile as sexual.

His longing for a mother's love felt so dirty to him, like he'd done something wrong. That was evil's voice to him. So he shut it down, only to force his search for a genuine mother's smile to show up in a shameful place: his porn use. That day in my office he risked being kind, and he wept for how his mom had used him. And I saw a boy returning to his innocent hunger for a mother's smile.

Healing Through Self-Compassion

This journey of kindness can end in healing only if you are willing to turn the corner toward self-compassion. If you can't be kind to yourself, you can't change. You need to reclaim the innocent longings within your sin, within your pain, within your story.

Often this involves a willingness to weep. It's where we come to recognize that, as Allender says, often what we've done to escape shame rivals the depth of abuse we've suffered.

Dacher Keltner, in his research on awe, says the emotion closest to awe is grace. And he described this grace emotion as "the feeling of the Divine provenance of the kindness and goodness of life."[8] I love that. Every single one of our stories reveals glimpses of our original goodness. And one of the greatest acts of kindness is to listen close for those moments. It's the very innocence Jesus wants to recover in us.

You have these stories.

I can still remember the shock on Chris's face the day he told me about his conversation with Joy on the playground. As you may recall, someone overheard them both talking about sex. And his teacher angrily chastised him, all while Chris's mother sat by, her silence condoning this scolding.

Chris told me this whole story as a confession that surely something about his sexual desire was perverted. He had believed this was exhibit A of his twisted sexuality.

When he told that story to me, out of my own shock I gasped in pain on his behalf. My heart broke for him, especially that boy with his innocent desire to be curious about sex in conversation. This could have been a young Adam and Eve talking in the garden.

I shared my pain for him and the image I saw instead.

His eyes grew big as he reeled back. He saw it for the first time for himself, and he welled up with tears. "I thought I needed to hate that boy. No one has ever told me I could like him." And he wept with a newfound love for his lover heart.

He wept, too, for all the ways he'd been so flippant with his sexuality since then.

Through sobs he said, "It's so good to have him back."

———

That's the work before you now. You must end your relationship with contempt. Break it off. The tryst has gone on long enough. Call out your shame for the lie that it is.

Instead breathe; welcome kindness. And with that kindness, walk the terrain of your story to hear the places haunted by pain and shame. Learn to welcome back your innocent wonder and curiosity.

I said at the outset of this book that though we've all fallen from

Eden, your sexuality has never lost its original blessing. It was the artwork of God. It still is the artwork of God. You can use it for harmful ends, yes, for sure. But it's never lost its original brilliance. You can be brilliant at sin. Or you can be brilliant at the worship of God. You get to decide. Once you've broken up with contempt and embraced kindness, you can finally reopen yourself to the wonder and beauty of your sexuality again. You get to live an aroused life.

EIGHT

The Aroused Life

To be alive: not just the carcass
But the spark.
That's crudely put, but . . .
If we're not supposed to dance,
Why all this music?
—GREGORY ORR

Down the road and across the street from our house sits a large open space called Ute Valley Park. Thank the city planning powers that be for their forethought in saving wild places in suburbia. And that's the thing about the park: it's surrounded by neighborhoods. But you wouldn't really know it once you're there. You can get lost in it. Most of the time, you won't see a single house. It's our mini-Yellowstone, complete with bears and mountain lions and mule deer galore. The earth pushed up a giant slab of granite here that makes a picturesque ridge and a meandering canyon. I sought God for the name of our middle son on that ridge two days before his birth. I've met God in many places on this trail. It's our little taste of Eden.

My family and I have developed a ritual to get us there. On summer nights after dinner, while the light still bids us play, we grab popsicles or ice cream cones and head down the street. Sure, it's great exercise, quality time together as a family, and relationship with nature and the earth. But that's not really why I push to get us out the door. I've got a slightly more subversive motivation. And this park is its propaganda.

I hope to teach my boys a lot about life. But near the top of my list, just below Jesus and learning to walk, is the ability to see and enjoy beauty. I know learning to say you're sorry and developing a taste for vegetables are really important life lessons. But not more important than the capacity to revel in beauty.

So we walk Ute Valley Park looking for wildflowers and insects and whatever beauty we can behold while the last light fades west over the foothills. I've heard it called beauty hunting but I'm pretty sure it's the beholder who gets captured.

On our walks, Simon is sure to exclaim, "Dad, some prairie fire!" A common wildflower here—he's fallen for the stuff. With its vibrant, almost dripping orange towering bud, I don't blame him. He always asks to pick one for his mother. "Dad, I love coming here this time of night. It's so peaceful," said Brandt, my oldest son, one night. We call him Hawk Eyes because he always seems to spot the deer feeding along the stream bed before dusk. We stop and watch the sunset painting the backdrop. It's piercing. Westley, our youngest, used to say when he was two, "Fun, Daddy! Happy!" It's poetry.

I learned along the way that there's only one way to teach this virtue. I have to truly love the beauty myself. It's the power of the "Wow." To which my boys say, "Ah Dad, you always do that when you see sunsets." But then the other day, Simon said, "Dad, look at that sunset. It's so beautiful!" "Yes it is!" I replied as I pumped a hidden fist from the front seat of our minivan, excited that he was getting the eyes to see.

You might think seeing beauty is hardwired. I sort of agree. But if so, then most of us have lost that ability. And while I'm helping my boys not lose theirs, it sure is good to get mine back.

This is a form of giving the sex talk to my sons. As I said, at the bedrock of all sexuality is sensuality and especially the capacity to take in beauty. And if you are ever going to heal your sexuality, you must recover your capacity to be moved by beauty.

Resurrected Innocence

You would never know the guy had just died and come back to life the way Jesus goes about playing after the resurrection. The Gospels reveal a man who almost can't help himself. He plays the element of surprise with just about everyone he sees.

First, it's Mary at the tomb. In John 20 she mistakes him for the gardener, and he plays along until he can't take it anymore. "Mary!" he exclaims, although it may as well have been, "Surprise!" She, of course, rushes to embrace him.

Next, in Luke 24, it's the two men travelling on the road to Emmaus, with whom Jesus uses some Jedi mind trick to cloak his presence. He plays dumb until they are exasperated and then blows their minds and sets their hearts ablaze with his teaching on the story of the Messiah. And the moment he breaks bread, they see him. Really see him. And poof, he's gone.

And on and on it goes. Jesus shows up behind locked doors (John 20:19–23) and asks his shocked disciples to bum some food (Luke 24:41–43). He jokes with them while they're fishing, ribbing them for having no fish before he overloads their nets. And only then do they realize it's Jesus, and they've been tricked again (John 21).

All this is to say that Jesus does not simply rise again from the dead. He comes back to *play*. This is a man who had experienced utter darkness, the deepest haunting of evil, hell itself in every way, the full weight of every sin ever committed. That is truly staggering and unimaginable. And he comes back as lighthearted and playful as a child.

It's Jesus' playfulness after the resurrection that gives me the greatest confidence in the victory of God over sin and evil. And I glimpse in Jesus the life God wants to give me. He does not simply want to save me from sin and leave me somber and pious. God does not want you simply to be good and behaved. He wants you to be alive and free and full of play.

This God has convinced me he wants to help us all recover a healthy and alive sexuality. And it's deeply possible.

Cultivating the Lover Within

This chapter is on sexual self-care. How can you live alive to your sexuality? What will cultivate a healthy sexuality within you? This is not simply for those who are sexually active but for all men. This is where we own our sexuality with dignity and honor. This is where we begin to pursue our own sexual nurture and the life of the lover within.

I said at the outset of this book that we are all oversexualized yet sexually undernurtured. That reality will make you feel crazy. This is not about needing more sex or pornography. That's not really how we feed, nurture, and develop our sexual self. Our sexuality is not fed by making food of sex and simply getting more of it. Remember, it's desire, not drive.

We must cultivate the lover within. To do that we must live an aroused life. No, I don't mean that everything becomes sexual and your life becomes a Viagra disclaimer. You won't need to see a doctor after four hours.

What I mean here is the broader definition of arousal. *Sexual* arousal in medical terms is about blood flow to your genitals as your body responds to sexual stimuli. Over the course of sexual experience, it follows a set arousal cycle, as we discussed earlier. *General* arousal is a body state of being awake, embodied, regulated, present, and alive to the moment. Sexual arousal fits within this general arousal but it's only a subset.

Arousal derives from a medieval falconry term for the act of a hawk shaking its feathers and rousing itself to life.[1] Arousal involves activation of your brain on every level (brain stem, limbic middle, and neocortex, via the ascending reticular activating system and five different neurotransmitters). It turns on all your sensory organs and awakens desire, mobility, and readiness.[2]

Can you already hear how much of your whole being is involved in arousal? Even in sex, it's not simply what happens in your genitals. This arousal encompasses all of life. As I said before, all of life is not sexual, but all of life is sensual. And sensuality is the bedrock of your sexuality.

I'm inviting you to live an aroused life as an act of self-love and self-nurture. The sex talk you never got left you neglected, exposed, wounded, and, yes, immature. It's time you rise to fight for the goodness of your sexual self.

I do not find this in our culture's construction of masculinity. I feel every man is suffering for lack of it. We need to recover our craving for the romantic—that intimacy and adventure that fills our lives with relatedness and aliveness.[3] Most men live in poverty of those two things. We suffer lonely, numb lives, which—ironically and tragically—is exactly what so many of us absorbed as the definition of being a man. We don't need anyone and don't let stuff get to us. That gets you a man card and a life cursed with what Henry David Thoreau called the life of "quiet desperation."[4]

You aren't going to be that man. You stuck around for this chapter, and I know you want more. You want to care for the lover within.

Recovering Your Sense of Embodiment

Caring for the lover starts with recovering your sense of embodiment. Let me state the obvious. Sex happens between bodies. And I hope you see now that it's about much more than bodies. But bodies are the context, the interface, the entry point into the rest of the story of what is happening. Sex is a form of play, and play involves the movement of bodies.

To be in your body—to know your body and to be well in it—is essential to living a lover's life and being sexually healthy.

The difficulty comes because trauma and shame also play out in our bodies. Trauma and shame *disconnect* us from our bodies, and this is the fundamental way they disrupt healthy sexuality. When we suffer abuse, even if the abuse did not involve the touching or harming of our bodies, we suffer in our bodies. Trauma involves the overwhelming of our capacity to stay present in our bodies. And shame as trauma does the same.

You might ask, "How could someone not be in his body?" It might seem like a given, that of course we live life in our bodies. No one can actually leave their body unless they're dead, right?

I sat with a man who had been the victim of sexual assault as a boy. To even remember it was horror itself. And when I asked him what he felt in his body, he said, "I don't know. I was not in my body. I hovered on the ceiling and watched." That may sound wild, strange, and mystical. But this is an example of extreme dissociation. God designed our bodies to be able to shut down or play dead (freeze) when experiencing the worst pain. When we suffer emotional or physical pain that overwhelms our ability to stay present, we dissociate. At its worst, the actual neural dendrite connections in our brain disconnect from the parts screaming in pain.[5] It's a survival technique.

You don't need this depth of trauma to invoke a flight from your body. Trauma of any kind can cause you to disconnect from your feelings and sensations. Remember, trauma is not simply about what something looks like on paper. It's the meaning of the event for our heart. Trauma always leaves an imprint on the brain and leaves people with an emotional limp. Some people may show intense changes in personality. Others recover to the point of feeling that they're functioning normally on the outside.

Shame fragments the brain in much the same way that trauma does. Trauma and shame work in tandem to keep us disconnected from our bodies. We don't feel alive. We feel numb from our senses. It's a struggle, a battle for all of us to recover a sense of embodiment we lost along the way.

This is why it's vital, for your body's sake as much as for your heart's, that you acknowledge your trauma and shame and do the work we discussed in the previous chapters.

How do we return to our bodies on a daily basis?

We simply pay attention. You do not have miles and miles of land to travel to get back to your body. You simply need to cross the nanometer gap between neurons. That's the distance. And we do that by simply asking, What is going on in my body? We just turn our focus to the sensations there. Attention is a form of care. It's our first act of loving our bodies again.

When your body gets loud enough, I guarantee you already do this. Throw out your back and your body will scream. You will hear that loud and clear. Eat bad food and the nausea will force you to listen to your body too. But apart from this, most of us have learned to tune out our bodies. It's our masculine inheritance. Warriors push through pain for the greater good. Work asks us to suffer the heavy lifting, the long days, the bad weather, the survival of the moment. Athletes train themselves to push through injury on the field. And there are moments for this. But we are rarely invited back into our bodies after the fact.

"What are you feeling in your body?" When I first ask this question of men in counseling, I usually get a cockeyed stare, like, *I don't even know what you just asked.* This stare is followed by either "I don't know" or "Nothing, I guess. I'm fine." We are not practiced at this bodily exploration.

A man with a healthy sexuality must learn to hear what his body is saying to him. It's not simply to work through pain; *all* of life is a felt experience. As James K. A. Smith makes clear, we are not bobblehead brains on a stick. "We inhabit the world not primarily as thinkers, or even believers, but as more affective, embodied creatures who make our way in the world more by feeling our way around it."[6] Feelings and emotions are the language of our inner world. All the thoughts you've ever pondered, the emotions you've ever felt, and the pleasures you've ever loved are embodied states. And if you numb your body to avoid pain, you end up numbing yourself to all the pleasures of life too.

Two effective ways I've found to recover my body's feelings are journaling and developing deeper relationships. I always journal as conversation with God (writing as relationship versus a "Dear

Journal . . .”). I write very honestly about my feelings and look for connections to my present circumstances. This helps me see how much life actually plays on my heart. And I've learned to feel by cultivating deep friendships and relationships. Pursuing someone's heart is far different from shooting the bull. I first learned I even had a heart and how to talk about it by going to therapy.

Tuning into your body and learning to recognize when it's talking to you will help prevent the overwhelm reactions (fight, flight, shutdown) that take you away from being alive. If you've ever watched a child get more and more distressed when they can't reach their parents, you get a little taste of what goes on in your body when you don't listen to it. It will get your attention, probably in ways you least want.

We return to our bodies because a lover needs to know how to sit with his emotions. He turns a brave eye toward his inner world. But along with awareness, all sensuality and bodily pleasures require another thing: that you can handle what you feel.

Body Regulation and Handling Sexual Tension

Arousal in the body happens in this window between too little stimulation and too much. That's where we feel most alive. Too little brain arousal leaves us checked out and too much makes us reactive and alarmed. Keeping yourself in that sweet spot between these two is where life feels alive and well in our bodies. We may still cycle between excited and bored, stressed and relaxed. But we feel it in a way that we can handle. We aren't going to lose ourselves.

Keeping ourselves in this “alive and well” place is called emotional regulation. It's not a passive experience. We have a lot of power to engage our nervous systems with care. You're doing it already, whether you know it or not. You've found a way to cope with life and show up, even if it feels halfhearted, poorly done, or costly. We all eventually find our way out of being overwhelmed. It just depends at what cost.

If you're stressed, you can regulate your nervous system by blowing off some anger at another driver on the road with an F-bomb and middle finger. That anger-release combination fuels the madness of domestic abuse. Often an abuser feels soothed after hitting a child or partner, making him oddly calm and even apologetic to the very person he's just hit. It's not repentance. Just a calmer body. Downing a few drinks every night to relieve anxiety will regulate you. Alcohol is a vasodilator. Watch anyone who vapes or smokes and you can see them calm down before your eyes. Maybe it's simply scrolling your phone to disconnect from being stressed or bored. These all relieve stress but at what cost? You pay for these with bad side effects.

Porn has fast become the soothe du jour. When you're stressed or bored, just pull out your phone with endless porn videos on it. Research has begun to show that chronic use of porn is probably linked more to affect dysregulation—meaning overwhelmed emotions—than sex drive. Porn use becomes an attempt at self-soothing (autoregulation).[7] We've talked about all the symbolism present in our porn use. But often what gets us there is boredom, stress, or some other emotion in our body we don't know how to care for or regulate.

Masturbation itself can soothe and comfort the body. This is not wrong. But if it becomes our only or primary way of soothing, we wire our brains to need sexual release whenever we're stressed. Sex can be a stress reliever. But mixing sex and stress is not a great long-term solution, especially if it's the primary thing that leads you to sex. Too much anxiety is linked to sexual dysfunction. Alexandra Katehakis calls it the "comfort without contact" strategy for regulation. "It makes other people not sources of relational comfort but objects to assist autoregulation."[8] We seek self-focused release rather than intimate connection for soothing.

When men say they need sex, I believe most often they actually need emotional regulation. Comfort. Connection. To be soothed. But they've never been taught about this. And we have a culture that permits men to demand sex, which allows them to use sex this way. As I said before, men are often taught in Christian circles that they cannot handle sexual desire in their bodies without release, that it's actually *every* man's battle to cope with, and that they are destined to always be just a hairbreadth from sinful lust. That perspective makes sexual desire an emergency in our bodies. We begin to think that if we don't take care of it, we'll explode or automatically fall into uncontrollable sin. But you don't have a sex problem. You have an emotional regulation problem that leads to a sex problem if misunderstood. You don't need sex, but you *do* need to find soothing.

Amy always knew when her husband had a stressful day by how he had sex that night. He would become really pushy and urgent about making sure they had sex. And the act itself was very driven. "It's like he needed to conquer me, not make love to me," she said. Amy always felt overlooked and tuned out. Sex became something to endure rather than an experience of connection and romance. The story of sex became release, not love.

Remember what David Schnarch said: "Seeing sex as a drive makes us focus on relieving sexual tension rather than wanting our partner."[9] It's very, very possible to get lost in the self-absorption of your own bodily needs and completely miss your partner. It happens all the time. And it's often felt by a partner as violating. It will keep you stunted and immature. You'll feel young to your partner, like a child that needs soothing.

It's best to come to sex regulated. Not too tired or bored, distant or checked out. And not too stressed or angry, anxious or alarmed. Be present and alive and ready for connection and the play of the moment. Sex is a place our love plays after all. What athlete or actor ever shows up checked out? Those guys get kicked off the team. That actor never gets callbacks.

Good sex happens when we can effectively hold sexual tension in our bodies until we or our partner are ready for release. This allows us to care for our partner's pleasure as well as our own (reducing the orgasm gap I mentioned in chapter 3). The arousal cycle requires the ability to regulate yourself between too much stimulation and too little. Too little and you'll check out, lose your erection, and get bored. Too much and, well, you'll reach orgasm or crash into shutdown and lose your arousal. Sex is meant to build and create climax when you're ready for it.

This same skill applies if you're single, dating, divorced, celibate, or if your partner just had a baby and can't have sex for a few months. We learn to hold sexual desire in our bodies, stay regulated, and find other ways of releasing our tension.

Regulating our sexual desire is really an act of learning how to steward our desire. Can you be okay with sexual desire in your body over hours or days or months or years? What I mean is: are you responsible with (i.e., able to respond to) the arousal in your body? Your arousal is your own responsibility and no one else's. No one is required to meet your sexual desires. Sex is a gift, not a right.

When the doctor confirmed for us that we were pregnant again, she said, "Out of an abundance of caution, consider not having sex until your baby is born." We had just suffered two miscarriages, and that experience had left our hearts pretty shredded. Sex can cause contractions of the uterus, which in our case could lead to another miscarriage. It was a no-brainer for us. We would follow the doctor's orders for the life of this child.

So, we fasted from sex together for nearly a year. I learned a whole lot about growing my capacity to hold desire in my body without feeling it as an emergency. And without losing myself to it or shutting it down.

Regulating our sexual tension during sex uses the identical skills we hone in the normal tensions of our lives. But in case you don't have any good regulation methods, here are a few that work well. We all have our things we use to soothe, good and bad. Your work will be finding ones that don't wreak worse havoc in the process.

Just simply bringing attention to our bodies is half the work of regulation. Beyond simple attention, we all need to learn things that soothe us effectively. If we are tired, bored, or shut down, we probably need something to stimulate us (activate our sympathetic nervous system). Or if we are stressed, angry, or irritated, we need to find something that relaxes us (activates our parasympathetic nervous system).

Breathing is a massively important part of how we regulate our bodies. Based on your stress levels, your body naturally speeds up or slows down your breathing. Literally every time you inhale, your heart rate increases and your sympathetic nervous system ramps you up. And when you exhale, your body does the reverse by slowing your heart and turning on your parasympathetic calming system. If you can learn to take deep breaths with a quick inhale and slow exhale, you can soothe your body. And if you need to wake yourself up, fast breaths or long inhales can help you get more alert.[10]

But by far the most effective way to regulate your body is by connecting with another person. We desperately need self-soothing skills (autoregulation) when no one is available and we have to fight our inner battles alone. But nothing is as quick and effective at calming a person down than human connection. It's called co-regulation and our brains are literally wired for this.[11] Talking and relating with another person actually soothes us when we are stressed or awakens us when we are numb.

How does a mother soothe a crying baby? By holding him. How do you calm a child when they've crashed their bike or skinned their knee? You simply hold them, rub their back, or reassure them. We never, ever outgrow that wiring. As John Bowlby, the father of attachment theory, once said, "Being alone doth make cowards of us all."[12] Life is too difficult alone. No one is as strong in life as when he has companionship. In a study on World War II vets, researchers found that those who had formed friendships with their compatriots had lower PTSD symptoms from the trauma of war.[13]

Why do lovers talk before sex? Of course, it creates intimacy. But it's also a great way to regulate your nervous system to prepare your body. Between three boys and two jobs, our sex life cannot be all that spontaneous right now and often gets shoehorned into the schedule. That's not ideal and takes some effort to maintain the playfulness and freedom. Talking and holding each other has been vital for my wife and me to relax from the stress of schedules before we enter into the play of lovemaking. We've even combined talking with a hot bath together.

Sex needs presence. And to have presence we need to regulate our nervous system.

The more you learn to regulate your own body, the more you will be able to offer care and empathy to others who aren't regulated. It's one of the most revolutionary things you can do for those around you. You'll be able to sense what others feel and intuit when they aren't well, because your body will start to feel what they feel. This is the heart of what your lover offers the world. And it will revolutionize not only your sex life but also your capacity to love.

———————

Evan and his wife had always known sex to be a place of mutual joy and play. And then she suffered the traumatic birth of their first child. The birth wrecked her body with the pain of physical scars and plagued her with the symptoms of PTSD. And to make it worse, it surfaced all the symptoms of her past sexual abuse. Yep, trauma can trigger other long-buried trauma. Whenever her husband touched her, her body would lock up and push him away.

She fought very hard to recover her body, getting therapy and care for both her body and heart. She wanted her body back and made it clear that she was not trying to reject him at all. It was such a tender area in their marriage. They both missed the sexual romantic play they had known.

But Evan did feel rejected. He wanted to lash out at her and blame her. But he had stood in that delivery room witnessing all the agony she had suffered. He knew it was not personal, but his body did not. So he came to counseling to grapple with his reaction to her and found within it the memories of his own sexual harm.

Slowly over time as he healed, he grew to regulate the triggered parts of him. He learned to regulate his body when his wife went through body triggers. As they began to explore sex again after more than a year, she needed to know he would stop whenever she said so. He stopped in those moments because he didn't want to just have sex with body parts. He wanted to make love to his wife. And that meant he wanted her present. So they stopped often, regularly ending sex for the night and enjoying what they could recover with each other. That took his body being able to recognize the emotions and felt experience of his wife. Being in his body had let his lover heart truly make love to her, even when it didn't involve sex.

Distinct Selves in Communion

We've really botched the idea of oneness in marriage. After describing how Adam poured out his poetic awe in meeting Eve, Genesis includes this equally poetic, albeit cryptic, phrase: "That is why a man leaves his father and mother and is united to his wife, and they become one flesh" (Genesis 2:24). Jesus quoted this exact verse to the Pharisees in a debate about divorce and added, "So they are no longer two, but one flesh. Therefore what God has joined together, let no one separate" (Matthew 19:6).

But what is meant here by "one flesh"? Do these two wedded lovers actually lose themselves to some new hybrid existence?

In our early years of dating and marriage, our friends often referred to Amanda and me simply as "Samanda." Okay, yes, we spent a lot of time together and got lost in each other's company. We left every date for six months absolutely starving because we talked so much we didn't actually eat our food. We reveled in each other's presence, and it fueled a lot of erotic attraction too. But that which often brings us together cannot sustain us forever.

A few years ago, I said to Amanda, "I think we need to properly hold the funeral for Samanda." Samanda had come to mean something far worse than the cute thing it was at the beginning. Call it codependence or enmeshment; we had lost ourselves to each other. And ending Samanda was an act of reclaiming our oneness.

The oneness God describes of married lovers is another way we image God himself. The Jewish prayer and declaration known as the Shema describes God as one and only one. "Hear, O Israel: The Lord our God, the Lord is *one*" (Deuteronomy 6:4). Yet we know that the Godhead is in fact three distinct persons—Father, Son, and Holy Spirit—that never merge with one another. God is one in union but not in person. This is oneness. Distinct selves in communion with each other. In giving ourselves to each other we never lose ourselves. Laying down your life by serving and submitting to each other is anni-hilation of your *selfishness* but not your *self.* Some take "one flesh" very literally to mean the sex act itself, the way intercourse melds bodies. And I think that could be a poetic picture of this. But even in the commingling of bodies, they never actually become one body.

You would be hard-pressed to hear this distinction being honored at a wedding. Quite the opposite. The betrothed often light a unity candle from separate candles and then blow these separate ones out. What does this communicate if not a snuffing out of their separate lives? And okay, I get it. This is a day to celebrate the beauty of union! We are so right to revel in this picture of two lives being joined. But where do you hear the pastor charging them to uphold their sense of identity and self, even as they promise their lives to each other?

It is the lovers' enduring separate sense of self that fuels sexual passion. Sex therapist and author Esther Perel says, "Eroticism requires separateness. In other words, eroticism thrives in the space between the self and the other. In order to commune with the one we love, we must be able to tolerate this void and its pall of uncertainties."[14]

Romantic married love thrives in the rhythm between the familiar and the adventurous, the known and the unknown, the comfortable and the risky. This is the rhythm of attachment we talked about before, the way we feel bonded to the closest people we love. We care for each other when together and then separately go explore the world, carrying each other's love and anticipating our return together.

According to John Bowlby, the more securely attached a child feels, the more confidently and freely he explores his world.[15] This is because they know they will be welcomed back when they return. If you watch children, you'll see them follow this explore-return rhythm. It's the cadence of love that we were never meant to outgrow. In the words of Bowlby, "All of us, from the cradle to the grave, are happiest when life is organized as a series of daring ventures from a secure base."[16]

Emotional connection can be wrecked with too little closeness but also suffocated with too much. Good full-bodied, full-hearted sexual connection needs both the familiar and the unknown. It thrives in the tension of both. To be familiar with your partner, to know her heart, and to feel closeness creates the safety necessary to disrobe both body and heart with freedom. But conversely, sexual desire thrives in the experience of otherness within the wild unknown and the vast mystery of another person. No matter how long you know your partner, you will never plumb the depths of her being and glory and heart. She is fundamentally wild and separate from you. The degree to which you can handle and even cultivate this fundamental separateness, freedom, and otherness is the degree to which your sexual desire can thrive. Indeed, it is how love itself thrives.

This is not easy work. You must garner the courage of an explorer setting off in the vast wilderness, leaving the known and comfortable, to allow the inherent wildness of your lover to truly overtake you. As Esther Perel says, "Faced with the irrefutable otherness of our partner, we can respond with fear or with curiosity. We can try to reduce the other to a knowable entity, or we can embrace her persistent mystery."[17]

Psychologist David Schnarch observed that your sexual prime is not actually in your hormonal twenties but during midlife and beyond. Why? "They have more self to bring to sex, and the differentiation to disclose themselves, unvarnished. A mature man no longer needs to have all the answers in bed and is less threatened by a partner who is a sexual equal. And he can let someone hold him."[18]

Skip the magazine articles on how to make fireworks in bed with toys and positions and supplements. Grow your sense of self instead.

Create a thriving life. The more work you do to develop your sense of self, the greater your sexual potential. Every man must own his life and become someone. This does not mean becoming a personality with a big ego. A personality and a self are vastly different.

A self means you are self-aware enough to be responsible with your life. You've spent time reflecting on your story, your impact on the world, catching glimpses of your glory and knowing your strengths and weaknesses. It's your true self. It's developing friendships and hobbies and constructing your soul with God. A person with a self knows where they've come from and is investing their life in the greater good of the world. A person with a self can suffer solitude with peace and yet revel in the togetherness of belonging to friends and family and community. He can (and does) give and receive love.

A person with a self empowers others to become whole people. His wife does not feel forced to conform to his wishes and ego and whims, let alone his sexual demands. She is free to be herself, too, and become all she was made to be. Indeed, she feels encouraged and empowered to be this. A man with a self revels in a woman who stands as his peer, his mental equal, his friend. A man with a self empowers his kids, celebrates them without getting lost in their successes, and challenges them without needing them to behave. This is a man who has grasped the deep value of his own sexuality and, even more so, of his own glory. Indeed, he knows how to "love his neighbor as himself" because he *has* a self.

In sex, a man with a self has depth to offer his wife to explore. He, too, is an infinite mystery to be explored by his beloved. Deep calls out to deep because he has a heart he's cultivated. Sex isn't reduced to a body function or getting off. Remember, sex begins in the heart, not the loins. He can express his sexual desire without demand or avoidance. And he can give her space for an authentic yes or no because she knows his self is not on the line. He doesn't bring his core questions to sex.

Here is the paradox of being a person. Having a self is exactly what allows you to lose yourself to the moment of pleasure and play. I know that sounds crazy. A person with a self can enjoy wonderful moments of self-forgetfulness. A hollow personality without a self needs constant primping, admiration, attention, and self-reflection. There's too much self-absorption to get lost in a moment. They exist only in the gleam of their own reflection. Having a self means you don't fear that you'll cease to exist when you're lost in the moment.

Sex is just such a moment. Its pleasures and movements become absorbing. And at the climax of pleasure, of orgasm, a person with a self can be undone without feeling annihilated. You can get lost in the moment. As Diane Ackerman says of all good play, "In rare moments of deep play, we can lay aside our sense of self, shed time's continuum, ignore pain, and sit quietly in the absolute present, watching the world's ordinary miracles. No mind or heart hobbles. No analyzing or explaining. No questioning of logic. No promises. No goals. No relationships. No worry. One is completely open to whatever drama may unfold."[19] There's no longer the chatter of our inner dialogue. We can get lost in the place where, Ackerman says, "acting and thinking become one."[20]

All genuine play allows for this. And so does awe.

Capacity for Wonder

This capacity for reverencing and enjoying the mystery and otherness of another person is really the capacity for awe. And by now you know that healthy sexuality is built on the stuff. You can't experience the full pleasure of another if you cannot respect and reverence them. So you need a robust capacity for wonder.

My family used to live by a Saturday morning ritual that went something like this. After a lazy breakfast, my wife, my oldest son (then a toddler), and I all piled in our standard-Colorado-issue Subaru to drop my wife off at her art class. My son and I would then carry on in search of a new park to explore until it was time to reverse the process and pick her back up. Once home, my wife would declare, "Want to see my drawings?" And slowly she would flip open her giant sketch book, full of freshly minted nude drawings of a man or a woman in some form of repose. She was asking for an audience in me.

If you know anything about art education, you know many artists train their skills through the ritual of live nude drawing classes. It's just like it sounds. A paid model disrobes, assumes a statuesque pose in the middle of a classroom, and freezes for as long as his or her muscles allow. The students then busily interpret on the blank page the one whom they've just beheld until the model fatigues and needs to reposition. And it starts all over, giving artists time to work their craft from a different angle. And my wife had pages of work to show.

While our son played with his toys in the other room, we sat and studied every drawing for the flow of its lines and awe of its subject. She paused at most drawings to retrace with me her line work. She described the importance of keeping the pencil in motion and attempting long, curving lines versus short, tight ones to mimic the movement and grace of the human body.

She ended the ritual almost always the same way. She quieted in silence, trancelike, passing back through her sketches. She would then shut the book and declare, "The human body is just so amazing! I love drawing it so much." And life moved on to Saturday chores.

That ritual changed my life. As I shared earlier, there was a time when I struggled with looking at pornography. It had taken much from me. But most enduringly, I had lost my capacity for awe. And our slow, Saturday morning sit-and-study liturgy gave me back the gift of beholding the human form. In many ways, it gave me eyes to see again. Yes, I was getting back the window to my soul.

Some might say that lust involves looking too long and is solved by simply turning one's gaze away. But I know now the real need is to look with different eyes. Not longer but deeper. Not to stare but to behold. The thing missing in my sexual desire was awe—a reverence for what I was beholding.

What if what our sex needs most is not more techniques or accountability, but new eyes, fresh eyes? Maybe we don't need less arousal, but more and fuller arousal. Not simply to look away, but to look with awe. Does it require staring at nude sketches? That was my spit and mud in the eyes from Jesus. But maybe that's not yours. Maybe it's letting yourself read and imagine the slow lines in Song of Songs. Or taking a longer minute with the next sunset, long enough to let the "Thank you!" rise in your heart. But that's for you to search out. The whole earth holds his glory.

It's easy to think that awe is a rare experience, reserved for a few moments where our breath is taken away. But awe is far more accessible than we may realize.[21] Everyday awe can be found all around us, in nature, music, art, film, and, again, most often in the people we live with. It just takes a little practice.

I find poet Mary Oliver's words often occupy my mind.

> Instructions for living a life:
> Pay attention.
> Be astonished.
> Tell about it.[22]

There's no real magic here. One must simply go out in the world with childlike wonder and pay attention. Every day when I drive my boys to school, we take some time to pray. One day Brandt prayed, "God, I ask to be overwhelmed today in a good way." I had never heard a prayer like that. He was praying for awe. I marveled at his fullhearted trust in God.

Fall in love with the world. It's full of glory. Learn to fish so you can feel a trout slip through your hands. Plant wildflowers. Study poetry. Just find something in the world to fall in love with. Whatever it is that fills you with awe, make sure you pay attention for at least fifteen seconds. Our brains are so disposed toward the negative experiences of life that it takes fifteen seconds of savoring a moment of awe for it to change our brains for the better.[23]

Here's the amazing thing about awe: The more you do it, the more pleasure it brings you. This is wildly unique. Due to something called hedonic adaptation, most pleasures—like imbibing a tasty beer or habitual porn use—only *decrease* the more we do them. We adapt to the experience and it takes more to feel the same pleasure. "Not so with awe," writes researcher Dacher Keltner. "The more we practice awe, the richer it gets."[24]

Awe also regulates our nervous system, lowers inflammation in the body, reduces PTSD symptoms, increases reasoning skills, and, as noted earlier, links heart rates with those around us.[25] Keltner concluded, "It is hard to imagine a single thing you can do that is better for your body and mind than finding awe outdoors."[26]

Relationally alive, regulated sex is an experience of awe too. And that would be a great thing to work for in your life. But sex cannot be your only source of awe. It cannot be the only place you practice beauty and the transcendent.

The world is not just something pretty to look at. It invites our engagement. The invitation of all awe is to go further in, to pursue its beauty.

While you may not need sex to live, I believe you do need beauty. Toni Morrison once said, "I think of beauty as an absolute necessity. I don't think it's a privilege or an indulgence. . . . The state and the wonder of being in this place. This overwhelming beauty—some of it is natural, some of it is man-made, some of it is casual, some of it is a mere glance—is an absolute necessity. I don't think we can do without it any more than we can do without dreams or oxygen."[27]

John Eldredge said that a man needs a beauty to rescue.[28] And there is something good about a man who will fight to protect the beauty of this world. It's the very glory of God, after all. That could be the way he fights for his wife's heart or the way he cultivates a garden. Our strength was made to fight for the beauty of the world. But the reverse is also true.

We all need beauty to rescue us.

I still remember the day I heard cellist Yo-Yo Ma for the first time, in an intro to music course in college. I sat in my chair, pierced solid through. His way with music put a foot in the door of my heart and held some place open I really wanted to shut. God often uses the beauty of music to rescue me. Time and again, music has a way of melting my defenses and keeping me openhearted.

It seems some men use sex as their own source of beauty. But that leaves a man undernourished at best. Some use pornography and find themselves even more emaciated. There is a whole world of beauty waiting for you.

"We recognize unmistakably the imperishable need of man to live in beauty," said Johan Huizinga. "There is no satisfying this need save in play."[29] Yes, it is not simply as a spectator that we receive beauty. Beauty bids us come and play. Beauty is born from play.

Real Versus Vicarious Play

Among all the things that bloom in springtime near us, soccer season may be the most robust. With three boys, I stand on the sidelines and watch a lot of soccer games. And there's nowhere else I'd rather be when my boys are playing. But at a game recently, I had the epiphany that for all the tug and pull of emotion I feel while watching, I am not playing. I am right there with my sons in the win or loss, but I don't make a single play. It's not my game. And Lord knows all those instructions I yell accomplish diddly squat. My smiles and cheers are the best I can do.

Have you ever heard a die-hard sports fan exclaim "We won!" after his team wins a game? You didn't win. Your team won. They put it all on the field. You watched, drank beer, and ate nachos, which is fine and good and even inspiring of awe in moments. But the danger in getting lost in the play of another is you forget to play yourself. This is known as vicarious play, which Dan Allender would call another way evil may cast its spell on your life.[30]

Watching pornography is vicarious play too. You experienced nothing of the sensuality, pursuit, romance, attunement, hard conversations, courtship, or commitment it took to be in that moment. And honestly, most of the performers did nothing but pop erection medication and show up on the set to get paid. Sex was never meant to be a spectator sport. It leaves you on the outside of something you were meant to be on the inside of. You were meant to experience sex for all its exertion and risks and thrills and relational sweeps. Your heart and body were meant to be on the line, not sitting behind a screen. That diminishes you because it shapes you to find pleasure in the effortless.

I took my sons to a fly-fishing film festival recently. We felt the excitement of the adventure, held our breath in the missed casts, reveled in the snap of tight lines, and wowed at the absolute hogs these guys pulled from the water. We had a great time. And guess what? The next day, though it was twenty degrees and windy, they wanted to go fishing.

Of course they did!

I looked out the window and cringed at the cold. But I knew I had to say yes because I knew this was the absolute healthiest response to watching a movie on fishing. So we went. It was miserably cold. But then we started landing trout. "Got one, Dad!" said son after son. And it brings me to tears even now. We shivered the whole time, but our hearts burned with the joy of the real.

Real play is much messier and more confusing and exhausting than anything you just watch. Oh, but the glory and the thrill and the full-body elation. Nothing could be sweeter. Same with sex.

To live a healthy sexuality, you must play. I mean no less than the labor toward having really good sex, if that's your lot in life. Like really, really work for it, which means accepting that like all play, it has its suffering. In the words of poet Rainer Rilke, "Sex is difficult; yes. But it is the difficult that is enjoined upon us, almost everything serious is difficult, and everything is serious."[31] That's not to say it's not also extremely amazing. But it requires becoming a student of sex, of your body and hers, of your hearts too. It's way more nuanced and complicated than a porn star makes it seem.

Sex cannot be the only place you play. That's too much pressure for sex alone to bear. And you won't be practiced in the art of play. Cultivate play in your life. Mountain biking is one place I give my nervous system a workout. It's pure joy. And yet my heart travels the terror and elation rhythm with every up and down of the hills. It's wild and engrossing and fun.

Even our marriages need other forms of play. This is the gift dating can give us, a long season of playing at other things than sex. Literally, your bodies will learn to trust each other as long-practiced dance partners or teammates. It's been found that long-term marriage partners actually have their heartbeats sync up when they are in close proximity to each other. Your bodies tune in to each other.

For Valentine's Day this year, my wife and I took a couples yoga class together. It was really sweaty and intense, and just about every sinew in my body popped. But I found it so amazing to relate with Amanda's body in a nonsexual yet very sensual way. We even had to coordinate poses together. That was such a wonderful way to practice togetherness. And it was a beautiful neural engagement that gave more body awareness to our sex life.

So where will you play?

———

There should be a warning on this chapter. You may have mistaken it for self-help advice. But if you become a man who regulates his body, knows himself enough to stand in the world, develops the capacity for awe, and learns to play well, you will become a wildly good man. And your life will be drawn into a story far more expansive than your own sexual pleasure.

You will find your sexuality can help change the world.

How Your Sexuality Can Change the World

*The very nature of true play is that we get to stand
on the neck of evil. Meaningful play invites us into a
deeper revelation of who we were created to be, and the
opportunity to evoke goodness in others.*
—DAN ALLENDER

*Be wise about what is good, and innocent about what is evil.
The God of peace will soon crush Satan under your feet.*
—PAUL (ROMANS 16:19–20)

During the summer of '69, the one immortalized in a song by
Bryan Adams while Neil Armstrong took his one small step
and Woodstock kicked off its free-love experiment, two fifteen-year-
old girls stood on the side of a sunbaked highway with thumbs in the
air, hoping to hitchhike to who knows where. Maybe it was teenage
rebellion or maybe it was a grasp at freedom. But it worked.

A couple of men wheeled their vehicle to a stop and beckoned them in. But once inside they learned real quick it was not to give them a ride. They would not be dropped off anytime soon. They had been abducted. They both swallowed hard against the death of that dream of freedom. For the next several weeks, the men trafficked both friends across state lines from Michigan to Illinois to Missouri to who knows where. The details are all hazy and hard to talk about. Trauma will do that. And they were often drugged. These savage men forced them into prostitution, gave them money to turn tricks in seedy hotels, and threatened their lives constantly.

After weeks of unspeakable horror, one of the girls sobered to the reality they were not going to make it out alive. They had seen too much and knew too much. Their captors were organized criminals, after all, not about to lose that standing to a couple of disposable girls.

One night the men dropped them both off at another motel in a forgotten part of an unknown town. Both were told the guy at the front desk had a gun and would kill them if they attempted to escape. Once in the room, one girl told the other, "We're getting out of here. We have to try. We are as good as dead if we don't." She hatched a plan and conjured the nerve to call a taxi. They would use the little money they had to get away. "Once we see the taxi, we have to run. If we get shot, we get shot."

The taxi pulled up. And run they did. Oh, they ran. Breathing beyond panic, they jumped in that back seat, only to realize no gun had gone off. No shots rang out. It was a ruse. "Take us as far as twenty dollars will get us!" they said. The man obliged and drove them to a truck stop in the middle of Missouri. Once there, they did an unbelievably brave thing and hitched another ride. A truck driver at the stop took interest in their plight and agreed to take them as far as his route would go toward home. "He was a kind man and a Christian," one girl recalled. "He didn't ask any questions. He just let us sleep in the back of his cab." And he drove them to Indiana.

They called home to get a ride the rest of the way. But there was little fanfare to their return. Treated as returned runaways by their families, they buried all the pain in the silence of an unspoken past, where it stayed for nearly fifty years.

I heard this story a couple of years ago while sitting in my own living room, my mom in the chair across from me. That girl, the one that devised the taxi plan, was my mom. She had only just begun to unbury this story in the last couple of years and wanted me to know. I had no words. My eyes full of tears, my chest swelled with grief for her. I was wrecked for her and raged in my heart at these men. Her life had been blown to bits. I stood in awe of her courage, the boldness of a fifteen-year-old girl in the midst of unspeakable horror, finding it in her heart to want to live, to escape, and to actually brave the dangerous journey. I gasped when I realized that, had she not escaped, I would never have existed. She is to me a hero.

Your Sexual Legacy

I told you a few chapters ago that it would be decades before I made sense of her laughter that day in her friend's kitchen. But now sitting in my own living room, witnessing my mother's trauma, gave me eyes to see what it must have felt like to have her son come of age, his sexuality awakened and alive and curious. I can only guess that her laughter held back a profound amount of fear. Male sexuality represented the worst horror of her life. That day in the kitchen, my story crashed into hers.

This story is my mother's to tell. And she gave me permission to share it with you. My story of sexuality began before I was born.

You, too, need to know that your story began before you were born. You have a sexual inheritance. You were born into sexual and relational forces already in motion long before you arrived, right up to the moment of passion in which you were conceived. And more than simply the events in the lives of our loved ones, we inherit the masculine culture around us and the sexual tides of the world.

And your story of sexuality will live on beyond you to be inherited by the next generation. Perhaps this inheritance will pass to your children. But the impact of the story of your sexuality is far bigger than childbearing. Your story of sexuality extends to how you loved the world around you. You were meant to be fruitful in ways that go beyond having children. Your sexuality is about far more than your personal happiness. Your personal pleasure is for sure a part of it. But your sexuality existed, as your whole life exists, to impact the world for good. How you live your sexuality in the world will change the world.

Your lover heart was meant to run the whole show. It's meant to be the beginning and end of your sex life. But deeper still, you will be known for how you loved and whom you loved and what you loved. Were you bighearted and generous or cold and stingy?

You will be known as a lover . . . or not.

The Tale of Two Male Sexualities

My mother's story shines her glory so bright. She is the hero here. But it stands amid the tale of two masculinities. We meet first the men of great darkness, her abductors. God made only one breed of men—those wired to reflect his very image and treat everyone with the awe worthy of their dignity. He didn't make monsters. Monsters are made here in the hell of the human condition and in the recesses of the human heart.

These abductors had turned the lover into a savage. You'd be hard-pressed to find an ounce of human glory within them anymore. This is sexuality fueled by absolute harm, abuse, greed, and contempt, the near total rejection of love. Surely they suffered, too, outside of Eden, and surely they've turned that suffering into utter revenge. I can only imagine what my mother saw in the face of a man who was meant to shine God's image and yet bore horrifying contempt.

But thank God, they were not the only men present.

There were the getaway drivers.

I know nothing of the taxi driver. I imagine him as a man—a good guess I'd say for late-1960s America. You could say he just did his job and drove the twenty-dollar trip. But I sense he had a safe destination in mind. God only knows what he really thought. Maybe it was just good customer service; but maybe he saw two terrified teenage girls desperate for help. I am forever grateful he followed their urgent request and found them a safe place.

And then, of course, the kindest of all: the truck driver. I want to hug that man. How did he know to not ask questions and let them sleep? That rest is a sensation my mother can still recall. There were no trauma-informed trainings back then. Few people knew about human trafficking. Organizations like Truckers Against Trafficking did not exist. He was just a good man in the right spot.

Yes, a good man in the right spot. No one's wearing capes here or swinging a Jedi lightsaber. Neither the taxi driver nor the truck driver accomplished the heroic. I daresay the world does not need the heroic man right now. We need a revolution of good men who just show up. We need men with lover hearts.

This is the tale of two different *sexualities*. That may seem odd to say at first, but it's true. How these men related to their sexuality made all the difference in this story. These men give us the picture of two different hearts, yes. But even more, they embody two different sexualities. One type of sexuality is found in the abductors, a picture of sexualizing violation, of savage abuse. It scripted sexuality as a weapon of power and contempt. And the other, embodied in the getaway drivers, almost looks like no sexuality at all—because they *weren't sexualizing* my mother and her friend. Sexuality was not in the script, because that was not a sexual moment. But the lover heart was there—human, alive, empathetic, and reverent.

Your sexuality will impact far more than just you. People can feel what it's like to be around you. This work of recovering and coming alive to a healthy sexuality will impact your world. You don't have to go looking for the heroic. Being a sexually alive and good man in the world will bring you face-to-face with the darkness in it. And you will get to stand on the neck of evil.

I want to introduce you to Peter Jonsson and Carl-Fredrik Arndt. You probably don't recognize those names. But there is one woman who considers them her heroes. And I think you would do well to hear their story and hers.

Late one night, these two graduate students took a bike ride on Stanford University's campus when they came upon two people behind a dumpster. Something wasn't right here because one person was not moving and half naked. When they asked the man what was going on, he fled. On instinct, Peter took chase, outran the fleeing man, and tackled and pinned him until the police arrived.

When they gave their account of events to the police, the reality of what they'd just interrupted overcame them both. This was a sexual assault. Carl-Fredrik could not even speak he wept so hard. They'd witnessed the truly awful of broken male sexuality, and it wrecked both their hearts.

The woman they helped was Chanel Miller, and she wanted you to know her name and her story, so she wrote a memoir.[1] She went unnamed throughout the trial of her rapist, Stanford swimmer Brock Turner, a name that may ring a bell, known as the guy who got off with a light sentence. But her victim impact statement went viral and for good reason. She addressed her statement in court almost entirely to her assailant, forcing him to witness the power of unyielding human dignity as she spoke to the lost lover in him.

In her statement she said this to Peter and Carl-Fredrik: "Thank you to the two men who saved me, who I have yet to meet. I sleep with two bicycles that I drew taped above my bed to remind myself there are heroes in this story."[2]

Heroes.

This is yet another tale of two different male sexualities. One, in Turner, did violence in the name of the pleasure of power. The other, in the hearts of Peter and Carl-Fredrik, showed up with reverence to protect and rescue and weep. These two had hearts. Turner did not.

Peter and Carl-Fredrik did not seek out some hero fantasy. They just went for a bike ride. But they went out in the world as men with at least a basic embodied and reverent sexuality. I certainly don't know their character as a whole. But I know what they were like on that day. And it appears it wasn't just surface level. Throughout the trial, both men hung out near the courthouse—in coffee shops or the lobby of the judicial building—just to show solidarity.

I bought a shirt with a bike sketch on it to remind me of these men. And I'm wearing it while I write this. These men inspire me.

Again, at this point in the story of the world, if you live an embodied, reverent, alive sexuality as a man, you will be radical. You will find a bazillion moments to change the tide in our world *away* from sex as power, or sex as escape, or sex as irreverent—and *toward* sex as love. We have so few of these stories being told in our culture.

Let me say it again: this chapter is not about getting you to perform hero-level stuff. Trying to be a hero almost always means you will not be one. It's probably more about your ego. Peter and Carl-Fredrik just went for a bike ride, after all. But something was different about them. I need you to know that if you do this work, if you find a healthy, alive relationship to your sexuality, you will be different in the world. You will be capable of experiencing the awesome and, yes, the awful too. If you're a good man who shows up to his life, you will find yourself changing the world. Maybe you, too, will be someone's hero.

Shrewd and Innocent

When Jesus sent out his disciples in Matthew 10 to travel city to city and announce the coming of his kingdom, he gave them a sober speech, making clear they would disrupt the status quo and stir up a ruckus among their people to the point of being hated and even beaten. He compared it to sending them as sheep among wolves—hardly an encouraging picture to rally your troops around. These are the difficult but necessary words from a platoon leader before a hard battle.

But then it got weird.

Rather than charging them to ready themselves for the journey, he asked them to intentionally disarm themselves by bringing nothing along. The only weapons he asked them to wield are these: "Be as shrewd as snakes and as innocent as doves" (Matthew 10:16). That's it. Arm yourself with shrewdness and innocence. And when you're in a desperate place, the Spirit will show up to help. Bon voyage! Say hi to the wolves!

What in the world?

Jesus directly ripped off the saying "shrewd as snakes" from the description of Satan in the garden of Eden. "Now the serpent was more crafty than any of the wild animals" (Genesis 3:1). In fact, the author of Matthew made this connection overt by using the same Greek word for "shrewd" or "crafty" that the Septuagint (an ancient Greek translation of the Old Testament) uses in Genesis to describe the serpent. Jesus was telling his disciples to be as crafty and cunning and conniving as evil.

What a wild invitation.

Jesus wants us to look evil in the face. Beyond being simply sober-minded, he invites us to mirror the same guile and creativity. Be as shrewd and savvy as our enemy.

By recalling this scene in Eden, I sense Jesus also wants his disciples to remember something else: the early innocence of Adam and Eve. As we mentioned, innocence is not simply sinlessness but a way of living with aliveness and wonder in the world. By combining these two things, shrewdness and innocence, I hear Jesus saying your innocence better not be naivety. You cannot enter the world as a fool. You must learn to plot your goodness, and goodness you must plot.

Paul carried this picture even further when he tipped his hat to Jesus' words at the end of his letter to the Romans: "Be wise about what is good, and innocent about what is evil. The God of peace will soon crush Satan under your feet" (16:19–20). Paul wanted you back in that scene in Eden too. He wanted you to hold Eden in your heart, especially God's promise to Eve that one day her offspring would strike the head of evil. He seemed to believe that shrewdness and innocence are actually our way to "stand on the neck of evil," as Dan Allender says so poetically.[3]

To join God in defeating evil, Jesus says we must be shrewd and innocent. In other words, you need to be a warrior and a lover. That's the vision. A soft-hearted warrior. A cunning lover.

Look, the lover in you is not all of you. You work and you war in life through a lot of crap. You need love, yes, but you need grit too. Yet the lover is what holds you together. He is your center. It's not good if you are all lover and no grit or drive or fight. You become an empath with no boundaries, absorbed in the feelings of the world. But to have all grit and fight and no love is to be a savage, a marauder of the world. We cannot be one without the other. Be a good warrior. But be a really good lover too.

Being shrewd and innocent is obviously about far more than sexuality. But the invitation back to the garden by Jesus and Paul certainly invites us to remember the time when humanity lived "naked with no shame," when nakedness was met with awe and innocence, not shame and harm. To stand on the neck of evil is to fight for a world where, poetically speaking, nakedness knows no shame. Where we can embody our sexuality without sin and shame and shutdown. Where reverence reigns. Where everyone experiences this freedom and safety and joy. Your sexual innocence, aliveness, and sexual shrewdness can change the world.

Just like the disciples, you are being invited by God to participate in the redemption of the world. You get to stand on the neck of evil. You get to be in the story. With your sexuality no less. And your weapons? Be innocent. Be shrewd.

Jacob lives a double life. Here in the United States he's a white man with a job and kids and a wife. You couldn't pick him out of a crowd other than maybe because of his big smile and even bigger kindness. But a couple of weeks a year, he disappears to double as a sex tourist in Thailand. Not a *real* sex tourist but a fake one, an actor with a made-up alias, story, and job. It's all to help stop human trafficking in one of the darkest areas in the world.

He and a group of other men work with a local nonprofit to gather intel on sex traffickers and children in bondage. The hope is to support the local police to make arrests and free underage sex slaves. The work is brutal. Jacob needs to be in character and put on the personality of a sexual predator. He and his comrades sit in bars and get offered minors who they talk with enough to get ages and stories on video as evidence. They never cross any inappropriate lines, of course, but it's taxing to be in character.

This work requires such a shrewd *and* innocent relationship with their own sexualities. To be in the presence of such dark objectification, harm, and violation and try to act like it interests them is profoundly difficult. It always makes him weep after the fact. The whole team often weeps together in debriefs.

Last time we sat together, he celebrated a recent police bust and arrest. He got to see a picture of a group of girls set free and safe in a recovery house. On one occasion, he had been invited to visit a recovery house and see firsthand the healing work. And as a pastor, he was asked to perform baptisms. He said at one point he looked at his hands and wept. "On this trip, a minor girl had tried to hold my hand in a brothel. And those same hands got to hold another victim's hand as I immersed her in the baptism waters. It all felt like holy work."

Jacob, a man living with shrewd and innocent sexuality, standing on the neck of evil.

Write a Better Story

So far I've shared some heavy stories where men play roles bordering on the heroic. These stories of their heroism are real. And so are the stories of sexual harm. And there are a billion more like them.

You don't need to try and be anyone's hero in the dramatic sense displayed in these stories. Most times, as I said, pursuing heroics will only push you into the realm of ego and away from your good heart.

I need to make sure I don't mislead you here. I said earlier that there are two ways to embody sexuality: the lover or the savage. And I mean every word of that. But what needs to be clear is that every single one of us is *both* men. We've all been the savage and the lover. No one lives so fully alive as the lover that we are never given over to the madness of selfish lust (even beyond sexual lust). Nor is a man ever so lost to his savage nature that he can't find the pulse of love. And our stories always involve messy moments of both.

This is not about perfection or getting it right. This is about starting wherever you are and moving toward your lover heart.

You may remember Cory from chapter 5, the one who was coercively pinned down and forced to look at porn. The poison arrow of shame shot in his heart that day, making him feel every bit perverted for looking and feeling aroused at what he saw. The temptation of his relief-revenge cycle led him into a regular habit of looking at porn and hating himself for it. That boy became a man, got married, and took a job as an elementary PE teacher.

Every year, the school gave one student the chance to pick a teacher to shadow for a day. And the winner, a little girl named Maddie, picked Mr. Cory. She was elated and, on that day, came eager and ready. Cory felt the weight of her joy and it truly melted his heart. At lunch she even gave him a picture she'd drawn of the two of them together. He saw just enough of how big a deal this was for her, and it brought him to tears. *Why me?* his heart said to God. And God simply answered, *You are a lover of women.*

All the shame of his porn use hit him hard, making God's words feel impossible. But Maddie's trust and that name from God gripped him more than his shame. Little did he know it was also foreshadowing— he's now the father of three girls. And he's courageously engaging his own story and heart work to truly become the lover God named him.

Want to know the best way to change the world for good with your sexuality?

Let the lover in you live better stories. Let him show up more. Cory didn't look for this story, but he showed up in it well, making Maddie's day as a safe and good man, and he will change the trajectory of his three daughters' hearts. As I've said, all sexuality lives in a story. There is no such thing as storyless sexuality. It always follows a script and a plot. Is it the stuff of romance and love? What script does it follow? Your sexuality will thrive only if it lives in the right story. It will suffer and malform in anything else.

That's what I mean when I say you don't have to go looking for these stories. If you live with an alive sexuality, better stories will find you. And I guarantee if you do this work and really foster an alive and virile sexuality, one capable of deep eroticism, sensuality, and awe, you will find yourself fighting against the abuse, misogyny, and other forms of harm that are done in the name of male sexual arousal.

Be shrewd. Be innocent. When I stood on that roof while the men mutilated the college women with their lust, I did not ask for that story. But I had a chance to speak up. I turned around in silence. I've wondered, what more could I have done? How could I have stood on the neck of evil to help write a different story? I wish I'd said something.

How about the next sex joke someone makes with you: What

could we do as men? There's always a subtext to those jokes that degrades women. I've taken advice I heard from Heather Thompson Day: simply look confused and tell them you don't get it. It'll make them have to explain the joke, which will expose them in it.[4] Nothing kills the laughter more than intentionally missing the punch line. Let it be awkward.

Not long ago, I stood on the sidelines of my son's soccer game and heard a dad make a joke about how he no longer needed his wife now that he had a bidet. It was a dumb joke that only exposed him. And he said it in mixed company, within earshot of his wife. I'll admit my masculine-culture training pulled on me to rescue him and laugh right along. But I knew the best thing to do was let the joke fall flat and embarrass him.

Sometimes the moment may call for a direct confrontation, like telling a friend he's a fool for pursuing an affair. Been there. Or reporting sexual abuse to authorities. Been there too. Shrewd sometimes means going right through the front door and confronting harm because the evil you're facing cannot simply be outflanked.

If you are married, you absolutely must be curious about your partner's story too. Remember, one in four women has suffered overt sexual abuse. But I say with confidence that all women have suffered harm to their sexuality. To know your wife is to know her story. But be shrewd. This is not something to barge through the front door on. Stay kind, curious, and patient. The evil one does not want to give up ground in Eve's story either.

———

You'll also find yourself participating in beautiful stories. The awesome. After reading Song of Songs a few years ago, I had the idea of trying my hand at the craft of erotic love poetry. I shaped a few lines for my wife and tucked them in my heart. My wife came home from work late one night and I offered her a massage, which she gladly accepted since her job had her on her feet for hours on end. And I surely hoped this might lead to sex. Armed with strong hands and my freshly minted verses, I worked her muscles and spoke words over her body.

"Wait," she said, "are you going full Song of Songs on me?"

"Um, maybe?"

We both burst out laughing.

It's not that this couldn't have been a beautiful moment, a meaningful blessing of her body. But knowing my wife, it's likely that my hands said what I hoped my words would say. She just wanted me to show loving affection to her and her body. That's her love language. I reflect back now and realize that the poetry helped *my* heart by giving me new eyes for the glory of every square inch of her body.

Sometimes we swing and miss. Other times we get it right.

Once while hanging out with my good friend Dan talking in his living room, his nine-year-old daughter came in and whispered something in his ear. He smiled and said, "Sure, we can do that." He turned to me. "She wonders if she can dance for you while I play guitar. We do this a lot together."

"I'd be honored," I said.

And while Dan set the stage for her with his acoustic guitar, she twirled and bowed and animated the song with her body. I could sense her trying on the power of her femininity. She seemed to know she embodied something well and good and powerful. Dance is by no means the only place femininity shines, but this was her place, her passion, her stage for the moment. And it was powerful and moving to witness a girl finding the glory and power of her presence in the world. And she shined.

After she bowed and I applauded her performance, she burrowed her head into her dad as he hugged her. And it struck me how much Dan's presence had made space for her growing glory and femininity. They did this often. He made the stage with far more than simply his guitar songs. The safety of a good father had hollowed out a safe place in the world for her growing beauty—yes, that power of presence—to radiate. He had a heart to recognize and reverence the growing glory in his daughter.

For some, it may be hard to even imagine this scene with Dan and his daughter because it's hard to catch the vision for safe and good men who know how to awe well. We don't have a lot of pictures of safe yet still affectionate and sensual men. But we must begin to let our minds hold both together.

There's a story of Jesus I didn't share in the last chapter on his kindness to the sexually broken because it's really possible we got it wrong. Luke told this story in Luke 7. Jesus was invited to eat a meal at a Pharisee's house when a woman of the city, known to be a sinner, came to find him. The host recoiled at this woman's presence and what she did with Jesus. I've always heard she was a prostitute. And while this may be true, it's not clearly spelled out in the text and may be a further way she has been mistreated over the years.

The woman didn't seem deterred by the snubbed nose of the Pharisee. She went right to Jesus with an alabaster jar of perfumed oil, intent to anoint him. So overcome with gratitude and awe for him as her Messiah, she began to weep, kiss his feet, and wipe them with her hair. She anointed his feet and the oil commingled with her tears.

This scene is wildly sensual.

Imagine the smell of essential oils filling the room. See her kissing and rubbing his feet and notice the intimacy of the woman using her hair to wipe them. Hear her weeping aloud with deep love for him.

And Jesus rebuked her accusers and instead welcomed and blessed *all* that she was doing. He was clearly receiving this deep act of affection with an even deeper gratitude for her.

I absolutely love this scene of healthy, alive sexuality for Jesus. Yes, Jesus was a sexually alive man. Some might say that this scene is only safe precisely because Jesus is *not* sexual. But I think he knows exactly the edge where sensuality ends and sexuality would begin. He was not sexualizing her, true. He was receiving this deep, affectionate, *sensual* love from a woman, and it stayed completely safe and reverent. But I would say that this is true only because he *is* sexually alive and well.

That's the safe, reverent awe we can all embody.

Invitation to Play

To write a new story for the lover in you is really an invitation to play. It's not simply to sit with pen and paper but to strum a guitar, ride a bike, work your hands in massage, or drive a truck with a different heart and different eyes. Go have savvy and innocent sex with your wife. Make mad passionate love in a field like the lovers in Song of Songs. Go plant a flower bed. Tell that story of sexual abuse to a counselor. Pursue your wife's heart. Talk to your son about sex. Or maybe do find a pen and paper and write good poetry. Either way, we write by participation and acting. If the true nature of sex is play, then play we must if we are to be alive sexually.

But we do well to remember that play carries a weight to it, a seriousness: playful always but never frivolous. We are playing, as C. S. Lewis said, "with possible gods and goddesses."[5] That ought to make you shake in your boots a bit.

Dan Allender describes this play best:

Conclusion

The kind of play we're talking about isn't just play in a game, it's not fundamentally a way of distracting yourself from life. It actually is an entry into the richness, the mystery, the ambiguity of life itself. The very nature of true play is that we get to stand on the neck of evil. Meaningful play invites us into a deeper revelation of who we were created to be, and the opportunity to evoke goodness in others.[6]

Here now, at the end of this book, I remind you of what German philosopher and playwright Frederick Schiller said: all good play produces beauty.[7]

You get to beautify the world.

There is an entire planet waiting for your participation, full of beauty and glory that has been desecrated, marred, harmed, and opposed. It's within everyone you meet; dare I say, around every corner you turn: new places that need the love and care and reverence of good men. God's world needs mending. But it also needs awe. We are called not just to fix but enjoy. The true heart of your sexuality is square in your chest, not your loins. And the more you cultivate your lover self, the more true libido (love capacity) you'll live with.

The world is dying for more innocents. More men capable of awe, reverence, and a capacity for the erotic. There are stories that you and only you can write with your sexuality. There are places only you can play. The lover in you has been handed a life and a world full of the glory of God. Go fall in love with it and write that better story.

For our last moments together, can I invite you to put your hand on your chest as you read these words? Here is my blessing for you.

You, my friend, are the artwork of God. God dreamed you up— your body and your being. He imagined the shape of your heart

Conclusion

and the salience of your sexuality. And then he made you. Fearfully and wonderfully. You are a thing of awe. You will never lose this marveling ability, no matter how much happens to you or what choices you make in life. And more, God blessed you. He "saw all that he had made and called it good" (Genesis 1:31). He did good work when he made you, including your sexuality.

You've lived much past the shimmering moment of your birth. Enough to meet me here in the final pages of this book. I don't know what your journey with your sexuality has held to this moment. I'm sure that evil has haunted your innocence, though I don't know where or when or why. And I know one other thing about you: You read this book to its beautiful—or bitter—end. You've wrung the towel of these pages. You clearly have a blood-red pulse beating in your chest. You want an alive sexuality. You are a virile man. You are resurrecting the lover already.

I hope you're beginning to see the path forward, however hard it may be. May you find kind places to heal your sexual harm, the stories that haunt, and the shame that shuts you down. Whatever you struggle with, big or small, may you remember that you will never lose that original shimmer of God. It can be recovered. May you know good sex and much beauty and the romance of God, the lover whose image you bear.

I hope you get to experience the passionate play of sex. And I hope it brings life to your romance. And I hope for all of you that you come to know the romance of God, the awe of his good world, and his passionate love for you.

All I know is an adventure awaits. With your hand on your chest, know that the most virile and potent place sits squarely within it: your lover heart. Go be virile in the world.

Acknowledgments

When I began writing this book, I printed off stock images of men (and women) reading books and taped them to the wall so I could envision and pray for you, reader. I felt the weight of your time and trust and, most of all, how my writing would impact you and your sexuality. It gave me a welcome affection for you and your life. Thank you for your trust. I hope this book has spoken to something important in your story. That has been my prayer.

To my love, my bride, Amanda, the one who pierced my heart with her beauty and still does every day: Thank you for rousing me to reckon with my uninitiated lover heart—and for loving that young man despite my fits and starts and misses and failures. It's quite a story we're caught up in. I love exploring and knowing the limitless mystery of your heart. Let's keep this romance going. And thank you for supporting me through all the early mornings, anxious pacings, and fist-pump victories of this writing journey.

My boys, Brandt, Simon, and Westley: You have hearts of absolute gold. You inspired this whole book. I love you so much. Thanks for putting up with a distracted dad who disappeared to write a lot these last few years.

Acknowledgments

Deep gratitude to my Friday men's group, Ben Day, PJ Musilli, and Nathan Johnson—the most virile and good men I know. Your encouragement, listening ear, feedback, and help have changed my life. All of that is written in these pages.

Thank you, Mike Winkler, for the years of friendship and hours of conversation that let me wrestle out my life and this book. To Jared and Megan Anderson, thank you for always caring enough to ask about the creative journey in all its mess and cheering me on.

I never trusted you, Ruth Buchanan, when you told me I would get here. But here I am finishing a book, humbled by your coaching wisdom. I don't know why you care so much about us authors, but thank you. I would not be here save your fierce and unrelenting encouragement.

John Blase, literally no other agent would have fit this book. From the sole of your crap kickers to your ponytail, you are a damn good man. Thank you for your friendship and poetry and riding shotgun in this rodeo called publishing. You protected the salience and sexual goodness of this book through and through. Long live your lover heart.

To my prayer team: God only knows how much your prayers have rescued me. I thought of you often as I wrote and could feel you carrying me through.

Thank you to all the clients and friends and family who gave me permission to write their stories in this book. Your courageous hard work has left me in awe. It's brought me such joy to introduce you to readers.

Thank you to John Eldredge for naming me a poet twenty-five years ago and always being a generous and good man. Your fathering of me is in these pages. To Chuck Degroat, thank you for your grace to me as a zealous student of therapy and all your early support and encouragement. And special thanks to Sheila Wray Gregoire, for risking a Zoom call on a random man wanting to write a book on sex and all the time you took to read that book. Your integrity and care for this topic and the church has my utmost respect and gratitude.

To all those who encouraged me in the content of this book, I'm here because of you. Thank you, Cory Smith and the Training Ground community—the most authentic men I know. And to all those who've followed my newsletter and let me try my hand at some of these ideas: you are the best.

Daniel Marrs: Beyond your wisdom and keen editing eye, your heart shines the brightest. Your openness and risk on this nervous writer have meant the world. Thank you! Things you've said will stay with me always. To Natalie Nyquist, most gracious and kind, and John Andrade, the sincerest, and Andrew Stoddard and Lisa Beech and all the team at Nelson Books, a heartfelt thank you. You all bring such commitment and care to your work. Thank you to Blake Jergens, for edits that rescued parts of this book, and Margot Starbuck, for your savvy and generosity.

To all those healers (counselors) who helped me wrestle out my own sexual journey: I'm crying as I write this. Thank you. To Peter Everts, the magician. And Brad and Becky Young, for the truest scalpels and caring eyes. To Lottie Hillard, the velvet hammer, for the fiercest kindness I've ever met. You are missed. To Trapper for your stone-cold, straight-faced approach to all BS always, thank you. To Dan Allender for the hour on my birthday. To Andy Ide for your wily way with stories and for blessing the virility within me that wrote this book. To Robin Wall for the calmest presence when I wrote too brave and stirred up my own story.

To the God who said, "Hope!" every time I prayed about this book, thank you! Something that I can't explain carried me through

this process. I never thought I would cry this much over writing a
book on sex. But you helped me see the heart of it—and changed me
through the journey. Thank you. May you romance in the same way
every man who reads this book.

Notes

Introduction: The Most Neglected Part of a Man's Life

1. Peggy Orenstein, "'Boys & Sex' Reveals That Young Men Feel 'Cut Off from Their Hearts,'" January 7, 2020, in *Fresh Air*, produced by Terry Gross, podcast, MP3 audio, 35:00, https://www.npr.org/sections/health-shots/2020/01/07/794182826/boys-sex-reveals-that-young-men-feel-cut-off-from-their-hearts.

2. Peggy Orenstein, "When Did Porn Become Sex Ed?," *New York Times*, March 19, 2016, https://www.nytimes.com/2016/03/20/opinion/sunday/when-did-porn-become-sex-ed.html.

3. "New Poll: Parents Are Talking with Their Kids About Sex but Often Not Tackling Harder Issues," Planned Parenthood, last modified October 30, 2016, https://www.plannedparenthood.org/about-us/newsroom/press-releases/new-poll-parents-talking-their-kids-about-sex-often-not-tackling-harder-issues.

4. Richard Weissbourd et al., *The Talk: How Adults Can Promote Young People's Healthy Relationships and Prevent Misogyny and Sexual Harassment* (Cambridge, MA: Harvard Graduate School of Education, 2017), 2, https://mcc.gse.harvard.edu/reports/the-talk.

5. *Quick Facts: Sexual Abuse Offenders*, United States Sentencing Commission, 2018, 1, https://www.ussc.gov/sites/default/files/pdf/research-and-publications/quick-facts/Sexual_Abuse_FY18.pdf.

6. Orenstein, "Boys & Sex."

7. Peggy Orenstein, *Boys & Sex: Young Men on Hookups, Love, Porn, Consent, and Navigating the New Masculinity* (New York: HarperCollins, 2020), 99.

8. Robert Bly, *A Little Book on the Human Shadow* (New York: HarperCollins, 1988), 20.

9. Bly, *Human Shadow*, 19.

10. Johan Huizinga, *Homo Ludens: A Study of the Play-Element in Culture* (New York: Roy, 1950), 205.

11. *The Century Dictionary: An Encyclopedic Lexicon of the English Language*, vol. 7, s.v. "savage" (New York: Century Company, 1914), 5357, https://www.google.com/books/edition/The_Century_Dictionary/SzAUAQAAMAAJ.

12. Esther Perel, *Mating in Captivity: Unlocking Erotic Intelligence* (New York: HarperCollins, 2006), xiv.

Chapter 1: You Are a Lover

1. Jay Stringer, *Unwanted: How Sexual Brokenness Reveals Our Way to Healing* (Colorado Springs: NavPress, 2018), 105.

2. John O'Donohue, "The Inner Landscape of Beauty," February 10, 2022, in *On Being with Krista Tippett*, produced by Krista Tippett, podcast, MP3 audio, 50:38, https://onbeing.org/programs/john-odonohue-the-inner-landscape-of-beauty/.

3. While women's arousal is equally visual and can trigger sexual desire, due to a lower arousal concordance, the self-awareness and expression of desire is more context dependent for women. Ekaterina Mitricheva et al., "Neural Substrates of Sexual Arousal Are Not Sex Dependent," *Proceedings of the National Academy of Sciences* 116, no. 31 (2019): 15671–76, https://doi.org/10.1073/pnas.1904975116.

4. Dacher Keltner, *Awe: The New Science of Everyday Wonder and How It Can Transform Your Life* (New York: Penguin Press, 2023), 11, 74.

5. Institute for Quality and Efficiency in Health Care, "How Does Our Sense of Taste Work?," InformedHealth.org, last modified January 24, 2023, https://www.informedhealth.org/how-does-our-sense-of-taste-work.html.

6. Rainer Maria Rilke, *Letters to a Young Poet* (Hawthorne, CA: BN Publishing, 2008), 21.

7. Maria Uloko, Erika P. Isabey, and Blair R. Peters, "How Many Nerve Fibers Innervate the Human Glans Clitoris: A Histomorphometric Evaluation of the Dorsal Nerve of the Clitoris," *Journal of Sexual Medicine* 20, no. 3 (2023): 247–52, https://doi.org/10.1093/jsxmed/qdac027; Elçin Tunçol et al., "Fiber Counts and Architecture of the Human Dorsal Penile Nerve," *Scientific Reports* 13, no. 1 (2023): 8862, http://doi: 10.1038/s41598-023-35030-w.

8. Jim Harrison, "The Man Who Gave Up His Name," in *Legends of the Fall* (New York: Grove, 1978), 150.

9. Robert Moore and Douglas Gillette, *King, Warrior, Magician, Lover: Rediscovering the Archetypes of the Mature Masculine* (New York: HarperCollins, 1990), 121, 140.

10. Alain Corbin, Jean-Jacques Courtine, and Georges Vigarello, eds., *A History of Virility* (New York: Columbia University Press, 2016), preface.

11. *Online Etymology Dictionary*, s.v. "romance," last modified September 16, 2021, https://www.etymonline.com/word/romance#etymonline_v_15175.

12. *Online Etymology Dictionary*, s.v. "romantic," last modified September 16, 2021, https://www.etymonline.com/word/romantic#etymonline_v_15180.

13. Moore and Gillette, *King, Warrior, Magician, Lover*, 140.

14. Frederick Buechner, *Beyond Words: Daily Readings in the ABC's of Faith* (New York: HarperOne, 2004), 139.

15. Augustine, *Confessions*, 13.9.10, in *Nicene and Post-Nicene Fathers*, series 1, vol. 1, trans. J. G. Pilkington, ed. Philip Schaff (Buffalo, NY: Christian Literature Publishing Co., 1887).

16. Moore and Douglas, *King, Warrior, Magician, Lover*, 137.

17. Moore and Douglas, *King, Warrior, Magician, Lover*, 140.

18. Rilke, *Letters to a Young Poet*, 19.

19. Rilke, *Letters to a Young Poet*, 20.

20. Emily Nagoski, *Come as You Are: The Surprising New Science That Will Transform Your Sex Life* (New York: Simon & Schuster, 2015), 226–32.

21. Nagoski, *Come as You Are*, 226.

22. Sheila Wray Gregoire, Rebecca Lindenbach, and Joanna Sawatsky, *The Great Sex Rescue: The Lies You've Been Taught and How to Recover What God Intended* (Grand Rapids: Baker, 2021), 158.

23. Sheila Wray Gregoire and Keith Gregoire, *The Good Guy's Guide to Great Sex: Because Good Guys Make the Best Lovers* (Grand Rapids: Zondervan, 2022), 163–64.

24. Gregoire and Gregoire, *Good Guy's Guide*, 166.

25. Dan Allender, *Leading Character* (Grand Rapids: Zondervan, 2008), 46.

26. Orenstein, *Boys & Sex*, 46.

27. Lisa Wade, *American Hookup: The New Culture of Sex on Campus* (New York: Norton, 2017), 134–35.

28. Quoted in Peggy Orenstein, *Girls & Sex: Navigating the Complicated New Landscape* (New York: HarperCollins, 2016), 117.

29. Wade, *American Hookup*, 41.

30. Portions of this section first appeared in my contribution to Sheila Wray Gregoire's blog: Sam Jolman, "What If Both Purity Culture and the Hookup Culture Are Teaching People to Treat Sex with Dissociation and Disconnection?," *Bare Marriage* (blog), May 18, 2022, https://baremarriage.com/2022/05/what-the-hookup-culture -and-purity-culture-have-in-common/.

31. Orenstein, *Girls & Sex*, 47.

32. Wade, *American Hookup*, 135.

33. Orenstein, *Girls & Sex*, 117.

34. Orenstein, *Girls & Sex*, 119.

35. Lisa Wade, quoted in Orenstein, *Girls & Sex*, 117.

36. Dan Allender, "Story of Sexuality Lecture: Weekend 3" (lecture presented at the Narrative Focused Trauma Care Certificate Program, Chicago, April 8, 2013).

Chapter 2: God Most Wants Your Awe (Not Your Purity)

1. Eugene Peterson, *Christ Plays in Ten Thousand Places: A Conversation in Spiritual Theology* (Grand Rapids: Eerdmans, 2005), 51–52.

2. Jennifer E. Stellar et al., "Awe and Humility," *Journal of Personality*

and Social Psychology 114, no. 2 (2018): 258–69, https://doi.org/10
1037/pspi0000109.

3. Paul K. Piff et al., "Awe, the Small Self, and Prosocial Behavior," *Journal of Personality and Social Psychology* 108, no. 6 (2015): 883–99, https://doi.org/10.1037/pspi0000018.

4. Paul Piff and Dacher Keltner, "Why Do We Experience Awe?," *New York Times*, May 22, 2015, https://www.nytimes.com/2015/05/24 /opinion/sunday/why-do-we-experience-awe.html.

5. Piff and Keltner, "Why Do We Experience Awe?"

6. Jonathan McPhetres and Janis H. Zickfield, "The Physiological Study of Emotional Piloerection: A Systematic Review and Guide for Future Research," *International Journal of Psychophysiology* 179 (2022): 6–20, https://doi.org/10.1016/j.ijpsycho.2022.06.010.

7. *Online Etymology Dictionary*, s.v. "awe," last modified October 2, 2022, https://www.etymonline.com/word/awe#etymonline_v_19020.

8. Dacher Keltner and Jonathan Haidt, "Approaching Awe, a Moral, Spiritual, and Aesthetic Emotion," *Cognition and Emotion* 17, no. 2 (2003): 297–314, https://doi.org/10.1080/02699930302297.

9. Tremper Longman, "Wisdom with Dr. Tremper Longman, Part One," April 13, 2018, in *Wisdom with Dr. Tremper Longman*, produced by Dan Allender, podcast, MP3 audio, 22:17, https://theallendercenter.org /2018/04/tremper-longman-wisdom-1/.

10. Concepción de León, "How to Rewire Your Traumatized Brain," *New York Times*, October 18, 2018, https://www.nytimes.com/2018/10/18 /books/review/how-to-rewire-your-traumatized-brain.html.

11. Eugene Peterson, *Living the Resurrection: The Risen Christ in Everyday Life* (2006; repr., Colorado Springs: NavPress, 2020), 20.

12. C. S. Lewis, *The Weight of Glory* (1949; repr., New York: HarperOne, 2001), 42.

13. Lewis, *Weight of Glory*, 45–46.

14. Tremper Longman III, *Song of Songs*, New International Commentary on the Old Testament (Grand Rapids: Eerdmans, 2001), 174.

15. Mike Mason, *The Mystery of Marriage: Meditations on the Miracle* (Sisters, OR: Multnomah, 1985), 125.

16. Mason, *Mystery of Marriage*, 126.

17. John Climacus, *The Ladder of Divine Ascent*, 15.58, quoted in Christopher West, *At the Heart of the Gospel: Reclaiming the Body for New Evangelization* (New York: Crown Publishing, 2012), 82.

18. Richard Chess, "When God Dreamed Eve Through Adam," *Image Journal* no. 85 (June 2015), https://imagejournal.org/article/when-god-dreamed-eve-through-adam/https://imagejournal.org/article/when-god-dreamed-eve-through-adam/.

19. Melanie Robson, "Sex and Awe," *Medium*, April 6, 2020, https://medium.com/pleasureadvocate/sex-and-awe-ade7f9985082.

20. Shaunti Feldhahn, "4 Truths You Need to Know About Your Son and Visual Temptation," *Shaunti Feldhahn* (blog), May 11, 2018, https://shaunti.com/2018/05/4-truths-you-need-to-know-about-your-son-and-visual-temptation/.

21. Winn Collier, "Holy," *Winn Collier* (blog), February 4, 2021, https://winncollier.com/holy/.

Chapter 3: What Is Sex?

1. Nagoski, *Come as You Are*, 136.

2. Diane Ackerman, *Deep Play* (New York: Vintage, 1999), 118.

3. Huizinga, *Homo Ludens*, 132.

4. Osmo Kontula and Anneli Miettinen, "Determinants of Female Sexual Orgasms," *Socioaffective Neuroscience & Psychology* 6, no. 31624 (October 2016), https://doi.org/10.3402/snp.v6.31624; T. Shirazi et al., "Women's Experience of Orgasm During Intercourse: Question Semantics Affect Women's Reports and Men's Estimates of Orgasm Occurrence," *Archives of Sexual Behavior* 47 (2018): 605–13, https://doi.org/10.1007/s10508-017-1102-6.

5. Huizinga, *Homo Luden*, 19–21.

6. Lewis, *Weight of Glory*, 46.

7. Gregoire, Lindenbach, and Sawatsky, *Great Sex Rescue*, 21.

8. Orenstein, *Boys & Sex*, 78.

9. Huizinga, *Homo Ludens*, 7.

10. Julius Frankenbach et al., "Sex Drive: Theoretical Conceptualization

and Meta-Analytic Review of Gender Differences," *Psychological Bulletin* 148, nos. 9–10 (October 2022): 621–61, https://doi.org /10.1037/bul0000366.

11. Nagoski, *Come As You Are*, 226, 227.

12. Quoted in Nagoski, *Come as You Are*, 45.

13. Ackerman, *Deep Play*, 118.

14. Huizinga, *Homo Ludens*, 14

15. Abigail Favale, *The Genesis of Gender: A Christian Theory* (San Francisco: Ignatius, 2022), 108.

16. Wade, *American Hookup*, 15.

17. Keltner and Haidt, "Approaching Awe."

18. Huizinga, *Homo Ludens*, 7.

19. Saul L. Miller and Jon K. Maner, "Scent of a Woman: Men's Testosterone Responses to Olfactory Ovulation Cues," *Psychological Science* 21, no. 2 (2010): 276–83, https://doi.org/10.1177/0956797609357733.

20. David Morris Schnarch, *Passionate Marriage: Love, Sex, and Intimacy in Emotionally Committed Relationships* (New York: Norton, 1997), 40.

21. Dan Allender, "Certificate Program, First Weekend, Friday Lecture" (lecture presented at the Allender Center, Seattle, September 24–28, 2012).

22. Frederick Schiller, *On the Aesthetic Education of Man*, trans. Keith Tribe (New York: Penguin Classics, 2016), 54, 58–59.

23. Gregoire, Lindenbach, and Sawatsky, *Great Sex Rescue*, 41–44.

24. Wade, *American Hookup*, 117.

25. Wade, *American Hookup*, 159–60.

26. Dacher Keltner, *Awe: The New Science of Everyday Wonder and How It Can Transform Your Life* (New York: Penguin, 2023), 99, 131.

27. Jonathan L. Helm et al., "Assessing Cross-Partner Associations in Physiological Responses via Coupled Oscillator Models," *Emotion* 12, no. 4 (2012): 748–62, https://doi.org/10.1037/a0025036.

28. Huizinga, *Homo Ludens*, 12.

29. Nagoski, *Come as You Are*, 136, 146.

30. Behnoush Behnia et al., "Differential Effects of Intranasal Oxytocin on Sexual Experiences and Partner Interactions in Couples," *Hormones*

and Behavior 65, no. 3 (2014): 308–18, https://doi.org/10.1016/j.yhbeh
.2014.01.009.

31. Nagoski, *Come as You Are*, 136.

32. Brené Brown, *Braving the Wilderness: The Quest for True Belonging and the Courage to Stand Alone* (New York: Random House, 2019), 154.

33. Mason, *Mystery of Marriage*, 129.

34. Dan Allender, "Play, Part 2," *The Allender Center Podcast*, August 8, 2015, https://theallendercenter.org/2015/08/play-podcast-2/.

35. Huizinga, *Homo Ludens*, 132.

36. *Oxford English Dictionary*, s.v. "petit mort," accessed December 4, 2023, https://www.oed.com/dictionary/petit-mort_n?tab=meaning_and_use.

37. Eugene Peterson, *Practice Resurrection: A Conversation on Growing Up in Christ* (Grand Rapids: Eerdmans, 2013).

Chapter 4: Your Real Sex Education

1. Jennie G. Noll et al., "Childhood Sexual Abuse and Early Timing of Puberty," *Journal of Adolescent Health* 60, no. 1 (2017): 65–71, https://doi.org/10.1016/j.jadohealth.2016.09.008.

2. Nagoski, *Come as You Are*, 165.

3. Peterson, *Christ Plays*, 51.

4. Brené Brown, "Listening to Shame," filmed March 2012 in Long Beach, CA, TED talk, 20:22, https://www.ted.com/talks/Brené _brown_listening_to_shame/.

5. Dan Allender, "Shame-Face," The Allender Center, February 14, 2018, https://theallendercenter.org/2018/02/shame-faced/.

6. Allender, "Shame-Face."

7. Curt Thompson, *The Soul of Shame: Retelling the Stories We Believe About Ourselves* (Westmont, IL: InterVarsity Press, 2015), 71.

Chapter 5: The Wounded Lover

1. Quoted in C. S. Lewis, *The Great Divorce* (1945; repr., New York: HarperOne, 2001), introduction.

2. Frederick Buechner, *Listen to Your Life: Daily Mediations with Frederick Buechner* (New York: HarperCollins, 1992), 2.

3. "US: Harmful Surgery on Intersex Children," Human Rights Watch, July 25, 2017, https://www.hrw.org/news/2017/07/25/us-harmful-surgery-intersex-children.

4. "Does ISNA Think Children with Intersex Should Be Raised Without a Gender, or in a Third Gender?," Intersex Society of North America, accessed January 10, 2024, https://isna.org/faq/third-gender/.

5. Michael Gurian, *The Wonder of Boys: What Parents, Mentors and Educators Can Do to Shape Boys into Exceptional Men* (New York: Putnam, 1997), 128.

6. I. Meizner, "Sonographic Observation of In Utero Fetal 'Masturbation,'" *Journal of Ultrasound in Medicine* 6, no. 2 (1987): 111, https://doi.org/10.7863/jum.1987.6.2.111.

7. Schnarch, *Passionate Marriage*, 186.

8. Nagoski, *Come as You Are*, 146.

9. Sue Johnson, *Hold Me Tight: Seven Conversations for a Lifetime of Love* (New York: Little, Brown, 2008), 192.

10. Shanta R. Dube et al., "Long-Term Consequences of Childhood Sexual Abuse by Gender of Victim," *American Journal of Preventive Medicine* 28, no. 5 (2005): 430–8, https://doi.org/10.1016/j.amepre.2005.01.015.

11. C. S. Widom and S. Morris, "Accuracy of Adult Recollections of Childhood Victimization, Part 2: Childhood Sexual Abuse," *Psychological Assessment* 9, no. 1 (1997): 34–46, https://doi.org/10.1037/1040-3590.9.1.34.

12. Howard N. Snyder, *Sexual Assault of Young Children as Reported to Law Enforcement: Victim, Incident, and Offender Characteristics* (Washington, DC: US Department of Justice, 2000), 13, PDF, https://bjs.ojp.gov/content/pub/pdf/saycrle.pdf.

13. M. B. Robb and S. Mann, *Teens and Pornography* (San Francisco: Common Sense Media, 2023), 5, https://www.commonsensemedia.org/sites/default/files/research/report/2022-teens-and-pornography-final-web.pdf.

14. Dan Allender, "What Is Shame? Healing the Wounded Heart with Dr. Dan Allender," The Allender Center, posted July 1, 2020, YouTube video, 2:44, https://youtu.be/ry5AFys5Pn8.

Chapter 6: Killing Our Innocence

1. Ming Zhang, Yuqi Zhang, and Yazhou Kong, "Interaction Between Social Pain and Physical Pain," *Brain Science Advances* 5, no. 4 (2019): 265–73, http://doi.org/10.26599/BSA.2019.9050023.

2. Marcela Matos and José Pinto-Gouveia, "Shame as a Traumatic Memory," *Clinical Psychology & Psychotherapy* 17, no. 4 (2010): 299–312, https://doi.org/10.1002/cpp.659.

3. Nagoski, *Come as You Are*, 165.

4. Dan Allender, *The Wounded Heart: Hope for Adult Victims of Childhood Sexual Abuse* (Colorado Springs, CO: NavPress, 1990), 79.

5. Allender, *Wounded Heart*, 164.

6. Valerie Voon et al., "Neural Correlates of Sexual Cue Reactivity in Individuals with and Without Compulsive Sexual Behaviours," *PLoS ONE* 9, no. 7 (2014): e102419, https://doi.org/10.1371/journal.pone.0102419.

7. Robyn J. McQuaid et al., "Relations Between Plasma Oxytocin and Cortisol: The Stress Buffering Role of Social Support," *Neurobiology of Stress* 3 (2016): 52–60, https://doi.org/10.1016/j.ynstr.2016.01.001.

8. Mitricheva et al., "Neural Substrates of Sexual Arousal."

9. David A. Fahrenthold, "Trump Recorded Having Extremely Lewd Conversation About Women in 2005," *Washington Post*, October 8, 2016, https://www.washingtonpost.com/politics/trump-recorded -having-extremely-lewd-conversation-about-women-in-2005/2016 /10/07/3b9ce776-8cb4-11e6-bf8a-3d26847eeed4_story.html.

10. Cole Arthur Riley, *This Here Flesh: Spirituality, Liberation, and the Stories That Make Us* (New York: Convergent, 2022), 32.

11. Orenstein, *Boys & Sex*, 32.

12. Brian Wacker, "Tiger Woods 'Sorry' for Tampon Prank: Didn't 'Turn Out' Way I Meant," *New York Post*, February 17, 2023, https://nypost .com/2023/02/17/tiger-woods-sorry-for-tampon-prank-supposed -to-be-fun-and-games/.

13. Peter Leithart and Alastair Roberts, "Episode 199: Is Song of Songs an Allegory?," January 18, 2019, in *The Theopolis Podcast*, produced by Theopolis Institute, podcast, MP3 audio, 31:19, https://soundcloud.com /user-812874628/episode-199-is-song-of-songs-an-allegory.

14. Gail Dines, *Pornland: How Porn Has Hijacked Our Sexuality* (Boston: Beacon Press, 2010), xxiv, xxv, 121; Bedbible Research Center, "Pornhub Statistics—Analysis of +9,000 Hours of Porn [Shocking]," Bedbible.com, March 22, 2023, https://bedbible.com/pornhub -statistics/.

15. Dines, *Pornland*, xxiv.

16. Longman, *Song of Songs*, 150, 151.

17. Eusebius, *Church History*, 6.8; "Origen," *Christianity Today*, accessed December 4, 2023, https://www.christianitytoday.com/history/people /scholarsandscientists/origen.html.

18. Jerome, "A Letter from Jerome (383–384)," Center for Teaching and Learning at Columbia University, accessed December 5, 2023, https:// epistolae.ctl.columbia.edu/letter/447.html.

19. Giorgio Vasari, *The Temptation of St. Jerome*, 1548, oil on panel, 166.5 x 121.9 cm, Art Institute, Chicago, accessed December 4, 2023, https:// www.artic.edu/artworks/110242/the-temptation-of-saint-jerome; Albrecht Bouts, *The Penitence of St. Jerome*, 1520, oil on panel, 41 x 45.1 cm, Norton Simon Museum, Pasadena, CA, https://www.nortonsimon .org/art/detail/M.2009.2.P/.

20. Terrence G Kardong, *The Life of St. Benedict by Gregory the Great: Translation and Commentary* (Collegeville, MN: Liturgical Press, 2009), 13.

21. Albrecht Durer, *The Self Mortification of Saint Benedict*, c. 1496, stained glass, 22.5 x 16.3 cm, Isabella Stewart Gardner Museum, Nuremberg, Germany, https://www.gardnermuseum.org/experience /collection/11315.

22. Dan Allender, lecture, May 25, 2010, Abuse Helpers Workshop, Duke Divinity School, Durham, North Carolina.

23. Neil Strauss, "Howard Stern's Long Struggle and Neurotic Triumph," *Rolling Stone*, March 31, 2011, https://www.rollingstone.com/tv-movies/ tv-movie-news/howard-sterns-long-struggle-and-neurotic-triumph-97935/.

Chapter 7: The Only Path to Sexual Healing

1. John Eldredge and Brent Curtis, *The Sacred Romance: Drawing Closer to the Heart of God* (Nashville: Thomas Nelson, 2001), 19.

2. Lewis, *Great Divorce*, viii.

3. C. S. Widom and Suzanne Morris, "Accuracy of Adult Recollections of Childhood Victimization, Part 2: Childhood Sexual Abuse," *Psychological Assessment* 9, no. 1 (1997): 34–36, https://psycnet.apa.org /doi/10.1037/1040-3590.9.1.34.

4. Allender, lecture.

5. See his essay "On Forgiveness" in Lewis, *Weight of Glory*, 180.

6. Stringer, *Unwanted*, xix.

7. Richard Rohr, *A Spring Within Us: A Book of Daily Meditations* (Albuquerque: CAC Publishing, 2016), 199.

8. Keltner, *Awe*, 46.

Chapter 8: The Aroused Life

1. *Online Etymology Dictionary*, s.v. "rouse," last modified October 8, 2021, https://www.etymonline.com/word/rouse.

2. Mark Dingman, "Know Your Brain: Reticular Formation," Neuroscientifically Challenged, accessed December 4, 2023, https:// neuroscientificallychallenged.com/posts/know-your-brain-reticular -formation.

3. Eldredge and Curtis, *Sacred Romance*, 19; Stephen Bearman, "Why Men Are So Obsessed with Sex," in *Male Lust: Pleasure, Power, and Transformation*, ed. Kerwin Brook, Jill Nagle, and Baruch Gould, 2nd ed. (New York: Routledge, 2014), 218.

4. Henry David Thoreau, *Walden* (New York: Vintage, 2017), 7.

5. X. Chen et al., "Synapse Impairment Associated with Enhanced Apoptosis in Post-Traumatic Stress Disorder," *Synapse* 74 (2020): e22134, https://doi.org/10.1002/syn.22134.

6. James K. A. Smith, *Desiring the Kingdom: Worship, Worldview, and Cultural Formation* (Grand Rapids: Baker, 2009), 47, 57.

7. Alexandra Katehakis, *Sex Addiction as Affect Dysregulation: A Neurobiologically Informed Holistic Treatment* (New York: Norton, 2016), xv.

8. Katehakis, *Sex Addiction*, xv.

9. Schnarch, *Passionate Marriage*, 40.

10. Andrew Huberman, "How to Breathe Correctly for Optimal Health, Mood, Learning & Performance," February 19, 2023, in *Huberman Lab*, podcast, YouTube video, 2:18:50, https://www.hubermanlab.com/episode/how-to-breathe-correctly-for-optimal-health-mood-learning-and-performance.

11. Stephen Borges, quoted in Bonnie Badenoch, *The Heart of Trauma: Healing the Embodied Brain in the Context of Relationships* (New York: W. W. Norton & Co., 2018), xi.

12. Quoted in Veronica Kallos-Lilly and Jennifer Fitzgerald, *An Emotionally Focused Workbook for Couples: The Two of Us* (New York: Routledge, 2021), 10.

13. Michael D. Nevarez et al., "Friendship in War: Camaraderie and Prevention of Posttraumatic Stress Disorder Prevention," *Journal of Traumatic Stress* 30, no. 5 (2017): 512–20, https://doi.org/10.1002/jts.22224s.

14. Perel, *Mating in Captivity*, xv.

15. John Bowlby, *A Secure Base* (New York: Routledge, 1988), 137.

16. Bowlby, *Secure Base*, 69.

17. Perel, *Mating in Captivity*, 18.

18. Schnarch, *Passionate Marriage*, 77.

19. Ackerman, *Deep Play*, 23.

20. Ackerman, *Deep Play*, 118.

21. Keltner, *Awe*, 74.

22. Mary Oliver, "Sometimes," in *Red Bird* (Boston: Beacon, 2008), 1.

23. Richard Rohr, "Turning Towards the Good," Center for Action and Contemplation, February 18, 2016, https://cac.org/daily-meditations/turning-toward-the-good-2016-02-18/; Nate Klemp, "The Neuroscience of Breaking Out of Negative Thinking," *Inc.*, August 7, 2019, https://www.inc.com/nate-klemp/try-this-neuroscience-based-technique-to-shift-your-mindset-from-negative-to-positive-in-30-seconds.html.

24. Keltner, *Awe*, 106.

25. Keltner, *Awe*, 99, 118, 131, 135.

26. Keltner, *Awe*, 128.

27. This quote from Toni Morrison comes from an interview with

Claudia Brodsky Lacour first recorded in 1992 and aired in "Before the Light," October 23, 2019, in *The Paris Review Podcast*, produced by the Paris Review, MP3 audio, 34:58, https://www.theparisreview.org /podcast/6047/before-the-light.

28. John Eldredge, *Wild at Heart: Discovering the Secret of a Man's Soul* (Nashville: Thomas Nelson, 2001), 163.

29. Huizinga, *Homo Ludens*, 63.

30. Dan Allender, "Replay and Rest: The Cost of Rest," July 23, 2022, in *The Allender Center Podcast*, podcast, MP3 audio, 21:44, https:// theallendercenter.org/2022/07/replay-and-rest-the-cost-of-rest/.

31. Rilke, *Letters to a Young Poet*, 18.

Conclusion: How Your Sexuality Can Change the World

1. Chanel Miller, *Know My Name: A Memoir* (New York: Viking, 2019).

2. Miller, *Know My Name*, 363.

3. Dan Allender, "Play: Part Two," August 8, 2015, in *The Allender Center Podcast*, podcast, MP3 audio, 21:37, https://theallendercenter.org /2015/08/play-podcast-2/.

4. Heather Thompson Day (@heatherthompsonday), "Best advice my dad ever gave me," Instagram Reel, October 3, 2022, https://www.instagram .com/reel/Cx8iW9IxWAL/.

5. Lewis, *Weight of Glory*, 45.

6. Allender, "Play: Part Two."

7. Schiller, *Letters*, 58–59.

About the Author

Sam Jolman (MA LPC) is a professional therapist with over twenty years of experience specializing in men's issues and sexual trauma recovery. He seeks to help men and women know and heal their stories, and find greater sexual wholeness and aliveness. He received his master's in counseling from Reformed Theological Seminary and was further trained in Narrative Focused Trauma Care through the Allender Center at the Seattle School of Theology and Psychology. Sam lives in Colorado with his wife and three sons. Together they enjoy exploring the best camping spots in a pop-up camper. Sam goes to therapy, loves fly-fishing, and can often be found trying to catch his breath on the floor of his local CrossFit gym.

Notes

Notes

Notes

Notes

Notes

_____

_____

_____

_____

_____

_____

_____

_____

_____

_____

_____

_____

Notes

_____

_____

_____

_____

_____

_____

_____

_____

_____

_____

_____

_____

Notes

Notes

_____

_____

_____

_____

_____

_____

_____

_____

_____

_____

_____

Notes

_____

_____

_____

_____

_____

_____

_____

_____

_____

_____

_____

_____